CELT AND GREEK

Peter Berresford Ellis

CELT AND GREEK

Celts in the Hellenic World

CONSTABLE · LONDON

First published in Great Britain 1997
by Constable and Company Ltd
3 The Lanchesters, 162 Fulham Palace Road
London W6 9ER
Copyright © Peter Berresford Ellis 1997
ISBN 0 09 475580 9
The right of Peter Berresford Ellis to be identified
as the author of this work has been
asserted by him in accordance with
the Copyright, Designs and Patents Acts 1988
ISBN 0 09 475580 9

Set in Linotype Postscript Sabon by
Rowland Phototypesetting Ltd, Bury St Edmunds, Suffolk
Printed in Great Britain by
St Edmundsbury Press Ltd,
Bury St Edmunds, Suffolk

A CIP data catalogue record for this book
is available from the British Library

For Eleni and Orestes – to commemorate the trip with Dorothy and myself, from Delphi, through the gorges of Parnassos, to Thermopylae. There were no thunderbolts but the gods were much in evidence!

Contents

Illustrations

THRACE

Byzantium

Lysimacheia

Lampsacus
Abydus
Ilium
Alexandria

Cyzicus

Macestus
(Megistus)

Miletupolis

PERGAMUM

Pergamum
Source of
the Caicus

Aphrodisium

Myrina

Hermus

Thyateira

Battle of the Elephants
✕ 269 BC ?

Erythrae
Smyrna
Sardis

Cayster

Ephesos

Maeander

Priene
Magnesia
Miletus
Laodice
Didyma

CARIA

Themisonium

Halicarnassus

L

COS

Telmessus
Tlos

RHODES

0   50 *kms* 100

MEDITERRAN

8

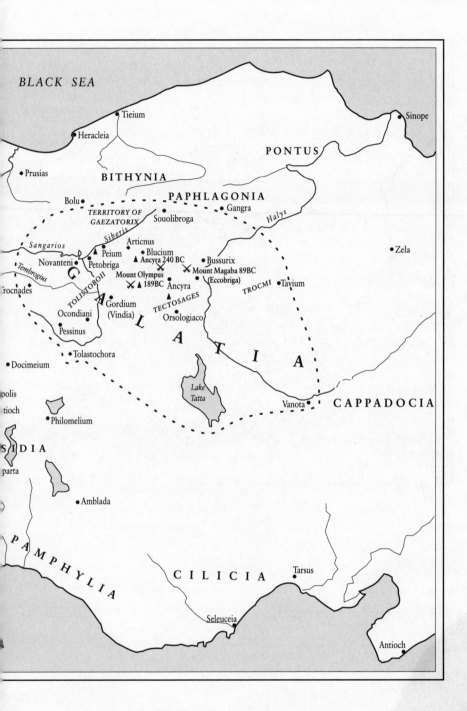

BLACK SEA

Tieium

Sinope

Heracleia

PONTUS

Prusias

BITHYNIA

PAPHLAGONIA

Bolu

*TERRITORY OF
GAEZATORIX*   Souolibroga   Gangra

Siberis   *Halys*

Sangarios   Articnus

Zela

Peium   Blucium

Novanteni   Petobriga   Ancyra 240 BC   Bussurix

Tembrogius   Mount Magaba 89BC
                (Eccobriga)

Crocnades   Mount Olympus   TROCMI   Tavium

TOLISTOBOII   189BC   Ancyra

G   Gordium   *TECTOSAGES*

Ocondiani   (Vindia)   Orsologiaco

Pessinus   A   L

Tolastochora   A   T   I   A

Docimeium

*Lake
Tatta*

polis

tioch   Vanota   CAPPADOCIA

Philomelium

SIDIA

parta

Amblada

PAMPHYLIA   CILICIA   Tarsus

Seleuceia

Antioch

9

[1]

The Battle of Thermopylae

THE sun was rising over Thermopylae that late summer morning in the year 279BC. Thermopylae lay between the cliffs of Mount Oeta and the waters of the Malian Gulf, a narrow pass linking the states of Thessaly and Locris, in east central Greece. The name meant 'hot gates' after the hot volcanic springs which had been famed for their healing qualities since time immemorial. Today, the sea has receded somewhat making it difficult for modern visitors to see just how narrow and strategic the coastal road used to be. It was the entrance from the north to the riches of southern Greece, a critical pass for whoever sought to control the power of the city states of the Peloponnese such as Corinth, Argos and Sparta. It was the pivotal route to the affluent Greek heartland; it gave access to the fertile plains of Boeotia, famous for its horse breeding as well as its great wheat fields, and to the mountains of Attica, where the great cultural centre of Athens lay, where the silver mines of Laurium, the lead mines and marble quarries were situated, and where many rich temples, such as those of Sunium, contained a fabulous treasure.

Invaders had fought hard to wrest control of Thermopylae on several occasions. It was here that Leonidas of Sparta had vainly tried to hold back the Persian invasion of Xerxes in 480BC, and the Athenians had succeeded in holding back Philip of Macedonia in 352BC. It would also be here that the legions of Rome would secure a decisive dominance over Greece and parts of Asia Minor by defeating the armies of Antiochos of Syria in 195BC.

This particular summer day in 279BC two armies were gathered at the pass once again to do combat and, as before, the riches of Greece were the prize. The defending army was commanded by Callippos, son of Moerocles of Athens. He had over 25,000 men at his command; the majority were infantry with perhaps 2000 cavalry, though there was little room for the use of cavalry in the pass. His army was made up of contingents from Athens, from Phocis, Aetolia, Boeotia and the island of Atalanta, and smaller contingents from Macedonia, Syria and the Greek cities of Asia Minor.

Facing the Greeks was an army of Celts commanded by Brennos and Acichorios. Brennos, a name recorded by the Greeks, might well have been simply a title rather than a proper name: *brenin* was the Celtic word for 'king', a word still surviving in modern Welsh. According to Strabo (64BC–after AD24) from Amasia in Pontus: 'Brennos, the man who led the attack on Delphi, is said by some to have been a Prausian, but I am unable to say of the Prausians where on earth they lived before.' There seems no other reference to the Celtic Prausi. If we are to believe Pausanias, the Celtic army was over 200,000 strong. However, this figure is more likely to be an overall estimate for all the Celts moving into the Greek peninsula at this time. Another source mentions some 40,000 around Thermopylae and this is a more creditable figure for those involved in the actual battle.

The Celtic invaders were no unknown quantity to the Greeks. While it was the Greeks who had first recorded the name Keltoi (Celt) as the name of the people who now confronted them, to most Greeks of that period they were better known as Galatae. Both names were used interchangeably. Pausanias, a doctor from Greek Asia Minor, living in the 2nd century AD, states: 'It was quite late on that "Gauls" became their agreed name; in ancient times they called each other Celts, and other people called them the same.' Greek travellers and writers had been describing the Celts in their works for centuries before that summer day at Thermopylae. Indeed, groups of Celts had been serving as mercenary troops in the Greek city states for over a century. In 366BC some 2000 Celtic mercenaries had distinguished themselves as cavalry in the Spartan army during the war against Thebes. They had played the decisive role in the battle of Maninea in 362BC.

The army of Callippos, general of the Athenians, was well aware that they were facing a fearsome fighting force. No less a person than Aristotle had once commented on Celtic bravery in battle, adding: 'We have no word for the man who is excessively fearless; perhaps one may call such a man mad, or bereft of feeling, who fears nothing, neither earthquakes nor waves, as they say of the Celts.'

This Celtic army of Brennos and Acichorios had already demonstrated its strength. For decades the Greeks had been aware of the
dangerous threat posed by the Celts on their northern borders. In
335/334BC Alexander of Macedon had decided to make a treaty
with them rather than attempt their conquest. It was in the turmoil
presented by the death of Alexander, and the disintegration of his
empire, that the Celts had started to move south into the Greek
peninsula.

According to Pausanias, who used earlier source material for his
Description of Greece, three Celtic armies, in loose confederation,
totalling 152,000 infantry and 61,200 cavalry, flooded into the Greek
states. The Sicilian Greek historian, Diodorus Siculus (c.60–30BC)
put the figures at 150,000 infantry and 10,000 cavalry, while Marcus
Junianus Justinus (Justin, in the 2nd/3rd century AD) says it was
150,000 infantry and 15,000 cavalry. While it has been accepted
that the Greek historians would have naturally inflated the figures
of the invasion force and deflated the numbers of the defenders, it
is worth pointing out that Justin's figures come from his abridgement
of the lost *Historiae Philippicae* by Pompeius Trogus, a Narbonese
Celt, albeit a 'Romanised' Celt, but who also used early Greek
sources.

The first of these three armies was commanded by a chieftain
called Cerethrios. The name is thought to be from the word *ceredig*
a rock. His army attacked through the country of the Triballi (now
Bulgaria). A western army led by Bolgios crossed into Macedonia
through Monastir. Bolgios had, at first, sent emissaries to negotiate
with the Macedon king, Ptolemy Ceraunnos, once a favourite cavalry
general of Alexander. Unwisely, the Macedon king treated the emissaries with contempt. Bolgios' army then descended into Macedonia
proper, defeated its army and slew Ptolemy Ceraunnos. Diodorus
Siculus claims that the Celts celebrated their victory by sacrificing
prisoners. The third and central army now entered Macedonia
through the hills of Haemos. This was the army of Brennos and
Acichorios.

Macedonia had fallen to the Celts. Then Thessaly fell. Still the
Celtic army moved resolutely southwards until they came to a halt
before the waters of the turbulent river Spercheios. As in all wars
since time began, atrocity stories were rife. According to Greek
sources, the Celts inflicted terrible outrages on the population. They

were even accused of cannibalism. It was said that they ate any hapless Greek child who fell into their clutches. Moreover, it was asserted that they did not even stop to bury the dead, not even their own dead. To Greek perceptions, this was inhuman as it meant that the souls of the unburied dead would become earthbound and haunt the land. Such stories were later refined into the Greek version of the invasion.

Pausanias observes:

> The Greek spirit had sunk right down, but the power of fear forced them to realise that Greece must fight. They saw that this struggle was not about freedom as it once was against Persia: it was not going to be enough now to offer earth and water. What had happened to Macedonia, to Thrace, to Paeonia, in the previous onslaught of the Celts, was still in their memory, and news came of the outrages that were now being committed in Thessaly. Every man as an individual and every city collectively had realised that the Greeks must overcome or be destroyed.

It was on the banks of the Spercheios that the advance units of the hastily gathered Greek confederated army of Callippos had their first encounter with the Celtic warriors. Callippos, having discovered that the Celts were already at Magnesia and at Phthia, ordered 1000 infantry and his main body of cavalry to the river. They destroyed the bridges across the tumultuous waters but then made the mistake of confidently camping on the opposite bank of the Spercheios, believing the rough waters would be enough to keep the *barbaroi* at bay.

But, as Pausanias admits: 'Brennos was not so barbarous as to be completely unsophisticated or wholly inexperienced in the contrivances of war.' Detachments of Celtic warriors – Pausanias puts their number at an incredible 10,000 – foraged downstream, finding calmer waters, and, using their long shields as rafts, they crossed and came up behind the Greek encampment.

Pausanias has it that the men picked by Brennos for this task were those who could swim or those who were tall, adding, 'Celts are the tallest people in the world.' The area where they crossed was where the Spercheios broadened out over level ground and formed a marshy lake instead of the narrow violent waters.

The Greeks were put to flight while the Celts then set about rebuilding the bridges. Brennos ordered several diversionary raids to encourage the Greeks to believe that his main army had already crossed the river. He did this so that his army would not suffer an attack during the actual crossing when it would be extremely vulnerable. His men now worked hard to accomplish the crossing. Had Callippos attacked at this dangerous point for the Celts then history might have been different. The Athenian general chose to keep his army at the pass of Thermopylae and regroup. Greek triremes, standard Greek warships with three banks of oars, were now moving north, along the coast, to protect the Athenian right flank from the seaward side.

With the withdrawal of the Greek army from the Spercheios, the nearby city of Heracleia lay at the mercy of Celtic attack. The citizens had shut the gates and prepared for a siege. At this point the general-ship of Brennos and Acichorios is shown to be excellent for, instead of wasting time in attempting to reduce Heracleia, they merely bypassed it, posting units of their army to keep the citizens penned in, but preferring to march forward to where the Athenian-led army were grouping.

Brennos and Acichorios reached the pass at Thermopylae within a few days of crossing the Spercheios and they took up positions at the northern end. Pausanias admits that Brennos knew the Greek order of battle from deserters.

The steep slopes of Otea and Callidromos and the rough terrain were not good from the Celtic point of view. The Celts were renowned as cavalry tacticians and they excelled in their use of war chariots. Horses were essential to most Celtic armies. Pausanias says: 'Cavalry was no use on either side because Thermopylae is a narrow pass and the ground is broken and slippery, a continuous series of streams among rocky outcrops.'

Pausanias knew that the Celts relied heavily on their cavalry and he describes the cavalry through Greek cultural perceptions in these terms:

To each mounted warrior were attached two servants, who were themselves skilled riders and, like their masters, had a horse. When the Celtic cavalry were in battle, the servants remained behind the ranks and proved useful in the following way. Should a horseman or his horse fall, the slave brought him a horse to mount; if the rider was killed, the slave mounted the horse in his master's place; if both rider and horse were killed, there was a mounted man ready. When a rider was wounded, one slave brought back to camp the wounded man, while the other took his vacant place in the ranks ... This organisation is called in their own language *trimarcisia*, for I would have you know that *marca* is the Celtic name for a horse.

This fighting unit did not consist of master and slaves. They were a coequal combat unit. Pausanias' description of its function, however, is quite accurate, and *marca* is still easily identifiable as the Celtic word for horse in *march* (Welsh), *margh* (Cornish) and *marc'h* (Breton).

At the battle of Thermopylae, the Celtic cavalry and war chariots were therefore rendered useless. The main fighting was to fall on the infantry. Apart from Brennos and Acichorios, we know the names of only two other Celtic commanders at Thermopylae. They were Comboutis and Orestorios. One wonders if Camboutis might be a mistranscription of Camboulos?

On the Greek side, Callippos and his Athenians, some 1000 infantry, took pride of place in the battle line. He had doubtless sent his 500 cavalry to the rear. The largest force in the army were Boeotians with 10,000 infantry and 500 cavalry commanded by Cephisodotos, Thearides, Diogenes and Lysander. It was, after all, the country of Boeotia which stood at the end of the pass if the Celts broke through. The Aetolians had 7000 infantry and 790 light infantry commanded by Polyarchos, Polyphron and Lacrates. They also had an unspecified number of cavalry. Phocis had sent the next largest contingent with 3000 infantry and 500 cavalry commanded by Critoboulos and Antiochos. The island of Atalante, between the mainland and north Euboea, had sent 700 infantry under Meidias. There were 500 Macedonians under Aristodemos, and a similar number from the Greek states in Asia Minor under Telesarchos.

It was Callippos who began the action on the first day. We are told that just after sunrise, he ordered his advance units to march, with spear and shield, on the Celtic formations. Pausanias seems to imply a curious criticism of Brennos when he says 'even supposing the Celts have some art of divination of their own, Brennos had no

Greek soothsayer and made no concession to local religious observ-
ance' before joining battle. Pausanias' sources for his description
could well include the works of Timaeus (c.356–260BC), who was
living in Athens at the time of the battle. Another source was
undoubtedly the contemporary writer Hieronymus of Cardia whose
lost histories are also quoted by many others such as Plutarch and
Diodorus Siculus.

These Greek historians observe that the Greek infantry advanced
quietly and in good order. Pausanias says that the Celts fought
impressively. Indeed, the Celtic warriors must have appeared fearsome to the Greeks. 'Their arms correspond in size with their
physique,' wrote Strabo. 'A long sword fastened on the right side
and a long shield, and spears of like dimension.'

Examples of Celtic shields, at this time, have been found to average
3 feet 9 inches in length and they were oval in shape. Spears have
been found as long as 8 feet while swords varied from the short
stabbing sword, later adopted by the Romans as the *gladius*, to the
long, slashing swords. By the 4th century BC, the weak bronze helmets of the Celts had given way to iron war helmets, often with
hinged cheek-pieces.

It was around 300BC that the Celts appear to have invented 'chain-
mail' and began to wear shirts made of individually forged inter-
locking iron rings, which required a high standard of the blacksmith's
craft. Being labour intensive, they were usually worn by leading
chieftains and warriors. Most warriors fought with no armour at all
and some Celts fought naked for religious reasons.

According to Diodorus Siculus:

Their armour includes man-sized shields decorated in individual
fashion. Some of them have projecting bronze animals of fine
workmanship . . . On their heads they wear bronze helmets which
possess large projecting figures lending the appearance of enormous stature to the wearer. In some cases horns form one part
with the helmet, while in other cases it is relief figures of the fore
parts of birds or quadrupeds. Their trumpets are again of a peculiar barbaric kind . . . and produce a harsh sound which suits the
tumult of war. Some have iron breastplates of chain-mail, while
others fight naked.

Pausanias, however, describing the battle at Thermopylae, is naturally biased:

> The Celts were worse armed than the Greeks. The traditional oblong shields were all the protection their bodies had ... they rushed on their enemies with the unreasoning fury and passion of wild beasts. They had no kind of reasoning at all. They slashed with axe or sword and blind fury never left them until they were killed. Some of them even pulled the spears they were hit with out of their wounds and threw them back at their enemies or used them in close fighting.

Leaving aside Pausanias' partisanship, the battle was certainly heated. Fighting lasted all day and casualties were heavy on both sides. At one point, Callippos ordered the Athenian naval force to row along the coast in shallow waters and attack the flank of the Celtic army using their bows, arrows and sling shots. According to Pausanias:

> The Athenian warships with some difficulty and danger sailed in through the mudbanks that stretched far out to sea, and held their ships close inshore, bombarding the flank of the Celtic army with arrows and sling shots.

For a while the Celts were hard pressed, Brennos ordering one section of his men to turn to face this new threat and advance towards them. This was a mistake. As the Celtic warriors moved down to the seashore to closely engage the Greek ships, the warriors stumbled into a coastal marshland, caused by the silting of the coast, and they became bogged down in its mud. Here they became easy targets and Brennos had to withdraw them.

Night fell and the Celtic and Greek armies retired to their camps to reassess their respective positions. Pausanias tries to give the Greeks an advantage.

> The Celts were indescribably tired, and, being in a narrow place, they had little effect while they suffered two or three times as much, so their commanders gave them the signal to retreat to camp. As they turned away in broken ranks and no kind of order,

many of them were trampled under each others' feet, and many went into the swamp and disappeared in the mud; as many of them perished in the retreat as died in the height of the battle.

Pausanias claims that only forty Greeks perished in the battle. If the Greeks had such a clear advantage then surely they would have followed up the Celtic retreat and taken advantage of the rout suggested by Pausanias. This did not happen. The battle of Thermopylae was not won on that first day. The Greeks were equally exhausted and also retreated to their encampment.

Callippos had retrieved the shield of a young Athenian named Cydias, who had fought with bravery in his first and last battle. Praising him as an icon of resistance, the Athenians took his shield and dedicated it to the resurgence of Greece in the temple of Zeus Eleuthrios in Athens. The dedication bore this inscription:

The shield of a brave man, Zeus's offspring, aches for the lost youth of Cydias: this is the first shield to hang on his left arm when the battle against the Celts was at its zenith.

The inscription was still in Athens in Pausanias' day but two centuries after the battle the shield itself was stolen by the Roman general Lucius Cornelius Sulla (c.138–78BC) when he was campaigning in Greece.

Pausanias says:

After the battle the Greeks buried their dead and stripped the barbarians, but the Celts sent no herald for the taking of their dead, not caring whether they were buried or fed wild animals and the birds who make war on corpses. This neglect of giving graves to those who had passed away was for two reasons I think: to astound their enemies, and because they have no natural pity for the dead.

Neither reason seems to fit in with what we know of the Celtic religious observances and their behaviour in battle. If they did leave their dead on the field of battle it was because the battle was not yet over. The first stage had simply been a draw. Neither side had gained any advantage.

There followed a week of raids, skirmishing and minor ambushes, during which both commanders probed for each other's weak points. Like Xerxes and his Persians before him, Brennos realised that the Greeks were in a strong position in the narrow pass. No matter how many warriors he could throw against them, a few Greeks could hold the narrow front of the pass protected by the sheer rocky outcrops of the mountains on one side and the mud-flats and sea on the other. Once again, the figure of the Celtic commander, Brennos, emerges as a strategist of no mean ability and one who obviously knew Greek politics. He knew that the union of the Greek city states in the face of the Celtic invasion was only a temporary phenomenon. After Alexander, the Greek states had once more fallen into warring factions, each distrusting the others. Brennos conceived a plan to split the alliance. He ordered Camboutis and Orestorios to take 40,000 infantry and 800 cavalry (Greek sources are curiously fond of using the figure of 40,000 for every division of the Celtic forces) and to return across the river Spercheios, striking west into Aetolia.

Aetolia, after Alexander's death, had re-emerged as a dominant military power in central Greece. The Aetolian Confederacy or League was governed by an assembly of all free citizens who annually elected a general as their leader; he ruled with a small council, the *apokletoi*. Aetolia had only a decade before occupied Delphi, the most sacred spot in Greece. For this, the Aetolians were not well liked by other Greek powers. Knowing that a large contingent of Aetolians were serving with Callippos, Brennos decided to ensure that news of his raids into Aetolia became known to them.

Pausanias was to relish the gory details of the stories which were now circulating:

It was Camboutis and Orestorios who committed the atrocities on the Callians, the most horrifying wickedness I have heard of, not the crimes of human beings at all.

The city of Calydon lay in western Aetolia, almost at the mouth of the Gulf of Corinth.

Every male they put to the sword, and there were butchered old men equally with children at their mothers' breasts. The more plump of these sucking babes the Celts killed, drinking their blood and eating their flesh.

As similar stories were told about the Persian invasions by the historian Herodotus (c.490–425BC), and later of the Roman invasions, one would not expect the Celts to be an exception to the propaganda rule.

However, stories reached Callippos' army that the women of Calydon were running themselves on to the Celts' swords rather than be taken alive. Again, the atrocity tales closely parallel those given by Herodotus for the Persian invasion. As Pausanias enthuses:

Any women and mature virgins with a spark of pride killed themselves as soon as the city fell; those who lived were subjected with wanton violence to every form of outrage by men as remote from mercy as they were remote from love. Women who came on a Celtic sword committed suicide with their own hands; it was not long before the others were to die by famishing hunger and sleeplessness, outraged in an endless succession by pitiless and barbarous men; they mated with the dying; they mated with the already dead.

The Celtic cavalry certainly plundered Aetolia with impunity. As Aetolia was one of the strongest military states of Greece at the time, this is a fact to be commented on. The main assembly of Aetolia (the *synhedrion*), totalling 1000 representatives, consisted of delegations in proportion to their military strength. The Aetolian military muster, therefore, was a large one. As news of the Celtic campaign came to their ears, Aetolians serving in Callippos' army immediately left and set out in defence of their homeland. These were the 8000 men commanded by Polyarchos, Polyphron and Lacrates.

Brennos had succeeded in substantially reducing the numbers of the Greek army opposing him.

The Aetolians, receiving news of the calamities in their own land, at once raced with speed from Thermopylae. They were outraged over the fate of Callian [Calydon] but anxious to preserve other cities which, never before in history, had been threatened by any army. From every part of Aetolia everyone able to bear arms came out to fight for every city, the very old mixed among them and even the women were willing to serve beside the men, driven by a deeper rage against the Celts than even their husbands.

As soon as Camboutis and Orestorios had set fire to Calydon, they turned back towards Thermopylae, presumably as instructed by Brennos. On the return, they met a small army of Patrians, members of the Achaean League, of which Aetolia was a member. 'This force suffered badly from the numbers and desperation of the Celts,' says Pausanias, presumably meaning that the Patrians were defeated. Again, however, he claims that Camboutis and Orestorios lost half of their force (20,000 men) on the return from Aetolia.

Elsewhere he makes this comment:

The Patrians alone of the Achaean League went into Aetolia on their own volition, out of friendship with the Aetolians, to help them against the Celts. But they fought battles more disastrous than I can describe, and most of the people were stricken by poverty, so that all but a few of them abandoned Patria. They scattered over the countryside in search of work.

Meanwhile Brennos' scouts had brought him news of a mountain pass which crossed Mount Oeta and which could only be traversed on foot. It was a narrow path leading behind Heracleia to the ruins of Trachis which was then a sanctuary to Athena. The place was actually the setting of *Trachiniae* by Sophocles (c.496–406BC), about the death of Heracles. The acropolis of Trachis had, in fact, become the town of Heracleia. If followed, this pass would enable the Celts to outflank Callippos. It was, indeed, the very same route which Xerxes and his Persians had used 200 years before when Hydarnes and the Persian Immortals were sent to outflank Leonidas and his Spartans. Leonidas and a rearguard of 300 Spartans made their heroic last stand to allow the rest of the Greek army to withdraw.

Whether Brennos led a detachment of his men in person over this route on Mount Oeta is unclear. However, the Celts moved up across the mountain and came to a temple of Athena. We are told that Callippos, doubtless remembering Xerxes' flanking movement, had posted a garrison there consisting of the volunteers from Asia Minor commanded by Telesarchos. The Celts assaulted the position and, it seems, Telesarchos did not have time to send warnings to Callippos. Once more Pausanias claims that 'Telesarchos defeated the barbarians in battle but Telesarchos fell fighting, he was devoted to Greece.' This 'victory' is a little hard to accept for the Celts were then able to continue unimpeded over the mountain pass and come down at the rear of the Greek army.

A second route had also been opened up for Brennos over Mount Oeta through the country of the Ainianians. This second route, Pausanias admits, was easier for the warriors to use than the one by Trachis. 'The Ainianians and Heracleians were induced to take Brennos by this route, not from ill-will to Greece but out of concern that the Celts should march out of their country and not hang about to ruin them. I think Pindar was right as usual about this when he said every man feels his own problems, but other people's problems do not bother them.' Pausanias claims that Brennos now left Acichorios in charge of the main army facing Callippos. Greek sources claim that 40,000 Celts (again that magical figure and a rather staggering achievement if it were true) moved along the narrow mountain tracks.

The Celtic descent behind the rear of Callippos' army was made in an early morning mist, which hid the warriors from the Greeks until the attack began. Pausanias says: 'It happened on that day that a mist rolled down the mountain and darkened the sun: so the Phocians who were guarding the paths [presumably Callippos had positioned a rearguard on the path at the back of his army] saw nothing until the Celts were upon them.' The fighting was fierce. Celtic war horns sounded the signal for the main attack. Acichorios began to push forward on the Greek front while Brennos led the attack on the rear.

'They put up a stiff resistance,' says Pausanias of the Greeks, 'but in the end they were forced to withdraw.'

Callippos, painfully aware of the disaster which had overwhelmed Leonidas and his Spartans, realised the perilousness of his position. He was encircled. Fighting every inch of the way, he managed to withdraw the majority of his army to the Athenian ships, which came in close to shore and evacuated the soldiers while trying to keep up a steady fire from bows and sling shots. The Celts followed them into the sea, fighting even as the Greeks clambered into the ships.

'The Athenian warships withdrew the Greek army from Thermopylae in time. The Greeks scattered to their own cities,' admits Pausanias, contradicting his previous claims of a Greek victory.

The Athenians turned their defeat into a rally symbol, calling for the unity of the city states against the invaders. Pausanias is emphatic in claiming victory at this point, glossing over Callippos' evacuation of the pass. It was a harsh fact for the Greeks that their army had been vanquished by the mere *barbaroi*. Even Callippos was honoured as a hero afterwards when his portrait was painted by one Olbiades, a painter of whom nothing is known, in the sanctuary of the temple of Athena at Athens. There was a graphic wall painting of the battle at Thermopylae, depicting it as a Greek victory, in the council chamber of Athens for many centuries.

The reality was that in the late summer of 279BC, the pass at Thermopylae lay open and undefended. The road to the rich Greek city states of the south was undefended. All Greece now lay helpless before the Celts.

The choice lay with Brennos and Acichorios. Would they, flushed with victory, now march on Athens?

[2]

Celt Meets Greek

A T the start of the 6th century BC two expanding European
cultures came into contact with one another. One had its
origins north of the Alps in west central Europe, the other in
the eastern Mediterranean. They were the Celts and the Greeks.

By this time a colonial expansion of the Greek states, both eastward into Asia Minor and westward to Italy, Sicily and along the
northern coast of Africa, had occurred. The expansion had been
motivated by trade and Greek merchants had established many
colonies which, in turn, became politically independent of their
mother-states. In the 7th century BC, the Greeks had opened Egypt
to world trade and settlers from Miletus founded a colony on the
Canopic (western) branch of the Nile, in the Egyptian Delta, which
they named Naucratis (sea queen). This became the seaport through
which trade with Egypt was conducted. Naucratis remained the principal *emporion*, or trading settlement, from c.620BC until Alexander
the Great founded the city of Alexandria in 332BC. The Greek colonists also moved west along the coast to Libya and founded another
important trading port at Cyrene in about 630BC.

It was during this expansion that the Greeks first began to encounter the Celtic civilisation.

According to Herodotus of Halicarnassus (c.490–c.425BC), it was
a merchant from Samos named Colaeus, trading along the African
coast, who first made contact. About the same year that Cyrene was
founded, 630BC, his ship was driven off course. The tides and winds
swept him beyond the Pillars of Heracles (Gibraltar) into the Atlantic
and he eventually made landfall at the mouth of the Tartessus, the
modern river Guadalquivir, in whose valley stand the modern cities
of Cordoba and Seville. The mouth of the river was just north of
Gades (Cadiz) a trading colony founded at the beginning of the first
millennium BC by the Phoenicians. Herodotus implies that the Celtic

lands were situated just north of Gades at this time, stating that 'the Celts are outside the Pillars of Heracles'.

The valley of the Tartessus was very rich in silver. The Celts, who had been settled in the area for at least three centuries, were exploiting the mines. Colaeus believed that he was the first to open this market to the Mediterranean world. We are told that he returned to Samos and, in celebration, gave a gift to the temple of Hera of a bronze mixing bowl in Argolic style with griffin heads around the rim, which was supported by three 10 foot tall figures in kneeling postures.

Shortly after Colaeus returned to Samos, merchants from Phocis, in central Greece, in which land was situated the great sanctuary of Delphi – 'the navel of the world', according to the Greeks – began to arrive at Tartessus. About 600BC they made a treaty with the local Celtic king who helped them build their settlements. This king's name was Arganthonios. The name obviously derives from the Celtic word for silver, *aganto*. According to Herodotus, he lived for 120 years and his name became a byword for longevity. He is said to have died in 564BC.

The Greek merchants of Phocis, using penteconters, swift galleys manned by fifty oars, began to take a leading part in opening up trade with the Iberian Celts. Herodotus comments that the Phocian merchants used these warships, rather than more cumbersome merchant ships, because they sought to dominate the trade routes. Warships rather than merchant ships thus kept rivals out of the trading colonies.

Through the western Mediterranean the ships of Phocis now set up colonies, including settlements in Sardinia and Corsica, but these colonies were quickly overrun by the more powerful Etruscans and Carthaginians. Carthage was a city founded on the North African coast in 814BC by Phoenician settlers from Tyre, in what is now Lebanon. One Phocian colony, founded at the start of the 6th century BC, was Massilia (Marseilles) on the southern coast of what is now France. It was built just east of the river Rhône in what became regarded as the Celtic heartland – Gaul.

Massilia lay in the land of the Segobrigai and there is some discussion as to whether they, in spite of their Celtic name, were a Celtic or Ligurian people. The element *sego* is much attested in Celtic names and means 'strength, vigour, boldness or daring'. The second element *briga* means 'exalted, high'. So we have a people who called themselves perhaps 'exalted for daring or strength'. The Ligurians were another branch of Indo-European peoples situated around what is now the Gulf of Genova. However, the story of the foundation of Massilia, given by Aristotle and in variation by Pompeius Trogus, gives names that are found among Celts and I believe we may take it that the Segobrigai were, indeed, Celts.

The story goes that Euxenes of Phocis, one of those founding the colony, was invited to be the guest of Namos (he who distributes), the king of the Segobrigai. His daughter, Petta, attending the feast, gave a bowl of wine mixed with water to Euxenes as a symbol that she had chosen him in marriage. Euxenes took her as his wife, changing her name to Aristoxene, and they had a son, Protos, who became progenitor of the leading family of Massilia. In this story we may have a foundation myth which has a parallel in the foundation myth of the Cruithin or Picti, where the king took his wife from outside his clan or group and received the alliance and blessing of his wife's clan.

When Namos died, however, he was succeeded by a king called Canamos (perhaps, he who loves to distribute) who became an enemy of the Greek Massiliots. On a Greek festival day he tried, unsuccessfully, to infiltrate his warriors into the city to overthrow it. After that, for a while, relations between the Greek colony and surrounding peoples seemed to be cordial and prosperous.

It is no coincidence that archaeologists have noticed that during the last phase of the Celtic Hallstatt D period (c.600–475BC) there is a new concentration of rich graves along the Rhône valley and adjacent Celtic areas. Dr Simon James, of the British Museum, argues that the reason for the increased riches was the establishment of Massilia. The Rhône gave access to the major waterway routes connecting the other Celtic territories along the Rhine, Seine, Loire and Danube. It is clear that the Celts were deriving great benefit from the trade with Greece. Luxury goods from Greece and other Mediterranean colonies begin to appear in Celtic graves as tokens of their owner's wealth and position.

The spectacular burial chamber at Vix, near Mont Lasois, in France, discovered in 1957, is one such example. It is a chariot burial of a female chieftain, probably of the Aedui tribe. She was thirty to thirty-five years old and her burial is dated about 500BC. She has a beautifully wrought gold torque, weighing 480 grams, which shows her position in life. Among the grave goods, and indicative of the new trade, stands a bronze *krater* which was for mixing and containing wine and which was made in Sparta. It is decorated with Spartan warriors, chariots and gorgons, and its manufacture is dated to 550BC. It stands 1.5 metres high and has a capacity of 1250 litres.

In turn, the Greek world bought minerals, gold, silver, lead, tin and iron, as well as agricultural produce, from the Celts. They also gained more knowledge of the Celts, and their mystic concepts of the Hypoboreans became more informed. It was from the work of Hecataeus of Miletus (*c*.500–476BC) and of Herodotus of Halicarnassus (*c*.490–425BC) that the Greeks first began to hear of the Keltoi. It is a curious coincidence that 300 years after Hecataeus had made the Greeks aware of the Celts, the Celts arrived at the very gates of his native city of Miletus in order to seek plunder. Miletus was mentioned in Homer's *Iliad*. It was a city near the mouth of the river Maeander in Asia Minor, monopolising trade in the Black Sea area. It was one of the most important of early Greek cities, founding colonies at Abydos, Cyzicus, Sinope, Diocurias, Panticapaeum and Oblia. Its trade extended throughout the known world and one of its citizens, Anaximander (*c*.610–545BC), the first Greek known to have written a book in prose, produced the first map of the world that we know of. The city produced many philosophers, poets and historians.

Hecataeus was born shortly after Anaximander's pioneering work and when he came to write his own *Histories* he used Anaximander as a source. Hecataeus also produced what is regarded as the second map of the world, in which he showed it as a flat, circular earth with a hole in the middle representing the 'middle earth' or Mediterranean. His *Histories* are now lost but we have some 331 fragments of his work and in these we find the first mention of the Celts.

Among these fragments, quoted in Strabo – who says they come from Hecataeus' work *Europe* – we find a reference to 'Nyrax, a Celtic city'. This has never been identified but various suggestions have been made such as Noreia, in central Austria, which was certainly in the Celtic heartland at this time. He also mentions the market city of the Celts, Narbon, which is probably Narbonne. Finally, he mentions the Greek colony of Massilia as being located near the territory of the Celts.

It was Herodotus of Halicarnassus, by coincidence another city in Asia Minor – this time on the south coast near the island of Cos – who mentions in his *Historiai* that 'the Danube traverses the whole of Europe, rising among the Celts . . .' He compared the Danube to the Nile and he also states elsewhere that the Celts were, during his day, already settled in Iberia, living outside the Pillars of Heracles. As separate pieces of intelligence, they are accurate enough.

The Greeks had some idea of the vast extent of the Celtic world. Ephoros of Cyme (*c*.405–330BC) described it as a territory the size of the Indian sub-continent, a fact criticised by Strabo. But Dr Rankin has dismissed Strabo's objection and believes that, at this time, Ephoros was not excessively exaggerating.

The first explorer to voyage to Britain and Ireland from the Hellenic sphere of influence was a Phoenician. He was a Carthaginian explorer named Himilco, about 500BC. The Greeks knew of his voyage and his account of it, which is now lost. Eratosthenes (*c*.275–195BC) of Cyrene, librarian to Ptolemy III, Pharaoh of Egypt, made a translation of the account into Greek. This, too, has been lost.

However, about AD366, the proconsul for Africa, one Rufus Festus Avienus, a native of Volsinii (Bolsena), wrote a work called *Ora Maritima*, a description of the shores of the known world, and this is regarded as being a reworking from Eratosthenes' translation, though some argue that Avienus used several sources and that it is basically a compendium of many works. Avienus had certainly translated other works before his *Ora Maritima*, such as those of the Greek Aratus, who spent some of his life under the patronage of Antigonus Gonatus of Macedonia. Most scholars believe that Avienus did copy Eratosthenes' work but not directly. It is argued that he used a copy made by Dionysius Periegtes in the 2nd century AD.

Dr H. D. Rankin has observed:

We shall not be incautious, I suggest, if we accept that Avienus is the carrier of some very early information about the Celts in the Classical world. I say this not so much in spite of his pompous and pawky style, as because of it: in concentrating on his own erudite image of himself and grasping with the technical problems of versification, he probably left himself less time for the pure distortion of facts, though we may possibly have to fear some parallax effect inherited from translators who in some instances came between the Greek originals and his staid iambics.

If we are looking at a record of Himilco's voyage in the late 6th century BC, and Dr Rankin is certainly of the opinion that Avienus' information 'has an atmosphere of the archaic', it is interesting that Himilco omits the Celts from his list of people on the western coast of the Iberian peninsula. Yet we know from Herodotus that some fifty years after Himilco's voyage the Celts were certainly in residence there. If the names have been transcribed correctly from Himilco's original text, it is from his voyage that we first learn of the Albiones (in Britain) and the Hierni (in Ireland). According to Avienus' version:

> ... the isles, Oestrymnides, raise their heads. Scattered they lie, and rich in metals, tin and lead. A vigorous race inhabits them, noble minded and skilful at their trades. All along the mountain range business is carried on. And in their well-known skiffs they widely plough the turbid sea. And the storm-pit of the monster-tenanted ocean. These folk indeed do not build their keels of pine, nor do they know how to fashion them, neither do they round their barks from fir as is the common practice, but with wondrous skill they make each skiff with skins bound together, and often in their hide-bound craft, skim o'er the mighty deep.

This sounds a remarkable early description of the Welsh coracle or Irish curragh.

> From here, a two-day sail, the sacred Island lies (for by this name the ancients knew it) rich in green sward amid the waves it lies, peopled thickly by the folk of the Hierni. Near them lies the broad isle of the Albiones.

The Greeks continued to build contacts through the Celtic world, opening trading links. Indeed, we are told by Strabo, Diodorus Siculus and the Elder Pliny that in the 4th century BC an explorer named Pytheas from Massilia also made a voyage along the west coast of Europe to the islands of Britain (Brettanike) and Ireland (Iverni) and circumnavigated them. He also named a land called Thule, six days' sail north of Britain, where, he said, the sun at midsummer did not set. Eratosthenes of Cyrene drew his Arctic circle through it while Ptolemy (c.AD 100–178) believed Thule to be the Shetlands.

Unfortunately the complete text of Pytheas' work is lost but scholars have argued that when Ptolemy around AD 100 came to do his survey of the British Isles, he based his account on Pytheas' work. There are several reasons for assuming this. In Ireland's case Ptolemy's geographical and tribal names do not seem modern enough for AD 100, as if Ptolemy was describing a more ancient period. Professor Thomas O'Rahilly believes that Ptolemy's use of Pytheas' information would explain matters. Pytheas was not sufficiently expert to make the detailed measurements of latitude and longitude which appear in Ptolemy's work, but O'Rahilly suggests that Pytheas' work contained a map or maps of the islands without parallels or meridians and that these were calculated by Ptolemy at a later period.

In fact, Dr H. Bradley (in *Archaeologia* vol. xlviii) suggested that Ptolemy had three early maps of the British Isles before him when he was drawing up his map. These would have been of southern Britain, northern Britain and of Ireland. Dr Bradley suggests that 'in fitting the three maps together Ptolemy (or his predecessor) fell into the mistake of turning the oblong map of Scotland the wrong way.' His is a reasonable suggestion as to why Scotland, on Ptolemy's map, moves off at 45 degrees from the rest of Britain, an obvious error.

From Pytheas' information, the Greek world became aware of these north-western extremities of the Celtic world and Pytheas spoke of trade links with Britain. In the 1st century BC, his fellow Greek, Diodorus Siculus, described a flourishing trade with the British Celts.

The inhabitants of that part of Britain which is called Belerion [perhaps Land's End] are very fond of strangers, and from their intercourse with foreign merchants, are civilised in their manner of life. They prepare the tin, working very carefully the earth in which it is produced. The ground is rock, but it contains earthy veins, the produce of which is ground down, smelted and purified. They beat the metal into masses like astragali and carry it to a certain island lying off Britain called Ictis ... here then the merchants buy the tin from the natives and carry it over to Gaul, and after travelling over land for about thirty days, they finally bring their loads on horse to the mouth of the Rhône.

In Dr Edward Gwynn's *Poems from the Dindshenchas* there is reference to a medieval Irish poem which speaks of foreign traders attending the great Fair of Carman and has the lines:

> *marggad mór na nGall nGrécach*
> *i mbid ór is ardd-étach*

which he translates as:

> the great market of the Greek Gauls
> where are gold and fine raiment.

Gwynn comments that this suggests 'a traditional memory of traders from Marseilles'. This would certainly be a fascinating folk memory but other scholars are not sure, believing that the words are actually mistranscriptions of *Gall* (foreigners) and *gréagach* (exquisite).

This trade with the Celts also brought early Greek 'ethnologists' with it, determined to report back to their fellows all the information they could gather.

The Greeks created their own Celtic origin myths. Timaeus (*c*.356–260BC), the Greek historian from Sicily, who settled in Athens and was there during the Celtic invasion, claimed the Celts were descendants of Polyphemus, an ugly Cyclops and son of the sea god Poseidon and a woman called Galatea (milk white). In some versions Polyphemus is replaced by a giant called Celtos. Ovid expands the story to say how Galatea loved a young shepherd named Acis. When Polyphemus discovered this, he hurled a great rock at Acis but to save him, before it fell, Galatea turned Acis into a river which henceforth bore his name. The versions given by Theocritus (*Idylls*), Virgil (*Eclogues*) and Ovid (*Metamorphoses*) all accord Galatea as the eponymous ancestor of the Celts. The English poet, John Gay, wrote a libretto to Handel's *Acis and Galatea*, which tells the story.

The theme of this myth is echoed by Diodorus Siculus, Pausanias and Ammianus Marcellinus (*c*.AD330–95), the Roman historian. They have a different version which seems older and is mentioned by Herodotus. They recount that Heracles, son of Zeus, in his wanderings in the west became the father of Celtos or Galatos.

This story was given poetic form by Pathenios of Apamea (1st century BC), a friend of the poet Gallus and the tutor of Virgil. Gallus was the scion of a Celtic family while Virgil, if not a Celt himself, was certainly raised in Celtic territory. Pathenios, in his *Erotica*, tells how Heracles was wandering through the Celtic country, performing his labour of bringing the cattle of Geryon from Erytheia. He was welcomed at the court of a Celtic king named Bretannos, at Alesia – the stronghold of the Mandubii on the plateau of Mont Auxois, some 30 miles north-west of Dijon. Bretannos had a daughter named Celtine. She fell in love with Heracles and hid his cattle. She would only reveal their whereabouts if Heracles made love to her. He did so and a son was born to them who was named Celtos and from whom the Celts were then said to have taken their name.

The Celts, thanks to the Greeks, became the first transalpine civilisation to take their place in recorded history. Strabo (*c.*64BC–AD21), who was from Pontus, next to Galatia, and who therefore must have known a great deal about his Celtic neighbours, points out that Celt or Keltoi was the ancient name for the Galatae whom the Romans also called Gauls and Galli. These names were all interchangeable.

The Celts lived in tribal societies as all Indo-European groups did. At the time when Celt and Greek first encountered one another, the Greeks were just emerging out of their tribal system (*phylai*). It was only in the 6th century BC that the reforms of Cleisthenes (*archon* of Athens from *c.*525BC to *c.*507BC) had begun to reform the Greek tribal system. Indeed, Poseidonius noted the similarities between the Celts of his day and the Homeric Greeks. They were divided into castes, as all Indo-Europeans were.

The Celtic tribes seem to have been more extensive than either the early Greek or Roman tribes. Diodorus Siculus says that Celtic tribes could vary from 50,000 to 200,000 *men*. If he is really enumerating just the men then we could be talking of tribes numbering in the millions. It has been estimated that the population of Gaul proper at the start of the Roman period was about 6–8 millions. Strabo comments that these tribes 'are wont to change their abode on slight provocation, migrating in bands with all their battle array, or rather setting out with their households when displaced by a stronger enemy.'

By the time they came into contact with Greek explorers and traders, the Celts were already spread in an arc from the Iberian peninsula through France, Belgium, Switzerland, Germany, Austria, northern Italy, Czechoslovakia, Hungary and touching the Balkans. It is generally agreed that the cradle of Celtic civilisation, their 'point of origin' as it were, was in the area around the headwaters of the Danube, the Rhine and the Rhône, all of which still bear their Celtic names. Here the Celtic names still proliferate. The Rhur, (roaring river), after which the Celtic tribe of the Raurici received their name, and the tributaries of most of the rivers within this area also retain their Celtic names. Labara means 'talking river'; Glan means 'clean river' and so on. Names of geographical features, mountains, rivers, forests, streams, territories and towns, indicate that the Celts had been living in this region for centuries.

By the start of the first millennium BC the Celts had become highly advanced in the art of metal working, particularly in smelting iron. Their formidable axes, billhooks and other tools allowed the Celts to open up roadways through the previously impenetrable north European forests. Such knowledge also provided the Celts with superior weapons to their neighbours. Not only did the new metal working allow the Celts to become more mobile and to excel in farming techniques, it provided them with a technological superiority which allowed them to settle as a ruling class among other peoples and gradually absorb them. By the 6th century, as they came in contact with the Greeks, Celtic civilisation dominated Europe outside the Mediterranean orbit.

Not everything the Greeks said about the Celts can be taken as accurate. Sometimes the archaeological evidence is in total contradiction. For example, Polybius, speaking of the Celts of northern Italy, says that 'their lives were very simple, and they had no knowledge whatsoever of any art or science'. One needs only a cursory knowledge of artefacts from the Hallstatt and La Tène periods to see how wrong such a statement is. Strabo, in particular, needs to be taken with a pinch of salt for his *Geographia* appears to be a pointed attack on the Celts. Even Nora K. Chadwick, who usually takes a vigorous pro-Graeco-Roman attitude, admits that it reads 'like a justification of Caesar's activities against their institutions'.

Later Greek writers were also influenced by their experiences with the Celts; for example, the invasion of the Greek homeland. They generally regarded them as nomadic tribes. Polybius says: 'Their possessions consisted of cattle and gold, because these were the only thing they could carry about with them everywhere according to circumstances and allowed them to shift when they chose.' The Greek vision of the Celts was as 'footloose' bands of marauders who would descend on a country, plunder it and move off again. Certainly one is not denying that this was one valid Greek experience of the Celts in their eastward movement.

These particular Celtic tribes were, however, as we shall see later, merely part of a population explosion, moving away from the settled Celtic areas in search of new 'living space'. In this respect, the Celts, in expelling their surplus population to seek out new lands, were practising something which might well have been part of an ancient Indo-European ritual for we find, in both Greek and Roman culture, a *ver sacrum* (sacred spring) when, at times of over-population or in emergencies occasioned by drought or famine, the young men and women, aged twenty years, were expelled from the country to go where they pleased to form new communities. By the time the Greeks were writing their accounts of the Celts, their own population explosions seem to have been adequately brought under control by the establishment of numerous Greek colonies around the Mediterranean and into Asia Minor. The aboriginal populations who witnessed the arrival of the Greek colonists might well have described the coming of the Greeks in the same way as the Greeks viewed the coming of the Celtic tribes, with their men, women, old folk, and their herds of livestock and baggage.

To Greek perception, these Celts lived solely by warfare, attempting to carve out their own kingdoms or selling their military services to those who would pay or give them land to settle in. At one time no Hellenist king would feel comfortable unless he had Celtic units in his army. Thus could Strabo observe: 'The whole race . . . is war mad, and both high-spirited and quick for battle, although otherwise simple and not ill-mannered.'

The Celts, when they settled, were excellent builders. Much work has recently been done on their fortresses, farmsteads and major settlements or townships. They were also excellent farmers. Even Strabo had to admit of Gaul proper: '. . . the country produces grain in large quantities, and millet, and nuts, and all kinds of livestock. And none of the country is untilled except parts where tilling is precluded by swamps and woods.' Livy also agreed, along with several other Greek and Roman observers, that the Celtic farmers were very industrious. In the Celtic kingdom of Noricum (modern Austria) the agricultural and mining trades flourished. In southern Gaul, not long after the establishment of Massilia, the Celts were growing their own vines and, indeed, the Saluvii were growing olives. The Saluvii, living around Entremont, were in close contact with the new Greek colonists and archaeology has shown that the Greeks supplied the Celts with many commodities. The Saluvii began to copy much from the Greeks, including their style of stone sculpture, with seated gods, chieftains and warriors. Their fortress in the hills above modern Aix-en-Provence was fortified around the 5th century BC and reveals a Greek-inspired street grid, sets of defences with projecting towers on the Greek model and several public buildings, one for the display of severed heads. The siege and destruction of the Celtic fortified town in 124/123BC was followed by the establishment of a Roman military stronghold at Aquae Sextiae (Aix).

Celtic farmers grew mostly cereals and pulses and various vegetables. They domesticated cattle, pigs, goats and sheep, bred dogs and hunted boar and deer. They even hunted birds and, of course, fished. The coastal tribes, such as the Venetii, had great skill with boat building. They also bred horses and are known to have introduced a four-pommel saddle, a key technical innovation, by which the rider could maintain a thoroughly secure seat when in battle. According to Livy, in his time the Romans would pay dearly for a highly prized breed of Gaulish horse called a *mannus*, a Celtic word borrowed into Latin, which was a small breed raised by the Gauls and renowned for its swiftness.

In warfare, the Greeks were the first to recognise the ability of the Celts as cavalrymen. The horse fulfilled a major role in Celtic life, as transport, for farming and as a military machine. Celtic graves often contain horse trappings, bridle bits, horse armour, spurs and harness. More importantly, the Celts used chariots expertly in their battles. Celtic chariot burials, where chieftains and warriors were buried with their favourite chariots, have been found throughout the Celtic world as far east as modern Turkey. The last time such vehicles were used on the Continent was at the battle of Telamon in 222BC, when Rome defeated a Celtic army in one of the great battles on the Italian peninsula. But Celtic war chariots continued to be used in Britain (and presumably Ireland) until the Christian epoch. Caesar encountered them in southern Britain. War chariots were also used in battle by the Celts of Asia Minor until a late period.

Caesar, in describing the chariot fighting in Britain, undoubtedly gives a good picture of the sort of fighting that the early Greeks and Romans would have encountered on the Continent and in Asia Minor.

In chariot fighting the Britons begin by driving all over the field hurling javelins, and generally the terror inspired by the horses and the noise of the wheels is sufficient to throw their opponents' ranks into disorder. Then, after making their way between the squadrons of their own cavalry, they jump down from the chariots and engage on foot. In the meantime their charioteers retire a short distance from the battle and place the chariots in such a position that their masters, if hard pressed by numbers, have an easy means of retreat to their own lines. Thus they combine the mobility of cavalry with the staying power of infantry; and by daily training and practice they attain such proficiency that even on a steep incline they are able to control the horses at full gallop, and to check and turn them in a moment. They can run along the chariot pole, stand on the yoke, and get back into the chariot as quick as lightning.

Celtic war chariots usually had two wheels and were drawn by two horses. Why the Celts of Gaul abandoned chariots in favour of cavalry before Caesar's conquest in the mid-1st century BC is hard to say. One thing that the prolonged use of heavy chariots demonstrates is that the Celts were no mean road builders and, in recent years, archaeologists have had to revise their ideas that the Romans were the road builders of Europe. In fact, the Romans borrowed Celtic names for practically every variety of wheeled vehicle they used – *carrus, carruca, carpentum* (from which derive our modern car, cart, chariot, carriage and even carpenter), *esseda, rheda* and *petorritum*. It obviously follows from this that the Celts also built roads.

It was a long-cherished belief that it was the Romans who built roads in northern Europe. The fact that Julius Caesar was able to march his legions rapidly over long distances in both Gaul and Britain, and that the British Celts were able to move at speed in heavy chariots to counter him, has long been seen as a sign of the existence of a good road network. It is only in recent years that archaeology has supported this deduction by the discovery of the remains of sophisticated Celtic roadways preserved in bogs. The roads were made of wood, the best material to hand. What the Romans did was simply build over the Celtic roadways with stonework.

Diodorus Siculus presents a typical view of how the Greeks saw the physical appearance of the Celtic male.

> The Celts are tall of body, with rippling muscles, and white of skin, and their hair is blond, and not only naturally so, but they also make it their practice by artificial means to increase the distinguishing colour which nature has given it. For they are always washing their hair in limewater, and they pull it back from the forehead to the top of the head and back to the nape of the neck, with the result that their appearance is like that of Satyrs and Pans, since the treatment of their hair makes it so heavy and coarse that it differs in no respect from the mane of horses. Some of them shave the beard but others let it grow a little; and the nobles shave their cheeks, but they let the moustache grow until it covers the mouth. Consequently, when they are eating, their moustaches become entangled in the food and when they are drinking the beverage passes as it were through a kind of strainer.

He also says that

> ... they amass a great amount of gold which is used for ornament not only by the women but also by the men. For around their wrists and arms they wear bracelets, around their necks heavy necklaces of solid gold, and huge rings they wear as well, and even corselets of gold.
>
> The clothing they wear is striking – shirts which have been dyed and embroidered in various colours, and breeches which they call in their tongue *braccae*; and they wear striped cloaks, fastened by a brooch on the shoulder, heavy for winter wear and light in summer, in which are set checks, close together and of varied hues.

As for the women:

> The women of the Celts are not only like men in their great stature but they are a match for them in courage as well.

But if one took the view of Athenaeus of Naucratis (c.AD 200), one would get a very curious view of Celtic society. In *Deipnosophistae* (men learned in the arts of the banquet) he says: 'And among barbarians the Celts also, though they have very beautiful women, enjoy boys more; so that some of them often have two lovers to sleep with on their beds of animal skins.'

Diodorus Siculus presents the Celts as 'exceedingly addicted to the use of wine . . . [They] fill themselves with the wine which is brought into their country by merchants, drinking it unmixed, and since they partake of this drink without moderation by reason of their craving for it, when they are drunken they fall into a stupor or a state of madness.' It is reminiscent of the 19th-century white settlers' conception of giving 'fire-water' to the native Americans. Poseidonius of Apamea (c.135–c.50BC), who would have been acquainted with the Galatian Celts, is quoted by Athenaeus, and states that wine was the drink of the wealthy classes only. They imported it either from Italy or from the Greek colony of Massilia. He says that sometimes the Celts added water to the wine. 'The lower classes drink wheaten beer prepared with honey (mead), but most people drink it plain. It is called *corma*. They use a common cup, drinking a little at a time, taking no more than a mouthful, but they do it rather frequently.'

Several Greeks remark on the Celtic banquet or feast. According to Poseidonius:

When a large number feast together they sit around in a circle with the most influential chieftain at the centre, like the leader of a chorus. His position is accorded on whether he surpasses the others in warlike skills, or nobility of his family, or his wealth. Beside him sits the person giving the feast and on either side of them sit the others in order of their distinction or merit. Their shield holders stand behind them while their weapon bearers are seated in a circle on the opposite side of the room and feast in common with their lords. The servers carried the drink in terracotta or silver jars like spouted jugs.

Diodorus adds that those partaking of the feast sit on skins of wolves. Usually the attendants are children, both male and female, who are of a suitable age to hand round the food and drink.

Importantly, the Greeks noticed that the Celts believed in a law of hospitality. 'They invite strangers to feast with them and do not inquire who they are or where they come from or what they want until the feast is over.' This was noted as an almost sacred law and one which, as we will see, Mithridates the Great of Pontus turned to his advantage.

Poseidonius states that at some feasts a dispute could break out as to who should be seated in the chief place. 'In former times,' he says, 'when the meat was served up, the bravest hero took the thigh piece, and if another man claimed it they stood up and fought in single combat until the death.' This sort of quarrel is also recounted in insular Celtic literature, in particular the story of Briccriu's Feast and the *Táin Bó Cuailgne* in Irish mythology.

Polybius, in spite of his obvious antipathy towards the Celts, says: 'They treat comradeship as of the greatest importance.'

According to Diodorus Siculus: 'Among them are also to be found lyric poets whom they called *bardoi*. These men sing to the accompaniment of instruments which are like lyres, and their songs may be either of praise or of criticism and disgrace.' Archaeological evidence supports the observations of Poseidonius, Athenaeus and Diodorus, that the Celts loved poetry, music and dance: a 7th-century BC Celtic pottery vase shows dancing figures. Instruments such as lyres, drums and pipes, and even a form of trumpet, are clearly depicted on a 7th-century BC pot from Sopron, Hungary. An anonymous Greek writer, claimed to be Seymnos, says that the Celts used music during public assemblies in order to soothe themselves.

The Greeks came to respect the warrior in Celtic society. They recognised Celtic warriors as being in the Homeric mould of Achilles, Hector, Agamemnon and Odysseus. They observed that the Celtic warriors believed in single combat between warriors of great renown even to settle warfare between tribes. In conflicts, the Celts would often challenge their opponents to settle matters by 'the truth of combat', a custom which appears frequently in the mythological texts of the insular Celts. In fact, at one stage, the Roman Senate had to forbid its generals and officers to accept challenges to single combat by Celtic warriors. Presumably the Romans were losing too many highly placed officers in such duels. Needless to observe, the result of the single combat, while binding to the Celt, was not binding to the Greek or Roman. If the Celt killed his Greek or Roman opponent, the Greek or Roman army did not abandon the conflict and disperse; they simply attacked the Celts *en masse*, much to Celtic amazement and outrage.

One aspect of the Celts in battle seemed to perturb the Greeks:

They cut off the heads of enemies slain in battle and attach them to the necks of their horses. The bloodstained spoils they hand over to their attendants to carry off as booty, while striking up a paean and singing a song of victory; and they nail up these fruits upon their houses, just as those who lay low wild animals in certain kinds of hunting.

They embalm in cedar oil the heads of the most distinguished enemies, and preserve them carefully in a chest and display them with pride to strangers, saying that for this head one of their ancestors, or his father or the man himself, refused the offer of a large sum of money. They say that some of them boast that they refused the weight of the head in gold; thus displaying what is only a barbarous kind of magnanimity, for it is not a sign of nobility to refrain from selling the proofs of one's valour.

Certainly, from insular Celtic sources and archaeological artefacts, we know that the cult of the head was part of the Celtic way of life. This was because the ancient Celts believed that the soul reposed in the head: to remove the head was a tribute to the enemy for a great soul enhanced a warrior's psyche or spirit. To the Celts, the idea that the soul was immortal was a very fundamental belief. Strabo pointed out that the Druids taught that souls as well as the universe were indestructible although both fire and water would eventually prevail over them. This seems like a variation of the teaching of Armageddon (Revelations xvi, 16) which also occurs in *Ragnarok*, or the better known *Götterdammerung* – the twilight of the gods. There would, for the Celts as well, come a time when all things would come to an end.

The Celts had a whole pantheon of gods and goddesses from whom they claimed descent. This is a particularly fascinating point, for the Celts did not believe in their deities as creators of humankind but as ancestors. They believed in a Mother Goddess. In this respect the Mother Goddess was Danu, the divine waters which flooded to earth from heaven, and from which Danuvius (the Danube) takes its name. The waters fertilised the sacred oak, Bíle, and from the joining of these two came forth The Dagda, the good god who was the progenitor of all the gods and goddesses, the children of Danu, from which the Celts descended. Danu, in Irish mythology, has her cognate in the Welsh Dôn. The name is also identified as Anu in Irish and Ana in British Celtic, and the word Anoniredi, 'the chariot of Anu', occurs in Gaulish. Numerous river and stream names throughout the Celtic world bear the stem of this name.

Polybius was one of the first Greeks to remark on the fact that some Celtic warriors fought naked. In describing the battle of Telamon, he says: 'The Insubres and the Boii wore trousers and light cloaks but the Gaesatae had been moved by their thirst for glory and their defiant spirit to throw away these garments, and so they took up their positions in front of the whole army naked and wearing nothing but their arms. They believed that they would be better equipped for action in this state . . .' Polybius believes that the term Gaesatae was a tribal one and that they were 'known as the Gaesatae because they serve as mercenaries'.

There are several mistakes here. Firstly, the Gaesatae were not a tribe. They were a band of professional warriors, an élite 'regiment' of fighting men. The name derives from the word *gaesum* – the Celtic name for a strong and heavy javelin or spear. The word *gae* appears in Irish as the word for a spear. So these 'spearmen' were an élite band of warriors who fought naked as a religious action by which they thought to enhance their psychic aura. Naked Celtic warriors have been attested in other places than the battle of Telamon, including the battle at Mount Olympus. That bands of professional élite warriors existed from early times among the Celtic peoples is also attested in insular Celtic literature. Perhaps the most famous of these were the Fianna of the High Kings of Ireland. However there were also the Red Branch (*craobh ruadha*) knights of Ulster – of which it is thought that the *ruadh* (red) might be a mistranscription of *rígh* (king) so 'king's branch' (*craobh rígh*); the *gamhanrhide* of Connacht; the *nasc niadh* (warriors of the golden torc or collar) of Munster and so on. Even the Knights of the Round Table of the original Celtic Arthur had their origins in the concept of a Celtic warrior élite.

So when the Greeks remarked on the Celts fighting naked they were witnessing special warrior élites in action, fighting under their religious laws and proscriptions.

It is from the 2nd century BC that the first Greek references to the Celtic intellectual caste occur – the *druidae*, from the Celtic word *druides*. One of the oldest references to the Celtic intelligentsia as Druids is made by a Greek writer (*c.*200BC) in a work quoted by Diogenes Laertius. The original work was attributed to Aristotle and while it is certainly not the work of *the* Aristotle (384–322BC) it is, perhaps, the work of a writer who shared the same name. It remains the earliest work to mention the philosophy of the Druids, and it says that the Druids taught in triads and that their tradition was 'to honour the gods, to do no evil and to practise bravery'.

At no time did any Classical writer call the Druids *sacredotos* or priests. Like most Indo-European societies, Celtic society was divided into its king/warrior caste (the equivalent of the Hindu *kshatriya*), the intellectual caste (*brahmins*), the farmers and craftsmen (*vaishya*) and the menials and labourers (*sudra*). Sometimes a member of the Druid caste could become king but a king could not become a Druid. It is in recent years that the popular myth of what a Druid is or was has become so entrenched in western folklore. The reality was very different.

Diodorus, having mentioned the Druids, goes on to say:

The Celts *also* [my italics] make use of soothsayers, accounting them worthy of high approval and these men foretell the future by means of the flight or cries of birds and from the slaughter of sacred animals and the Celts are subservient to them.

No soothsayer, says Diodorus, could perform a sacrifice without a member of the Druid caste being present, for offerings rendered to the gods should be approved by those who were experienced in the nature of the divine. Thus there is a great difference between the Druid caste and soothsayers and even priests. Indeed, we find the Greeks using other terms for Celtic priests such as *gutuatri, semnotheoi* and *saronides*.

The early contacts between the Celts and Greeks were to give rise to a controversy among Greek scholars in Alexandria some centuries later. Pythagoras, a Greek polymath and philosopher, lived in the 6th century BC. None of his writings survive, presupposing that he ever committed his ideas to paper. It is thought that he was born on the island of Samos *c.*580BC and migrated to Croton in Magna

Graecia (Italy). He taught a doctrine of reincarnation or transmigration of the soul. He claimed to be the Trojan Euphorbus, slain at Troy, in a previous reincarnation. Many of his contemporaries, such as Heracleitus and Xenophanes, regarded him simply as a fraud.

According to Diodorus Siculus it was Alexander Cornelius (b.c.105BC), nicknamed Polyhistor, who mentioned that 'the Pythagorean doctrine prevails among the Gauls'. Certainly the Celts believed in the immortality of the soul. Timagenes, an Alexandrian taken as a prisoner to Rome in 55BC, and often cited by others as an authority on the Celts, says: 'The Druids, men of loftier intellect, and united to the intimate fraternity of the followers of Pythagoras, were absorbed by investigations into matters secret and sublime, and unmindful of human affairs, declared souls to be immortal.'

But the Greek philosophers were divided as to whether the Celts had developed their doctrine from Pythagoras or whether they had developed it themselves and perhaps Pythagoras had borrowed it from them. It did not seem to have occurred to them that this was probably a case of parallel development for, as I have previously argued in *The Celtic Empire*, the philosophical concepts of Pythagoras and the Celts were not very similar.

Hippolytus (c.AD170–c.236) claimed that the Druids had adopted the teachings of Pythagoras through the intermediacy of Zalmoxis of Thrace who had been his slave. Herodotus had mentioned Zalmoxis being Pythagoras' slave when he lived on Samos. Hippolytus says that Zalmoxis 'eventually returned home to Thrace and promised his people immortality by teaching them this new philosophy'.

> The Druids among the Celts have profoundly examined the Pythagorean philosophy, Zalmoxis, a Thracian by race, the slave of Pythagoras, having become for them the founder of this discipline. He, after the death of Pythagoras, having made his way there, became the founder of this philosophy for them. The Celts honour the Druids as prophets and prognosticators because they foretell matters by ciphers and numbers according to the Pythagorean skill ... The Druids also practise magic arts, however.

The problem is that while Hippolytus knew that historically there were Celts in Thrace, they were not identified there until the 4th century BC. Therefore the 6th century BC is rather early for them to be placed in Thrace proper.

Clement of Alexandria (c.AD 150–211/216), with a wide knowledge of Greek literature and Stoic philosophy, puts the cat among the pigeons when he says that it was Pythagoras who adopted the philosophies of the Celtic Druids and he cites Polyhistor as his source. 'Pythagoras was one of those who harkened to the Celts and the Brahmins.'

Strabo seems to mention another apparently Celtic Pythagorean connection when he speaks of a Hyperborean, 'a dweller beyond the north wind', making a visit to the Greeks at this time. Hecataeus of Miletus had identified the Hyperboreans as dwelling in the region in which Himilco had found the Oestrymnides – the British Isles. It was more complicated than believing the Hyperboreans were simply another distant people because the Greeks believed they were a fabulous people who lived with Apollo. Those specially favoured by the gods could spend their afterlife with the Hyperboreans. It was Asclepiades of Tragilos who mentioned that there was a Celtic king named Boreas and that Cyprissa was his daughter. Boreas was, of course, the north wind, and Asclepiades is merely concerned to identify the Celts as living in northern climes. Strabo recounts that a Hyperborean named Abaris arrived in Athens while others have identified him as a Druid.

He came not clad in skins like a Scythian, but with a bow in his hand, a quiver hanging on his shoulders, a plaid wrapped about his body, a gilded belt encircling his loins, and trousers reaching down from the waist to the soles of his feet. He was easy in his address; agreeable in his conversation; active in his dispatch and secret in his management of great affairs; quick in the judging of present accuracies, and ready to take his part in any sudden emergency; provident withal in guarding against futility; diligent in the quest of wisdom; fond of friendship, trusting very little to fortune, yet having the entire confidence of others, and trusted with everything for his prudence. He spoke Greek with a fluency that you would have thought that he had been bred up in the Lyceum and conversed all his life with the academy of Athens.

In other words, from Greek perceptions, Abaris emerges as a typical Celt. But the idea that Abaris, whoever he was, came to Athens to discourse with Pythagoras is faulty in the extreme. Pythagoras, having left Samos, was actually living in Croton, which is in modern Italy, on the west coast of the Gulf of Tarentum (Taranto).

When the Celts collided with the Greek world, the Greeks realised that among them were philosophers and natural scientists and references to their reputation in these areas begin to survive from the 2nd century BC. Marcus Tullius Cicero (106–43BC), who numbered prominent Celts from several parts of the Celtic world – such as Diviciacus of Gaul and Deiotaros of Galatia – among his friends, says that the Druids were knowledgeable in natural philosophy and able to predict the future. Cicero says they had 'that knowledge of nature that the Greeks call *physiologia*'. Caesar, drawing his information mainly from Poseidonius, says that the Celts knew much about 'the size and shape of the world, the movements of the heavens and of the stars'. When Hippolytus says that the Druids could 'foretell certain events by the Pythagorean reckoning and calculations' it meant only one thing – that the Celts were advanced in astrology as well as astronomy. Pliny also acknowledges their astronomical calculations.

Dr Simon James has pointed out that the Celts stand favourable comparison with the Classical world in terms of their medical knowledge. Not only did they practise herbal medicine but they carried out surgery. Several graves containing medical instruments have been found. A 3rd-century BC grave at München-Obermenzing in Germany has revealed what has been called a Celtic 'warrior-surgeon'. Found in this grave were surgical instruments including retractors, probes and a trephining saw for cutting circular holes into the skull. Trephined skulls have been found in several places in the Celtic world, even in Britain, showing that not only did the Celts carry out such 'neurosurgery' but, in many cases, their patients survived for the bone has healed and grown after the operation.

In reconstructing the attitudes and perceptions of the early Celts towards the Greek and Roman world, we have one major problem. While the Celts had a rich and sophisticated oral tradition, they did not believe in committing their knowledge to writing. Julius Caesar comments that 'they consider it improper to commit their studies to writing, although they use the Greek alphabet for almost everything else . . .'

What we seem to be witnessing here is a religious proscription on committing Celtic philosophy and knowledge to a written form. But certainly from the 3rd century BC we begin to have surviving memorials in Continental Celtic languages written with Greek characters, exactly as Caesar says. Other inscriptions have been found in Etruscan and Iberian characters and finally in the forms we recognise as Latin. There are some 200 inscriptions and texts from northern Italy and southern and central Gaul. There are some seventy or more texts and inscriptions in which the Etruscan alphabet has been used, dating from between the 4th/3rd centuries BC and the 1st century BC, found around the lakes of Como, Lugano, Maggiore and Orta. There are around sixty inscriptions from the southern area of Gaul, some, like one inscription of Montagnac (preserved in Béziers), dated to the 3rd century BC. More than twenty more inscriptions, including potters' records, have been found in the north of Narbonesis using the Latin alphabet, notably the Coligny Calendar and the graffiti from La Graufesneque, in the Cévennes. These date from the first half of the 1st century BC to the turn of the millennium. The other big corpus of Continental Celtic materials comes from northern Spain in the area between Zaragoza and Burgos and here we have some rather extensive texts. The exact number of texts found in Eastern Europe and in Galatia has, as yet, not been calculated but we are probably speaking of a further one hundred or more. Celtic coins also supply a rich field of personal names.

Certainly, the Celts were beginning to break loose from the religious prohibition, and the popular historical dismissal of them as an illiterate society could not be further from the reality. As some of them moved into the Mediterranean orbit they started to use Latin both as a *lingua franca* and as a literary medium. As Dr Rankin has demonstrated, many writers whom we now think of as Roman, because they wrote in Latin, were in fact Celts. No study has yet been attempted of examining Greek written sources to ascertain if any authors were Celts writing in Greek as either a *lingua franca* or their adopted tongue.

This is rather like the modern confusion of who is an Irish writer and who is an English writer when the Irish writers are using English. Was Oscar Wilde an English writer because he wrote in English or, in reality, an Irish writer writing in English?

Yet the Celtic religious proscription on writting down a corpus of knowledge prior to the start of the Christian era has been the cause of much misunderstanding and allowed the Greek and Roman writers to spread their prejudicial interpretations about Celtic society without any necessary checks, balance or correctives. Only a few fascinating 'native knowledge texts' have emerged. In 1897 antiquarians discovered pieces of bronze tablet on which they found an intricate calendar written in Gaulish Celtic. It was dated to the 1st century BC. This not only confirmed the Celts' amazing astronomical observations and knowledge but was, at one time, thought to be the most extensive piece of written Celtic. Dr Garrett Olmsted has recently demonstrated that the computations of this famous calendar, the Coligny Calendar, were actually first compiled around 1100BC.

In 1887 a text was found at Rom (Deux-Sèvres) on a thin lead plate in Latin script and dated around the end of the 1st century BC. This was one of the most exciting Celtic literary finds for it was a poetic dedication to the Celtic horse goddess. Dr Garrett Olmsted has also recently rendered the inscription thus:

> Te voraimto esta, Atanta. Te sedto, Atanta.
> Te compriato sosio dertino, Eponina.
> Io ate sotiss, Epotia, te priavimo.
> Atanta, on te satimeto. ate te euraiimo.
>
> Are sosio dertin, Imona, demtisse, Epotia,
> are cialli carti eti seiont,
> Cati Catona, demtissie,
> clotu epasedemtition tibi cartaont, Dibonia,
> Sosio deeipia, sosio pura, soio govisa,
> sue ioti et sosio poura, te seiont,
> sua demti, Epotia dunna Vovesia.

He translates this as follows:

> It was set up for you, Sacred Mother. It was set out for you, Atanta.
> This sacrificial animal was purchased for you, horse goddess Eponina.
> So that it might satisfy, horse goddess Epotia; we will pay you,
> Atanta, so that you are satisfied; we will dedicate it to you.

By this sacrificial animal, swift Ipona, with a filly, goddess Epotia, for a propitious lustration they bind you, Catona of battle, with a filly, for the cleansing of riding horses which they cleanse for you, Dibonia.

This swift mare, this cauldron, this smith-work, besides fat and this cauldron, bind you, moreover with a filly, Epotia, noble and good Vovesia.

Dr Olmsted comments that the closest example to the Rom inscription is a Vedic hymn to Indra, demonstrating the common Indo-European root of the Celtic and Sanskrit literary traditions.

The discovery of an inscription on bronze at Peñalba de Villastar (near Teruel in northern Spain) and another at Luzaga (Guadalajara) have presented us with more lengthy texts. In 1971, a bronze tablet was found at Botorrita (south-east of Zaragoza) with a 200-word text from the 1st century BC. A further inscription was found at Chamalières (Puy-de-Dôme) and another at Larzac in 1983 which, inscribed on a lead tablet, contained forty-eight lines of Continental Celtic. Dr Olmsted has demonstrated that these more extensive inscriptions are all in poetic form. When analysing the Larzac inscription (dated to the 1st century AD) Dr Olmsted observed that compositions in poetic form are only to be expected, endorsing Greek references such as that of Poseidonios to the 'poets who deliver eulogies in song'.

As we follow the Celtic peoples in their eastward movement, we should bear in mind that the Greek perception of the Celts as a horde of war-hungry nomads, coming down from the north, raiding and plundering mindlessly, lacking art and science, and being only primitive in theological perceptions, is far from the reality.

[3]

Sparta's Celtic Warriors

THE Celts, according to Pompeius Trogus, had fought several wars with the Greek colony of Massilia by the start of the 4th century BC 'which increased the city's glory by the addition of victory to victory'. Massilia had also defeated the armies of Carthage, made alliances with the Celts of Iberia and was now the dominating trading and military force in the western Mediterranean.

It was during the first decade of the 4th century BC that the Celts of southern Gaul made another attempt to conquer the city. Trogus says they 'elected a leader by general agreement'. His name was Catumandus, 'he who directs the battle'; the element *catu* (battle) is still seen in the Irish *cath* and Welsh *cad*. While we are not sure which tribe Catumandus led, it seems likely that he was chieftain of the nearby Saluvii whose capital stood just behind Massilia at what is now Entremont.

Trogus says that while Catumandus was laying siege to Massilia he saw 'a vision of a menacing woman who told him that she was a goddess'. Catumandus took her to be one of the Celtic triune goddesses of death and battles, known collectively in ancient Ireland as the Mórrígú (great queen). The goddess warned him not to proceed with his attack.

Catumandus broke off his siege and asked for a peace treaty with the Massiliots. He also asked if he might enter the city to worship their gods. According to Trogus, he recognised a statue of a goddess at the portico of the temple of Minerva and claimed it was the very woman he had seen in his vision. He therefore presented his gold torque, his necklace symbolising his rank, as a sacrifice to the goddess and swore a treaty of perpetual friendship with the city.

Trogus says it was shortly after this that news reached the city of the defeat of a Roman and Etruscan army at Allia (390BC) and of the subsequent sack and burning of Rome itself by a Celtic army

from the Po valley. The Celts had been settled in the Po valley before
the 6th century BC. It has been argued that they had probably commenced their settlements in that area about the 9th century BC.
Warfare with the Etruscans, disputing the territory, had led to a
major battle near Ticino in 474BC where a Celtic army defeated the
Etruscans. This had placed the Celts in control of the plains of northern Italy north of the Apennine mountain range. Clashes continued
with the Etruscans, who had finally called upon the rising power of
Rome to help them. The result was a total defeat for the combined
Etruscan and Roman forces at the river Allia, 11 miles north of
Rome.

Significantly, the name of the Celtic leader who defeated the
Romans and Etruscans and went on to capture and sack Rome was
Brennos, the same as that of the leader who defeated the Greeks,
thereby reinforcing the idea that this name was a title – *brenin*, a
king. Apparently, Massiliot ambassadors had been sent to Delphi to
give thanks to Apollo and offer gifts, presumably for their safe deliv-
ery from the Celts of Catumandus, and these had just returned when
the news of Rome's defeat arrived. The implication is that they
brought the news with them. The Massiliots favoured Rome and
therefore the news was marked by a public mourning. The information that the Celts did not particularly want to occupy Rome but
had offered withdrawal if a ransom was paid caused the Massiliots
to establish public and private funds to help pay the tribute. For this
act of friendship, Rome concluded a treaty with the city, granting
them trade immunities and a senatorial seat in the auditorium for
the games.

Theopompus of Chios (c.376–323BC) claims that it was during
their attack on Rome that the Celts offered an alliance to the Greek
colony of Syracuse and its *tyrannos* or dictator, Dionysius I. Syracuse
(Syrakousai) had been founded by Corinth in 733BC on the south-
east coast of Sicily. The colony had become, over the centuries,
an independent and powerful state. An Athenian expedition led
by Nicias, designed to curb Syracuse' growing power, had proved a
disastrous venture. In the wake of this, Dionysius, a man of obscure
birth who had been a clerk in public office, swept to power in a
popular coup in which he deposed the city's generals. He was
appointed dictator, in 405BC. A man of demagogic power, he swiftly
made himself master of most of Sicily and then invaded southern

Italy, extending his rule over other Greek colonies which were collectively known as Magna Graecia. His oppressive imperial rule brought wealth and power to Syracuse. He even planned to sack the treasures of Delphi itself but this attack did not materialise. According to Livy, the further successful Celtic attacks on Rome, in 367BC and 365/3 BC, were financed and encouraged by Dionysius of Syracuse.

Dionysius I was also to play a major role in introducing the Celts to the Greek homeland. He was the first to use bands of Celtic warriors as mercenaries in his army. The practice of Celts fighting as mercenaries for the Hellenic states appears to have had its origins at this period, establishing a mercenary tradition which lasted among the Celts until comparatively modern times. Greek coinage and other forms of gold and silver from the period have been found extensively in the Celtic lands and indicate that young Celts saw mercenary work as a means to collect wealth and return to their homelands thereby boosting the native economies. As for Dionysius I, his policy of an alliance with the Celts was simply to enable him to use them against the Greeks of the mother country to enhance his own power base.

In 369BC, however, Sparta, capital of the Spartan state of Laconia in the Peloponnese, and an old ally of Syracuse, desperately needed military help. Spartan power was in decline and the city had been defeated by the hegemony of Thebes. So desperate were the Spartans that they had even sought aid from their old enemy, Athens. Sparta, with its ally Syracuse, had been the victor over Athens in the early Peloponnesian Wars (458–404BC). Sparta tended to stand for everything that Athens did not. Therefore it was an indication of just what straits Sparta now stood in, if they felt that they needed to invoke the help of Athens against the Theban alliance.

In the summer of 369BC the Spartans and Athenians were facing an army commanded by Epaminondas of Boeotia, the Theban alliance's most resourceful commander. He had already defeated a Spartan army in 371BC and invaded the Peloponnese during the following year to help the Arcadians throw off Spartan rule. He had broken through the Spartan and Athenian lines at Mount Oneion. Just at the crucial point of the battle, when the outcome hung in the balance, a fleet arrived from Sicily containing 2000 Celts and Celtiberian cavalry troops, paid for by Dionysius I of Syracuse as a *quid pro quo* for Sparta's former alliance.

The arrival of the Celtic troops was crucial in turning the tide against Epaminondas. But the conflict continued and in the summer of 368BC Dionysius sent a further contingent to aid Sparta against the Arcadians. Marching through Laconia to take ship at Gytheion for the return to Syracuse, this army was attacked. The Spartan commander Archidamus, in the rear, managed to disperse the attacking force with great loss. It was called 'the tearless battle' for no Spartans nor their allies were killed.

In spite of negotiations the wars among the Greeks continued. In 362BC Epaminondas once again marched against Athens and Sparta to assert Theban domination in the Peloponnese. He arrived at Tegea. The Spartan army under Agesilaus was expected to arrive at Mantinea. Epaminondas sent his Theban cavalry to attack the Athenian cavalry before they reached the city. In this battle, Gryllus the son of the historian Xenophon was killed. It was from Xenophon's *Hellenica* that we hear of the Celtic cavalry and their prowess in this war. In describing an action near Corinth, Xenophon, who had himself served in the Athenian cavalry, says of the Celts:

> Few though they were, they were scattered here and there. They charged towards the Thebans, threw their javelins, and then dashed away as the enemy moved towards them, often turning around and throwing more javelins. While pursuing these tactics, they sometimes dismounted for a rest. But if anyone charged upon them while they were resting, they would easily leap on to their horses and retreat. If enemy warriors pursued them far from the Theban army, these horsemen would then turn around and wrack them with their javelins. Thus they manipulated the entire Theban army, compelling it to advance or fall back at will.

Epaminondas launched his main attack on Mantinea. He feinted by marching his army obliquely towards the hills and, when the Spartans and Athenians thought that he was marching away and would not give battle, he turned to the attack. Epaminondas' cavalry routed the Athenian horse and the charge of the Theban left decided the battle. The battle was, in fact, a Theban victory. But as so often happens, the aftermath of the battle turned into a disaster for Thebes. Epaminondas, in pursuing his retreating enemies, was mortally wounded during a rearguard Celtic cavalry charge. The news quickly spread. In his dying moments Epaminondas asked for his lieutenants,

Iolaidas and Daiphantus, but they had both been slain. Despairing, he told his men to make peace with the enemy, knowing that they would regroup and take the advantage. The Thebans obeyed his advice. As Xenophon remarked: 'Greece was more unsettled and disturbed after the battle than before.'

This was the first time that the Celts had appeared in Greece and fought on the soil of the Greek homeland. Plato (427–347BC), a descendant of an early king of Athens, and eyewitness to these events, observed that these Celts were hard-drinking and warlike. Just the sort of remark one might have expected about mercenary soldiers even today. Xenophon remarks that they were worthy soldiers, and later Diodorus Siculus indicates that even the Spartans had admired the Celtic fighting qualities.

Spartans took pride in their courage, endurance, frugality and discipline. It was an aristocratic and militaristic state. Boys were taken from their mothers at the age of seven to live in barracks until the age of thirty. No deformed Spartan was allowed to live, and the newborn were washed in icy mountain streams to harden them to life. They were a people frugal in speech, which has given us the word laconic (from Laconia) as well as Spartan itself. Their praise of others' military abilities counted among the Greek historians.

Ironically, when one thinks of the Spartan regime, Aristotle (384–322BC), from Sageira, whose father had been physician to Amyntas II, father of Philip II of Macedonia, accused the Celts of imposing similar hardships on their children as if it were an un-Greek custom. He says that they hardened them to the cold by allowing them little clothing in cold weather.

It was Ephoros of Cyme who now acclaimed the Celts as one of the three great peoples who dwelt on the circumference of the world. He spoke of the Indians to the east, the Ethiopians to the south, the Scythians to the north and the Celts to the west. Ephoros stated that the Celts were philhellenes, lovers of everything Greek, were friendly to Greeks and were adopting many Greek habits. But at the very time when Ephoros was placing the *Celtike* safely in western Europe and enthusing on their love of Greece, some Celtic tribes were moving in an irresistible flood along the Danube valley and, even at the time he was writing, had already arrived within striking distance of the Macedonian border.

[4]

The Celts Move East

THE Roman historian, Livy, gives a reason for the sudden Celtic expansion which he places during the reign of the Roman king L. Tarquinius Priscus (616–579BC).

During the reign of Tarquinius Priscus in Rome, the Celts . . . were dominated by the Bituriges, and their king was consequently a member of that tribe. At the time we are concerned with, the king was one Ambigatus, who by his personal qualities, aided by the good luck which blessed both himself and his subjects, had attained to very considerable power; indeed, under his rule, Gaul became so rich and populous that the effective control of such large numbers was a matter of serious difficulty.

Since he had grown old and wished to relieve his kingdom of the burden of its excess population, he announced that he would send Bellovesus and Segovesus, his sister's sons, two adventurous and enterprising young men, to find such new homes as the gods might assign to them by augury.

He would give them as many followers as they thought would ensure that they could overcome any opposition they might encounter. The gods were duly consulted; Segovesus was assigned the Hercynian uplands [the Black Forest, Bohemia and the Hartz] but to Bellovesus the gods proposed a far pleasanter road, into Italy, whereupon, collecting the surplus population [of many tribes] he [Bellovesus] set out with a vast host, some mounted, some on foot, and reached the territory of the Tricastini at the foot of the Alps.

It is the eastward movement of Segovesus with which we are concerned.

The idea of over-population and an inability to cope with the economic and social tensions as the spark which prompted the vast migrations at this time is an acceptable as well as a likely one. It is an idea which is affirmed by the Greek, Plutarch, and the Vocontii Celt, Pompeius Trogus. Indeed, as we have mentioned, it was a solution that was employed by both the Greeks and the Romans to ease the population burden in earlier times.

Titus Livius, Livy (59BC–AD 17) was actually born in Patavium (Padua) among the Cisalpine Gauls, although his family were doubtless Roman colonists who had settled in the area after the conquest of the Celts there. His history of Rome, begun in 29BC, has frequently been remarked to be unlike the usual Latin forms, including many fabulous and epic stories that are obviously Celtic in origin. Livy, therefore, was using traditions that he had heard among the Celts of Cisalpine Gaul concerning their origins.

Whether the story of the Celtic chieftain Segovesus and his followers setting out eastward from the Celtic homelands is true or not in its particular, the Celts started the eastward movement long before the date given by Livy; in fact, around the 8/7th centuries BC the Celts were already reaching into the area of the modern Czech and Slovak republics, Austria was settled by them and they had moved into Hungary and south into what is now Slovenia, Croatia, Bosnia-Herzegovina and Serbia. The date of this movement is confirmed by archaeological evidence. Celtic graves, typical flat cemeteries, begin to appear in south-west Slovakia and western Hungary in considerable numbers before the end of the 7th century BC. According to Dr Elizabeth Jerem, currently Celtic Commissioner of the Austrian Academy of Sciences, some of the La Tène cemeteries overlie older Celtic cremations of the Hallstatt period. As the Celts moved on a broad eastward front they came up against an expansion in the opposite direction, westwards, by a people called the Agathyrsi. The Agathyrsi have been identified as partially Scythian in origin. The Celts halted this westward movement in the Slovakian region.

Dr Ralph F. Hoddinott, the Thracian expert, believes, along with Dr Stuart Piggott, that all central Europe was clearly Celtic in occupation by the beginning of the 4th century BC. In fact, they also both agree with the evidence presented by Dr B. Hänsel, arguing that 'the 8th-6th centuries are probable' for 'the early mingling of Celts and Thracians on the Pannonian (Hungarian) Plain'. The Thracians, an

Indo-European people who had developed their culture in the Bronze Age, stretched, at this point, from present-day Hungary to the Ukraine and from the Carpathians south to the Aegean. Herodotus described them as the most numerous of peoples. The Greeks had established colonies among them in order to exploit their rich gold and silver mines.

There are, however, Celtic artefacts from the 8th/7th centuries BC found in some profusion in the area, showing early settlements and links, as well as a strong intermingling of the two cultural forms of art – Celtic and Thracian. Dr Hoddinott observes:

> The Celts preferred the triskele to the tetraskele, but the strong impact of Thracian art is seen in the Celtic copy of a horsehead tetraskele from the Magdane Inska Gorain, Slovenia. It lacks the characteristic Thracian hatching and, with its central hole, is more like a garment *appliqué* than an ornament.
>
> Thracian influence on the craftsmanship of the Gundestrup Cauldron, unquestionably Celtic in spirit and symbolism, has been studied *inter alia*, by O. Klindt-Jenson (1950:1953), N. K. Sandars (1968) and T. G. E. Powell (1971). Parallels include the use of hatching for clothing, as on the Oguz plaque; as Sandars points out, this technique for smooth-coated animals stems from Sasanlu and earlier in the East.

Dr T. G. E. Powell observes that the Gundestrup cauldron was produced 'in a place where Thracian versions of ancient Orientalising art were still executed by craftsmen who were not perhaps exclusively Thracian or Celtic, and so their home can be narrowed down to those parts of Carpatho-Danube Europe where archaeology must continue to explore the interrelation of these peoples.'

So we are witnessing, in this area, as the Celts approach the Carpathian mountains, a mixing of the two peoples. We know that the Celts had established good relations with King Patraos of the Thracian kingdom of Paeonia (*c.*335–315BC). Certainly, by the 4th century BC, with steady expansion and occupation of the land, Celtic tribes were to be found along the entire course of the Danube and south of the river to the very borders of Macedonia.

Dr Elizabeth Jerem has published work revealing that whenever the Celts settled they were excellent farmers. They sowed a major crop of wheat, followed by rye, barley and millet. Vegetables were planted, mostly pulses such as beans, together with industrial crops such as flax. Animal husbandry was also a significant part of the Celtic economy during the eastward movement. Settlement debris reveals the predominance of the bones of the domestic pig and cow, followed by sheep and goats. Hunted animals, such as the wild boar and red deer, make up only a small portion of the refuse. Around the early La Tène period in the eastward progress, domestic fowl started to appear. Such evidence shows that the farming settlements of the Celts in eastern Europe were little different from those areas they had left behind in the west.

The settlement debris shows that the Celts were not, as many have imagined, vast hordes of nomadic tribes, hunting and plundering from local peoples.

According to Pompeius Trogus the Celts were guided by the flight of birds – a form of augury – into Illyria, basically modern Croatia and Bosnia and down towards Albania. Place-names are found combining Celtic geographical perceptions such as *vindo/uindo*, white; *seno*, old; *ritum*, ford; *uxellos*, height; *dunum*, fortress; *duro*, hard or tough; *magus*, plain; *maros*, big; *nementon*, sacred place; *broges*, country; *briga*, hill.

A major foundation named with a combination of the *vindo* stem was Vindobona (Vienna). The country of Upper Austria, Carinthia and Styria emerged to history in the 2nd century BC as *'regnum Noricum'*, the kingdom of Noricum, named after its major town of Noreia. The Celtic stem of *noro* is also seen in the place-name Noro-metus and the personal name Noros, this latter being the name of a potter. The tribes that settled here were the Taurisci, Ambidravi and Ambistones, while in Lower Austria, western Hungary and Croatia, the Osi (Osni) and Aravisii settled. Noricum emerges as a large kingdom basing its economy on agriculture and trading. Strabo praises its farming and its mining of iron ore and silver. It was incorporated as a Roman province in the time of Augustus about 16BC but, by then, the Celts of the area had already been overwhelmed by Germanic tribes.

As the Celts followed the Danube valley eastward we find the names of cities in antiquity which bear clear Celtic forms – we have already mentioned Vindobona (Vienna) but there was also Matucaim (Treibach), 'pig enclosure', Gabromagus (Windisch-Garstein), 'plain of goats', Carnuntum, Brigetio and Arrabona. Pliny mentions a place in what is now Hungary called Belgites, which name appears related to Belgae, Boii and Bolgios, while we also find Bononia (Vidin), Ratiaria (Artcher), Durostorum (Silistria) and Noviodunum (Isakcha). There was also a Carrodunum in South Russia on the Dneister and another in Croatia near Pitsmeza. The western part of what is now the Czech republic took its name from a large Celtic tribe which settled there – Bohemia, from the Boii. It is in this area that we have coin inscriptions with the names of two early Celtic kings, Nonnos and Biatec. Of Nonnos, it is worthy of note that the same name in feminine form, Nonna, is recorded as that of the mother of Dewi of Mynyw in Wales (St David). In fact, the inscriptions of this area supply us with a great number of Celtic personal names such as Broccus (the badger – cf. the Irish *brocc* and the Welsh *broch*), Enigenos (son of the tavern) and Nertomarus (powerful – cf. the Irish *neart*, strength, and *mhar*, great).

There had been much activity during this period as the various Celtic tribes pushed along the Danube valley looking for new territories to settle. Pompeius Trogus actually gives a date by which he says they had reached the Carpathians. He puts it around 358BC. Archaeological evidence, as we have seen, confirms their settlements even as far to the north-east as southern Poland. From the town of Olbia on the river Bug survives an inscription in praise of one Protogenes who distinguished himself when the town was attacked by Celts in the 3rd century BC. Olbia, also called Borysthenes, was founded in the 6th century BC by settlers from Miletus. Celtic hill-forts and settlements have been found as far north as Wroclaw (Breslau), and as eastward as Krakow (Cracow) and even further eastward along the Tisza river, beyond Kosice into the Ukraine. Celtic remains of the La Tène period have been found in the cemetery of Jarubinetz on the Dniper and as far as the Sea of Azoz (Maeotis) which Plutarch fixed as the furthest limit of the Celtic world in the east. In the 2nd century AD, Pausanias refers to 'the remotest Celts, the Cabares, who live on the edge of the ice-desert'. He adds:

In the country of the Celts is a wild beast called an elk, it is between a camel and a stag. It is the only beast which a human is unable to track but sometimes when a hunter is after other game the gods put the elk into his hands. Otherwise it is impossible for it picks up human scent from great distances and disappears into chasms or deep caves.

This is entirely possible as the elk, the largest of the deer family, was found across northern Europe into Asia and China.

It has been argued that the Tauri, mentioned by Euripides (*c.*485–406BC) in his *Iphigeneia in Tauris*, living in the Crimea, were Celts. But Dr Rankin says:

> . . . there is nothing to suggest that the Tauri, in spite of their name and their legendary predilection for human sacrifice to a sinister version of Artemis, were Celtic. These inhabitants of the Crimea, in the terms of the myth which Euripides has made so famous in his *Iphigeneia in Tauris*, were simply following old and respectable IE [Indo-European] traditions, as were the Celts themselves.

Celtic sites and even place-names are to be found north of the Danube along the Black Sea to the Sereth. Ptolemy mentions the towns of Britolagae, Aliobrix and Camodunum on the Dniester. But these settlements are sparse compared with the concentrations in what are now the Czech and Slovak republics and Hungary. Celtic settlements are also found in Romania and Bulgaria. In this area there also flourished a Getic culture which had an efficient technology and a good political system which was not easily dominated by the incoming Celts.

It is suggested that in many eastern areas, Celtic settlements did not impose a predominantly Celtic population in the landscape nor did they displace the native populations. The idea that the Celts arrived and established themselves as a 'ruling class' has been proposed. We must remember that this area of Celtic studies is only just being opened up to the West in view of the geopolitical divisions of eastern Europe which were in force since the establishment of Celtic studies, particularly archaeology, during this century.

We know that, as matters now stand, Pannonia (Hungary) was the easternmost fully Celticised territory of Europe. Herodotus places a people called the Sigynnae here before the arrival of the Celts and it has been argued that these were also Indo-European speakers with the name Sigynnae signifying 'merchants'. The Celts quickly absorbed them.

As early as the 4th century BC the Celtic tribes of the Scordisci, offshoots of the Boii and Taurisci, had settled in western Dacia, while other tribes reached as far as eastern Moldavia and Dobrudja. Celtic remains of this period have been found in Transylvania and Oltenia. Pompeius Trogus tells of a Dacian king, Oroles, who fought against the Celtic incursions. These incursions forced the Dacians to form a union of tribes under a king called Rubobostes. The Celts eventually settled and contributed to Dacian cultural development. They had brought with them skill in ironwork and pottery, contributing to the acceleration of the development of Dacia. The *Editura Enciclopedica Romana* acknowledges that the potter's wheel and advanced iron-smelting methods used by the Celts led to the rise of prosperous communities over the whole territory of modern Romania.

One important Celtic site was at the town of Zimnicea, Romania, a major Danube crossing point, on the north bank of the river. This was the point apparently reached by Alexander and it was destroyed by him. Speaking of the 4th century, Dr Hoddinott says: 'By the end of the century, it [Zimnicea] was probably under Celtic control. Cremation, adopted by the Celts, remained the burial ritual. Grave goods were poor; horse burials, either the complete skeleton or head and legs only, were separate from human burials. Fibulae in the 2nd century are all of Celtic type. The Celtic emphasis of this last phase could explain the city's destruction attributed to Burebista, in the first half of the 1st century BC.' We will deal with Burebista later.

As this is still a new area of Celtic studies, the exact relationship between the Celts and the Thracians, until the emergence of the Geto-Dacian kingdom of Burebista in the 1st century BC, is still a matter of contentious dispute. It has been agreed that the waves of Celtic invaders came to dominate the local populations, levying tribute in goods and services, and that they settled from the 4th century BC. Hoddinott says: 'By the early 3rd if not the late 4th century, they had established their domination over Slovakia, the middle and upper Tisza and the whole Transylvanian plateau.' Certainly there have been many discoveries of the Celtic occupation in Transylvania. A prime example is a hill-fort on Piatra Craivii situated on a peak near Alba Iulia which was found to have many metal Celtic artefacts from the 3rd to 1st centuries BC. The fortress appears to have been reduced by Burebista during his push against the Celts in the mid-1st century BC. Celtic cemeteries in the region show signs of long use.

According to Dr Vasile Parvan it was the much superior Celtic culture which enabled the Celts to exercise a decisive influence on Transylvanian and Thracian cultures. The exact size of the Celtic migration and its distribution of population still remains as a subject for much further work in the archaeological field.

Dr Hoddinott says:

The technological skills of the Celts and especially their introduction of iron agricultural, mining, metallurgical and domestic implements were an important factor in raising Transylvanian cultural and economic standards. Wheel-made pottery, although perhaps earlier introduced by Getic traders from the south, had not been locally manufactured. Under Celtic influence it came into general use. The traditional North Thracian handmade ware continued in use, but with the wheel new shapes, partly traditionally Thracian and partly deriving from Celtic and Greek models, slowly evolved along new lines towards a distinctive blend that was to characterise subsequent Geto-Dacian ware.

Celtic funereal cremation methods were used across the area. We know the Celts practised inhumation of their dead but it is difficult to know if the Thracians had also practised this or were simply influenced by the incoming Celts. Around Ciumesti, the Celtic cemeteries show signs of use by both Celts and Thracians without discrimination. Artefacts of both cultures are found in graves of Celts and Thracians.

According to Dr Hoddinott:

During the 3rd century BC Transylvania became part of the vast Celtic *koine* [commonwealth] which reached west to the Atlantic and south to territories dominated by Republican Rome, to Illyria and Macedonia, and, for two thirds of the century, through the kingdom of Tylis to Greece and Asia Minor. As a market opened to the Mediterranean lands it had enormous possibilities. Besides a source of agricultural produce and ores it would offer an inexhaustible supply of slaves and mercenaries.

In the area of Muntenia (Romania) on the north bank of the Danube, much Celtic influence has been noticed, especially in the making of agricultural and other iron tools by Celtic craftsmen. Celtic pottery, such as a hoard found at Ciolanestii din Deal, near Alexandria, has been noted as being similar to Celtic pottery in western Europe. Archaeologists digging in the forested hills of the upper Argess have also revealed a Celtic sanctuary with potsherds, ashes and fragments of 3000 bones, mainly domestic animals, deer and some birds. The bones have been exposed to fire and it has been argued that this may have been a deposit of ritually smashed relics of a feast. With these were unburnt iron objects – forty-five arrowheads, twelve knives, five spurs, twelve large nails, five fibulae – plus Celtic-style glassware and a silver coin dated to the late 3rd century B C.

The Muntenia area also shows extensive settlements and cremation sites whose contents include remnants of Celtic chain-mail, Celtic swords and much older Celtic war equipment. Dr Hoddinott observes that 'it is difficult not to conclude that these were graves of Celtic rulers'.

Sites at Negri, 40 kilometres north of Brad, on the Siret, in northern Romania have revealed Celtic chain-mail, iron bars and other arte-facts. The Serdi tribe had entered and settled in north-west Bulgaria and made Serdica (modern Sofia) their tribal capital. Other Celtic tribal settlements have been found as far as Plodiv along the upper Topolnitsa valley and the Panagyurishte.

So it is clear that even before Philip and Alexander of Macedonia led their punitive expeditions into Thrace, the Celts were already in place on the northern Macedonian border.

Theopompos of Chio, a friend of Philip II and later of Alexander, mentioned that the Celtic tribes, pushing along the Dalmatian coast opposite Pharos (Lesnia) and Corcyra Nigra (Curzola) somewhere near the mouth of the Naron (Narenta), came into violent collision with the Antariatae. These were the predominant people of Illyria at the time, whose lands extended into Bulgaria. The Antariatae had exerted their authority over Macedonia and made Amyntas II, father of Philip II, pay tribute to them. In 359 B C Bardulis of the Antariatae had defeated the army of Perdiccas III of Macedonia and killed him. Only Philip II had been successful in driving them back.

If Theopompos is right in his statement that the Celts were busy fighting the Antariatae at the time of Alexander's rise to power, perhaps Alexander did a deal with the Celtic chieftains. This would have kept the Antariatae out of Macedonia and thus explain why he apparently left it undefended when he embarked on his Asian conquests. The deal would have been that Alexander paid the Celtic chieftains to continue their warfare against the Antariatae on his behalf. This would explain why so many coins of Philip II and Alexander of Macedonia have been found at Celtic sites along the Danube valley. Was such an agreement the reason for the mysterious Celtic embassy to Alexander at Babylon? Had the Celts agreed to subdue the Antariatae on Alexander's northern border in order to allow his invasion of Persia? We shall come to this matter later.

We know that one major Celtic tribe, the Scordisci or Scordistae, built their capital at Singidunum on the Danube, which is present-day Belgrade. In fact, one of the first great Celtic female rulers to emerge in history was a lady named Onomaris, arguably meaning 'like a great mountain-ash or rowan tree'. Dr Rankin has pointed out: 'Onomaris was the woman leader of the Celts in their wanderings into south-eastern Europe.' In fact, as J. Weisweiler demonstrates, Onomaris led the Scordisci into their initial battles against the Illyrians, or Antariatae, who inhabited much of the Balkans. Celtic settlements and remains have been found throughout Bosnia-Herzegovina. Greek geographers mention that among the Illyrians were a people called the Hylli who appeared to have been Celticised by their Scordisci neighbours.

Indeed, Henri Hubert speaks of 'Celto-Illyrians'. Certainly ancient geographers, such as the unnamed 4th-century B C scribe who revised the 5th-century *Periplus* of Scylax of Caryanda, Scymnos of Chios and the authors of the *Etymologicum Magnum*, all mention the extensive Celtic settlements in this area.

Most historians believe that it was only after the Celts were pushed back out of Greece that the Celtic tribal kingdoms to the north were established. It is obvious, from archaeological finds, that these Celtic kingdoms had already been established and that they provided the bases for the massive Celtic invasion force. The Scordisci, for example, from their capital at Belgrade, certainly seemed to have spread into the country of the Triballi, and northern Macedonia, making permanent settlements between the Shar-Dagh (Mons Scordus) and the Danube. Their chieftain was called Bathanattos. The Triballi, said to have plundered Abdera with an army of

30,000 in 376BC, quickly disappeared after the Celtic settlement of their area. As Dr Hoddinott says: 'After more losses at the hands of the Illyrian Antariates and, in 295BC, the Celts, the Triballi gradually disappeared.'

However, Pompeius Trogus says that one Comantorios (Kommontorios), a general of Brennos' army, came to the area of Haemos after the invasion and that it was he, not Bathanattos or Cambaules, who formed the Thracian Celtic kingdom of Tylis on the west shore of the Black Sea north of Byzantium. Dr Mihailov has successfully demonstrated the boundaries of this kingdom. From the evidence, I believe that it is clear that the kingdom was already there and that Comantorios *returned* to it and did not create it.

Under Comantorios, the Celtic kingdom did come to the attention of Byzantium. At first the Celts exacted an annual tribute of eighty talents per year from Byzantium but then, it seems, they settled down to become good neighbours. Polybius writes in praise of one of their kings, Cauaros, whose coins still survive, and who mediated on Byzantium's behalf. We shall return to him later.

It is recorded that in 310BC a Celtic chieftain named Molistomos caused a large displacement of the Illyrian population, causing them to migrate *en masse* into northern Macedonia much to the alarm of the Macedonians. A Macedonian army had to be raised to push the Illyrians back out of the country.

In 298BC the Celts made a military feint towards Macedonia. They arrived at Mount Haemos, the very passes in which Alexander had defeated the Triballi. A harassed king, Cassander, seeing the threat to the northern border of Macedonia, took personal command of an army and managed to defeat the Celts in the same mountain passes. A year later, he was dead. Pausanias then records a Celtic chieftain called Cambaules, perhaps 'crooked hand', who moved his tribes into Thrace, no doubt while Lysimachos was trying to wrest power in Macedonia. Cambaules established a settlement there or perhaps reinforced other Celtic tribes. His movement might have been the arrival of the Dardani, who settled along both the north and south banks of the Danube. We might be seeing in this name an echo of 'the descendants of Danu', the goddess of the Danube.

That the Celtic settlements were permanent and stable after this movement is seen by the Celtic chieftain graves, hill-fortresses and native coinage. Coinage in Europe began to appear in Greece in the

6th century BC. The Celts encountered the use of coinage by their contact with Greeks. From the 4th century BC onward the Celtic mercenaries in the armies of Syracuse and later other Greek states were paid subsistence money in bronze coinage. Such 3rd-century BC bronze coins have been found in Gaul and even southern Britain. As bronze coins were not used in foreign trade, Dr Daphne Nash argues that the Greek and Punic coins arrived by means of mercenary soldiers returning to their homelands.

She says:

Many returning warriors of that epoch – particularly those from poor dependent groups in the payment of the dominant warlords of the Rhineland and northern Gaul – must have taken small change home with them at the end of their periods of service. Only communities very remote from the Mediterranean world are likely, however, to have set much value upon bronze coins, even as a class of exotic metalwork, and mercenary soldiers everywhere were paid their principal campaign fee in silver or gold coins instead.

The Celts were comparatively quick to start minting their own coins. Through the eastern Celtic settlements in Europe the coins of Philip II and Alexander, as we have mentioned, are found in Celtic graves and sites in large quantities, suggesting that both Philip and Alexander employed Celtic mercenaries in their armies. But as other Macedon kings, like Cassander and Antigonus Gonatus, minted coins with the heads of Philip and Alexander on them, in order to claim legitimacy as heirs, this may not be the case. The coinage of Philip and Alexander remained popular among the Celtic communities well after they had died.

By the 3rd century BC the Celts were minting their own coinage and, when they did so, they based it on Greek models. The Celtic tribes along the borders of Macedonia, Bosnia and Serbia were the first to produce coinage. They were imitations of the silver tetradrachms of Philip II. These coins became popular among the Celtic tribes in the Balkans and Lower Danube around 300BC. Celtic coinage in western Europe, especially in Gaul proper, started to emerge at the same time and was also based on Greek models, which arrived via the colonies of Massilia and Syracuse.

The eastern Celtic coinage carried many Celtic motifs, horses, severed heads and torques. It was not until the middle of the 1st century BC that these Celtic coins were generally abandoned in favour of the Roman *denarii* which indicates a change in the cultural climate of the area. The reason was that the Celts were beginning to be absorbed into the Dacian orbit and the Dacian king, Burebista, had become all-powerful.

By the mid-4th century BC, however, the Celts were firmly settled along the entire Danube valley. A short journey across the mountains to the south lay Greece.

[5]

A Meeting on the Danube

AFTER the battle of Mantinea, in 362BC, Athens emerged as the most important state in Greece. But in the north lay the semi-Hellenic kingdom of Macedonia, a land ruled by powerful kings, holding sway over the territory on the northern and northwestern coasts of the Thermaic Gulf. The Macedonians were a military people. The Macedonian kings had played prominent roles in the various Greek internal wars but not as a dominant power. King Archelaus (413–399BC) had made his reputation as a builder and road maker and created his court at Pella which became a centre of artists and poets.

In 359BC King Perdiccas III was slain by Illyrians (the Antariatae), over whom the Macedonians had tried to exercise an overlordship. His son, Amyntas, succeeded but was only a child. Therefore, his uncle Philip, who had been raised in Thebes as a hostage, became guardian of the child and regent. He was twenty-four years old. It was Philip who drove out the Illyrians, and defeated a fleet sent by Athens when they supported another claimant to the Macedon throne.

Philip now set out on a war of attrition, expanding Macedonia firstly into a strong kingdom and then into an empire. The fiction of being guardian to the young Amyntas was soon dispelled and Philip became Philip II of Macedonia. By his death in the summer of 336BC, Philip II had made Macedonia overlord of all the Greek states. He had invaded Thrace and also sent his forces into Asia Minor. In 341BC Philip II had conquered the Thracian kingdom of Odrisses and turned it into a Macedonian province. But two years later the Scythians of King Ateas and a Geto-Istrian coalition fought another battle with Philip on the Danube. Although Philip was victorious, while he was returning to Macedonia groups of tribes, identified as the Triballi, ambushed his army, made off with his spoils of war and left Philip himself wounded.

Pausanias observed cryptically:

If you measure one nation against another no people among mankind are as numerous as all the Thracians, except for the Celts; this is why no one before the Romans ever subdued the whole of Thrace. But all Thrace is in the hands of Rome. Part of the Celtic country Rome considers useless because of extreme cold and poverty of the soil, and deliberately overlooks it, but what the Celts had worth having belongs to Rome.

Unfortunately, we hear nothing of Philip's encounters with the Celts whom he must have confronted during his campaign in Thrace.

In 338BC Philip, having divorced his wife Olympias, married Cleopatra, the daughter of one of his generals, Attalos. During the wedding feast, Attalos, slightly drunk, proposed a toast inviting those present to pray to the gods for a *legitimate heir* to the throne. Attending this wedding feast was Philip's son, Alexander, just twenty years of age, who had been tutored by Aristotle and had already fought at his father's side at Chaeronea. Alexander had also been one of his father's trusted ambassadors to Athens.

Alexander stood up and threw his drinking cup at Attalos. Philip started up, trying to draw his sword, but he reeled and fell. Alexander jeered: 'Behold, the man who would pass from Europe to Asia, and trips passing from couch to couch!' This was a reference to the fact that Philip had been made captain-general of a Greek anti-Persian crusade. Plans had been drawn up for Philip to lead an army into Asia Minor to free the Greek city states from the rule of the Persian empire of Darius III, who had succeeded to the Persian throne in 336BC. With their lives at risk, Alexander and his mother, Olympias, left Pella immediately for Epiros where Olympias' brother, also an Alexander, was king.

Cleopatra bore Philip a son. Philip did not want to break with Alexander of Epiros and so offered him his daughter's hand in marriage. On the wedding day, as Philip moved in solemn procession in advance of his guards, a man named Pausanias, using, interestingly enough, a Celtic short sword, struck him down. It was not clear whether it was part of a plot; dark rumours blamed Alexander for his father's murder.

Alexander moved rapidly to strengthen his position. Just as rapidly Thessaly took the opportunity to rise up against Macedonian supremacy. Alexander, at the head of an army, took the field and out-manoeuvred the opposition without bloodshed and was therefore made *archon* of Thessaly. He continued to march south towards Thermopylae, in order to reassert his claim to be king of Macedonia. He was met by a repentant embassy from Athens which had previously supported the unrest against Macedonia. Alexander then called a meeting of the Hellenic League at Corinth and was confirmed as captain-general of the anti-Persian crusade in his father's stead. He now had to turn north to deal with the restless tribes on his northern borders. The Thracians and Illyrians were poised to take advantage of the dissensions in Greece.

The main source of restlessness was the Triballi, occupying the passes of Mount Haemos. At the news of the approach of Alexander's army, the Triballi, under their king Syrmos, had sent their wives and children and elderly to an island in the Danube called Peuce. The Triballi tried to halt the advance of the Macedonian army on the river Lyginus (Panega) by the use of chariots. Alexander had his men fall to their knees, holding locked shields, so forming a barrier which the chariots could not surmount. In spite of the shock of the chariot charge, not one Macedonian was killed. The counter-attack took the pass and the Macedonians marched on through the valleys of Mount Haemos as far as the Danube.

On the northern bank was the country of the Getae. In the river was the island garrison of Peuce. The Triballi were supported by Scythians. It is, perhaps, strange that we hear nothing of the Celtic tribes of this area who were obviously watching the conflict with interest. Alexander had warships, which he had ordered to move north along the Black Sea coast into the Danube, but he knew that he could not use them against Peuce until he had secured the farther shore. During one night, he collected fishing boats and tent skins filled with hay, managing to lead a band of horse and foot across the Danube. At dawn he attacked the Triballi and the Scythians. He did not bother to chase the fleeing warriors but marked the Danube as the border of his northern conquests. On the banks of the river, sacred to the Celtic Mother Goddess Danu, Alexander sacrificed to Zeus Soter and Heracles to honour his victory.

We hear that a decade later, in 325BC, Alexander's governor in Thrace, Zopyrion, sought to extend Macedonian authority north of the Danube. He was killed with most of his soldiers by an alliance of tribes led by the Getae. It was at this spot, a major Danube crossing, that the fortified city of Zimnicea, which was razed to the ground by Alexander, stood. We know that by the end of this century the city was firmly controlled by the Celts. The question is, how Celtic was Zimnicea when Alexander razed it? Probably not at all, and the Celts only occupied it after Alexander had left the area.

While he camped on the banks of the Danube, presumably within sight of the smouldering ruins of Zimnicea, in the early spring of 335BC, an official embassy from the Celts arrived at his camp. According to Strabo: 'The Celts who lived about the Adriatic joined Alexander for the sake of establishing friendship and hospitality . . . the king received them kindly . . .'

Arrian, quoting a lost work of Ptolemy, son of Lagus, who was one of Alexander's generals at the time and therefore an eyewitness, describes these Celts as 'men of haughty demeanour and tall in proportion'. The meeting was a meeting of equals. The Celts did not come to submit to Alexander but to offer an alliance. Alexander gave them a feast and during the course of this he asked them what they feared most. The reply he was probably expecting was: 'You, my lord!' Instead the Celts replied: 'We fear only that the sky will fall and crush us or the earth open and swallow us or the sea rise and overwhelm us.' In other words, they did not fear him.

Alexander, not understanding Celtic symbolism, felt the Celts had a high opinion of themselves. Indeed, Arrian and Aristotle seem to agree that 'the mutton-headed Celts did not understand diplomacy, and could only say they feared nothing, unless perhaps that the heavens might fall on them'.

However, the Greek historians have misunderstood the main thrust of the Celtic statement. They were actually using a ritual formula to emphasise their good intentions as well as a desire for Alexander to treat them as equals. The words were in fact a form of oath, committing the individual's corporeal integrity to keep a bargain but also invoking natural elements. The Irish law tracts of the medieval period still had the formula: 'We will keep faith unless the sky fall and crush us or the earth open and swallow us or the sea rise and overwhelm us.' In the *Táin Bó Cuailgne* the host of Conchobhar of Ulster vow: 'We shall hold this ground where we now stand. Unless the ground quakes beneath us, or the heavens fall down on us, we shall not flee from here.' In the *Leabhar na Nuacongbhala*, the Book of Leinster, there is an amplified form: 'We shall do so, for heaven is above us and earth beneath us and the sea all around us, and unless the firmament with its shower of stars fall upon the surface of the earth, or unless the blue bordered abounding sea come over the face of the world, or unless the earth quake, we shall never retreat one inch from this spot until such time as you come back to us again.'

Similar forms of oath are found in various other passages in the Irish texts and, indeed, we find the same motif in Welsh texts including a line from the *Canu Taliesin*: 'Look to the door, boy; listen, what is the noise? Does the earth quake? Or is it a sea incursion?'

Whether or not the Greeks, through cultural misunderstanding, thought the Celts merely braggarts, before two generations had passed, they were to show their mettle by coming crashing through Alexander's once mighty empire to the sacred centre of Greece itself. In support of the theory that the Celts did agree a treaty with Alexander to protect his northern border, the formula recorded by the Greeks could well have been simply the ritual agreement of the treaty, confirming that the Celts would keep faith until Alexander returned.

Although it is only a contention, I believe, as stated earlier, that the evidence of the Macedonian coinage among the Celtic settlements to the north of Greece at this time indicates that Alexander did come to an agreement with the Celtic chieftains. They would protect his northern borders while he was away campaigning from incursions by the Antariatae and Triballi, in return for payment.

Alexander was to turn from this meeting to lead his men to victories against the Illyrians and then find agitation against him springing up once again in Greece. This time he found himself fighting Thebes and the fall of Thebes marked the end of opposition to Alexander. He could finally set off for the conquests that made him famous – crossing the Hellespont into the Persian empire, marching as far as the western Himalayas and moving into what is now Pakistan, before returning east to march through Syria, Palestine and Judaea and into Egypt, bringing them all under his empire.

On 10/11 June 323 BC, aged thirty-three years, Alexander died in

Babylon. He was asked to whom he bequeathed his kingdom. On his death-bed he whispered: 'To the strongest ... I foresee a great funeral contest over me.'

His words were prophetic.

By coincidence, Arrian, quoting Ptolemy, mentions that a further embassy of Celts had made the journey to Babylon to meet with Alexander, arriving only to attend his funeral. One is intrigued. For what purpose did they want to speak with Alexander? What was their proposal? Perhaps they had come to ask for more money in order to keep his northern frontier safe? These Celtic ambassadors remained to attend his funeral and watched, undoubtedly with interest, as his generals began to squabble over the spoils of his empire.

Alexander had been survived by his ten-year-old son, Heracles. He had also left his new wife Roxana, the daughter of Darius, the defeated Persian emperor, pregnant with another son to be called Alexander. Neither son was of the age to inherit. His generals began forming factions and these rival factions eventually went to war over the division of the empire.

It is essential to understand the break-up of Alexander's empire in order to understand the Celtic invasion of Greece. The Wars of the Hellenistic Monarchies, as they became known, lasted for a couple of centuries until the Roman republic eventually established its rule over all the Greek kingdoms.

It was this dissension that the Celtic chieftains looked at with increasing speculation.

Alexander's senior cavalry officer, Perdiccas, had been appointed 'regent of the empire'. Areas of the empire were allotted to the governorship of the various generals. Egypt went to Ptolemy son of Lagus; western Asia Minor went to Antigonus; Thrace to Lysimachos; Cappadocia and Paphlagonia to Eumenes. For nearly half a century a complicated struggle for power evolved between these generals and their sons.

Perdiccas was murdered in Egypt in 320BC. Then Alexander's half-brother Philip Arrhidaeus was nominated as ruler by some of Alexander's officers. He was totally incompetent and Alexander's mother, Olympias, had him executed in 317BC. Antipatros (Antipater) (397–319BC), one of Alexander's most able commanders, had been made governor of Macedonia in Alexander's absence and declared himself regent of the empire. He had been able to put down an uprising from a league of Greek states encouraged by Alexander's old antagonist Demosthenes of Athens. When he died in 319BC, his son Cassander (Kassandros) (c.358–297BC) declared himself as regent of Macedonia. Cassander had been with Alexander when he died and persuaded Roxana and her infant son, Alexander, to place themselves under his protection. In 316BC, he had them executed together with Alexander's mother, declaring himself king of Macedonia.

Antipater, however, had declared Polyperchon, one of Philip II's former officers, as regent of the empire before he died. Another general, Antigonus, organised an alliance. This led to renewed warfare. By 311BC, a peace was settled on the basis of the status quo. However, in 307BC, when Cassander was absent from Macedonia, Antigonus declared himself king while his son Demetrius set off for Athens and took over its governorship for his father.

During the year 305BC the final collapse of Alexander's empire into totally separate kingdoms began. And in 301BC the final break-up was marked with the battle of Ipsus, in Phrygia, when Antigonus and his son, Demetrius, made an unsuccessful bid to hang on to the empire. Cassander, Lysimachos and Seleucus allied to overthrow Antigonus. Now four major spheres of power emerged – the kingdoms of Macedonia, Thrace, Egypt and Syria. In Macedonia, Cassander established his short-lived dynasty. In Thrace, Lysimachos became king. He sent his son, Agathocles, with an army to subdue the Getae tribes under Dromichaites. It is arguable that Dromichaites might well have been of Geto-Celtic stock. When Agathocles was defeated, he was taken prisoner and a ransom demanded. Lysimachos was put in the embarrassing position of ransoming his own son. He crossed the Danube in 291BC with a large army and suffered the same fate as Agathocles. Lysimachos was made the personal prisoner of Dromichaites. Lysimachos now offered not only to pay a ransom but to form an alliance with Dromichaites. Professor Otetea notes that the 'military democracy' was such that Dromichaites had to argue his case for releasing Lysimachos on payment of the ransom and for agreeing a treaty. Like most Celtic leaders the king was not absolute. An alliance was concluded which was consolidated by the marriage of Dromichaites and Lysimachos' daughter.

The two longest-lasting dynasties were created in Egypt and Syria. In Egypt, Ptolemy, son of Lagus, adopted the title of Pharaoh as

Ptolemy I Soter (saviour). He died in 283 BC. He founded the Ptolemy dynasty which survived three centuries until the death of the famous Cleopatra, the last of the Ptolemy rulers.

In Syria, Seleucus (c.358–280BC), a close friend of Alexander who initially had been governor of Babylonia, declared himself Seleucus I, with his capital at Babylon, ruling the Syrian empire. He built Seleucia on the Tigris and then made Antioch (modern Hataz Antakya) his capital. The Seleucid dynasty was to survive until the Romans annexed Syria to Rome in 65–63BC.

When Cassander died in 297BC, Demetrius, whose father Antigonus had been killed at Ipsus, re-emerged to claim the kingdom of Macedonia. Demetrius was unsuccessful as a king. He lost many of the Macedonian possessions and was finally expelled from Macedonia by Lysimachos of Thrace together with Pyrrhos of Epiros, who tried to claim the kingship of Macedonia but was driven back to Epiros by Lysimachos. Pyrrhos became an important figure in the subsequent history of the Celts as we will later see. Demetrius fled to Asia Minor and became a prisoner of Seleucus in 285BC but died two years later.

Lysimachos of Thrace now controlled Macedonia. He decided, unwisely, to invade Seleucus' territory in Asia Minor to expand his kingdom. The two old generals, now octogenarians, met at Corupedion, near Magnesia in Lydia, in 281BC. They decided to settle their differences by fighting in single combat. Seleucus slew Lysimachos and crossed into Macedonia to claim the spoils. But Ptolemy Ceraunnos, son of Ptolemy I of Egypt, excluded from the Egyptian throne but ambitious to create his own kingdom, slew Seleucos and drove the Syrian army back into Asia Minor. Ptolemy Ceraunnos was now Alexander's last surviving general. He had been a young cavalry commander. Now he was king of Macedonia and claiming to be heir to Alexander's empire.

It was at this point, having watched the forty years of internecine warfare among the heirs of Alexander, that the Celts made their move.

[6]

The Sack of Delphi

ACCORDING to Pausanias' *Description of Greece*, it was Brennos of the Pausi Celts who urged an invasion of Greece.

It was then that Brennos, both in public meetings and also in personal talks with individual Celtic chieftains, strongly argued a campaign against Greece, enlarging on the weaknesses of Greece at the time, on the wealth of the Greek states, and on the even greater wealth in sanctuaries, including votive offerings and coined silver and gold. So he induced the Celts to march against Greece . . .

What is certain is that the movement of three large Celtic armies into Greece from three different locations at the same time was no coincidence. It was undoubtedly part of a single plan. Pausanias gives the person of Brennos, whether title or name, credit for conceiving a plan to plunder Greece. The main historian of these events is Hieronymus of Cardia (c.323–272BC) whose original text is lost but is quoted extensively by Diodoros Siculus and Arrian. The other authority who lived at this time is Demetrios of Callatis, a reputed geographer and historian, who wrote a work *On Asia and Europe*. This is also lost, as is the work of Satyros, another native of Callatis, writing in Egypt in the 2nd century BC. Both these texts are known only in quotation.

The first Celtic army to cross into Macedonia was commanded by one Bolgios. His name is given as Belgius by Pompeius Trogus and Justin but as Bolgios by Pausanias. The name occurs in ancient Ireland in the Fir Bolg who are listed as early invaders of Ireland. It also appears in the *Historia Brittonum* of the Welsh 9th-century AD historian Nennius as Builc and in the work of the Irish chronicler

Eochaidh ua Flainn (d. 1004) who talks of the Tuath Bolc (people of Bolc). It has been argued by Eugene O'Curry that the name refers to 'bag' and thereby 'belly', the Fir Bolg being regarded as 'bag men'. But Professor O'Rahilly has demonstrated that the name derives from an Indo-European root *bhel*, flash, with *bheleg*/Bolg as 'lightning'. The same root is found in the Celtic tribe, the Belgae of Gaul (surviving in the name Belgium) and of southern Britain, which name would make them 'descendants of the lightning god'. The stem also occurs in other tribal names such as the Boii and the Tolistoboii, also given as Tolistobogii.

Therefore the first Celtic leader to cross into Macedonia was called 'lightning'. Curiously enough, the king of Macedonia, Ptolemy, was nicknamed Ceraunnos which meant 'thunderbolt'. Bolgios sent emissaries to the Macedonian king and offered to refrain from attacking his country if the Celts were paid a sufficient sum of money. Ptolemy Ceraunnos appears to have misread the situation. Perhaps he had not dealt with the Celts before and thought that the emissaries were suing for peace rather than giving him a choice to save Macedonia from plunder. Perhaps he was too arrogant to think that mere *barbaroi* could inflict any damage on the mighty army that had once conquered the known world for Alexander. Instead of offering money, he demanded that the Celts hand over their leaders as hostages for their good behaviour. Justin says that his reply greatly amused the Celts.

Bolgios led his army down on to the Macedonian plains where Ptolemy Ceraunnos hastily prepared his army for battle. While Celts had fought before in Greece, as mercenaries for Sparta, this was the first time that the Greeks had encountered a Celtic army fighting on its own terms and under its own commanders. Diodorus Siculus says:

> It is also their custom, when they are formed for battle, to step out in front of the line and to challenge the most valiant men from among their opponents into single combat, brandishing their weapons in front of them to terrify their adversaries. And when any man accepts the challenge to battle, they then break forth into a song of praise of the valiant deeds of their ancestors and in boast of their own high achievements, reviling all the while and belittling their opponent, and trying, in a word, by such talk to strip him of his bold spirit before the combat.

Whether this happened at the confrontation between Bolgios and Ptolemy we do not know. It is highly likely. The final result of the battle was that the pride of the Macedon army, unnerved by the Celtic onslaught, broke and were annihilated. Ptolemy was slain and his head cut off. In traditional Celtic style, it was placed on a javelin before being carried in triumph through the country. The Celts moved through Macedonia, burning and pillaging.

A Macedonian officer named Sosthenes managed to regroup the remnants of the Macedonian army and conduct a small-scale guerrilla war which kept Bolgios pinned down in the area. Sosthenes, we are told by Justin, was a man of modest origins. His activities merely held up Bolgios while Macedonian messengers went to find Antigonus Gonatus. He was the exiled son of Demetrius Poliocretes, in turn the son of Antigonus, who had once laid claim to the kingdom of Macedonia. Antigonus, who took his second name after the city in which he had been born, decided to accept the offer the messenger brought – that he return to Macedonia and seize the kingship. To do so, however, he would have to save Macedonia from the Celts.

Meanwhile, other Celtic armies were on the move. An army commanded by Cerethrios was moving along the northern border, through the country of the Triballi, towards the city of Byzantium and the Bosporus. We know that soon after 281BC the Celts descended on the city of Seuthopolis, near modern Kazanluk in Bulgaria, and presumably this was the same army. Excavations of the town, where a sanctuary of Kabeiroi, the gods of Samothrace, was situated, show that the Celts burnt the city during their attack. They then occupied it for a couple of generations before abandoning it.

In 279BC the large army of Brennos and Acichorios descended into Greece. The Greek chroniclers give the date as 'in the magistracy of Anaxikrates at Athens, in the second year after the hundred and twenty-fifth Olympics, when Ladas of Aigion won in the stadium.' We have already dealt with the meaning of the name of Brennos. His co-general, Acichorios, has a name which might mean 'his sister's dog'. There seems no doubt in the Greek chroniclers' minds that Brennos was the major player in the invasion – the supreme battle leader.

Pausanias offers only one reason as to why the Greeks were unable to successfully turn back this invasion. He says:

Greece had been badly damaged first of all by Philip and Alexander, and then by Antipater and Cassander who had utterly worn it out; now everyone was so weak that none of them were ashamed their help should be missing. The Athenians were more exhausted than anyone else in Greece, by the long Macedonian war and by losing a lot of battles; all the same they went off to Thermopylae with any other Greeks who wished to come with them . . .

The numbers of the Celts given by Pausanias, Pompeius Trogus and Justin imply that with the armies came a whole nation on the move. Justin indicates some 300,000 in the initial movement into Macedonia alone. Pausanias, in estimating the figures at Thermopylae, gives 152,000 infantry and 20,400 cavalry, with the two mounted attendants to one mounted warrior putting the total cavalry at 61,200. Justin and Diodorus keep to the figure of 150,000 infantry but estimate the cavalry at variously 15,000 and 10,000. According to Dr Stephen Mitchell: 'These figures are high but not necessarily far from the truth if they are taken as an assessment of the total Celtic manpower.'

We now learn the names of the main chieftains of this vast Celtic tribal confederation which had planned the attack on Greece: Bolgios, Brennos and Acichorios as well as Cambaules, Cerethrios (which might be identical with Polyaenus' Ciderios, also placed in the Thrace region), Commontorios (Rhŷs thought the *comm* element suggested 'one dressed in fine clothes'), Leonnorios, which seems more Greek than Celtic, and Luturios, 'mouse' (although some have suggested it might be the same as Louernius, 'fox').

Their ultimate object was new lands to settle but their intermediate objective was plunder.

Pompeius Trogus observes: 'Triumphant, Brennos ravaged the whole of Macedonia without hindrance. Then, as if the treasures of men had no further attraction for him, he turned his eyes to the temples of the immortal gods, joking that they, who were rich, must make largess to mortals.'

With the armies of Bolgios and Cerethrios behind them in Macedonia, the army of Brennos and Acichorios marched southwards through Thessaly, sweeping aside any opposition. Thus they came to the pass at Thermopylae and the final stand of Callippos' Greek confederated army. The Celtic victory here left all the Greek city states vulnerable to the Celtic invaders. It was now that Brennos was faced with the decision of moving southward on Athens and the rich lands of the Peloponnese.

It has been asked why so few Greeks joined the federated army to defend the country against the Celts, especially from the rich city states of the Peloponnese which had much to lose. Pausanias actually provides an answer:

The expedition to Thermopylae against the Celtic army was ignored by all the Peloponnesians alike; as the barbarians had no ships the Peloponnesians reckoned on suffering nothing terrible from them, providing they walled off the isthmus of Corinth from one sea at Lechaion to the other at Cenchreai. This was the plan of the whole Peloponnese at the time but when the Celts somehow or other crossed over by ship to Asia, the condition of Greece was so depressed that no Greek people were left with the strength to take the lead.

But the Peloponnese was safe. Brennos made his historic decision to turn directly southward through the gorges of Parnassos to Delphi, the shrine of Apollo and centre of the Greek universe, situated in the former kingdom of Phocis but now claimed by Aetolia. Delphi lay on the southern slope of Mount Parnassos, high up in a narrow valley in a great natural amphitheatre. Behind the town flowed the Castalian stream between two peaks of rock. There had been a small settlement there in Mycenaean times (about 1400BC) but this had been destroyed. It had been in the 8th century BC that the city had risen while, above the town, lay the sanctuary of Apollo with its oracle, the Sacred Way leading from the Castalian spring to the principal entrance.

Here was the sacred *omphalos*, the navel stone, which marked the mid-point of the Greek world, determined by the god Zeus as the place at which two eagles met, after flying one from the eastern and one from the western boundaries of the world. Presiding over the oracle was the high priestess and prophetess of Apollo, the Pythia (python). In the innermost sanctuary (the *adyton*) the Pythia would give her oracular responses to those who came to consult her.

The idea of the Pythia seems to go back to Mycenaean times. Apollo is said to have slain the Python, the serpent of the earth goddess who was originally worshipped there. Terracotta figures of the 11th century BC have been found in Delphi. The Pythia had to be over fifty years old when appointed. Her oracles were delivered from a tall tripod on which she sat.

Over the centuries the Delphic temples had gathered great wealth. With every Greek victory, tributes were brought there and memorials built such as the Serpent Column commemorating the Greek victory over the Persians at Plataea in 479BC, memorials of Lysander of Sparta who destroyed the Athenian navy at Aegospotamu in 405BC, the gold tripods of Syracuse and many other tokens of conquest.

Kings, emperors and dictators throughout the Hellenic world, and later Rome – for Delphi did not decline until the 4th century AD – came to hear the oracles.

Brennos had undoubtedly heard of the riches of Delphi and probably of its religious symbolism in the Hellenic world. Leaving Acichorios and part of the Celtic army at Heracleia to protect his rear, Brennos moved on to Parnassos, moving among the towering mountain peaks, and coming by way of the gorges to Delphi itself. Pausanias' account has some interesting observations, although he is clearly dramatising events for his Greek readership.

The Greeks at Delphi, hearing of the advance of the Celtic army, demanded an oracle from the Pythia. Through her the god Apollo is said to have told his people: 'I will defend what is mine.' He told the people of Delphi not to remove the treasure. In fact, Pausanias is following a motif from Herodotus concerning the Persian attack on Delphi. In Callimachos' *Hymn to Delos*, we have Apollo pointing out that the Celts were 'already beside my tripods' when the oracle was given.

He also has Apollo making a prophecy from his mother's womb, aeons before the attack on Delphi:

I say that there will come to us in the future a struggle we all wage together, when, raising the barbaric sword and Celtic war, latter-day Titans will rush upon us like snow from the very far West; or as numerous as the stars when at their thickest they pasture the sky. And forts and [villages of Locris and the Delphic high places], the Crisean plain and narrow [valleys] of the mainland will be crowded all around and we shall see smoke from a neighbour's house burning, not simply hear of it; soon beside the temple they will see the armies of hostile men, and next to my

81

tripods swords and vicious sword belts. And their hated spears which will lead their owners, the mindless tribe of Celts, on a journey which comes to no good.

The complex at Delphi, we are told, was defended by 400 Phocians from Amphissa, some Aetolians and some Philomelos numbering 1200 warriors.
The Greek 'secret weapon' was Apollo.
Says Pausanias:

Brennos and his Celts were faced at Delphi by the hostile portents of the god, which were swift and conspicuous to a degree that to my knowledge has no other instance. All the ground where the Celtic army marched quaked violently all day, with continuous thundering and lightning. The Celts were dumbfounded by this lightning, and unable to hear when officers gave them orders; flashes from heaven would strike warriors down and set fire to others in spite of their shields.

Even Pompeius Trogus repeats this dramatic motif, although he also has men inflicting some physical damage:

The Celts hurled themselves in battle without considering the danger. The Delphians fought back, trusting more in their god than their own forces. But Apollo's presence was soon apparent; rocks, split from the mountain by an earth tremor, came crushing down on the Celtic army and scattered the strongest units, which at the same time broke under the blows of the defenders. Finally, a storm broke and hail and cold put an end to the Celtic wounded.

In spite of Apollo, one famous warrior from Delphi named Aleximachos was killed in the battle and the Phocians afterwards sent a portrait of him to Delphi where it was kept in the sacred shrine.
Some 40,000 Celts are said to have accompanied Brennos to Delphi. This is an exaggeration. We can be sure that as they moved through the narrow mountain passes the Aetolians and Phocians lost no opportunity to attack the Celtic column for the passes are so narrow that, at points, no more than two or three can march abreast. Rocks would have been hurled down on them. In this, perhaps, we

have the basis of the divine earthquakes, thunder and lightning. Pausanias says that ancient Greek heroes now appeared. 'Nightmare figures stood in arms against the Celtic army.' They included Hyperochos and Amadokos, who were said to be Hyperboreans, 'dwellers from beyond the north wind', by which it was generally assumed that the Greeks were referring to the Celts themselves. It is an odd choice of heroes to conjure to defend Delphi against the Celts. Laocon of Calydon, the Argonaut, also appears and Pyrrhos, son of Achilles, accompanies him. Pyrrhos was another interesting choice of ghostly defender. Pyrrhos was the nickname given to Neoptolemos, the son of the hero Achilles by Deidameia. He was at one time regarded as a rival to Apollo in terms of worship. But because Pyrrhos appears against the Celts Pausanias says: 'The Delphians pay Pyrrhos the honours due to a divine hero's tumulus, though they used not even to honour his monument, since he was an enemy of theirs.' Yet another hero mentioned is Phylacus of Delphi itself.

Delphi had only recently been incorporated into Aetolia. Pausanias points out: 'When Brennos led his army of Celts against Delphi, the Phocians went to war with more enthusiasm than anyone else in Greece and through doing so joined the Amphiktionian league of Greek states and completely restored their ancient prestige.' Elsewhere he says: 'They resisted the Celtic army with more vigour than anyone else in Greece, avenging the god of Delphi and, I think, trying to justify themselves over the old charges.'

He says that the cold weather, frost and snow debilitated the Celts. He even says that they started to kill their own wounded. During the retreat, when they were attacked at night, in their panic they did not recognise each other, and they started killing their comrades by mistake. He says that Brennos was wounded and carried from the battlefield on his own shield.

All day long the Celts were gripped by disaster and by horror; but a much more calamitous night was waiting for them. There was a fierce frost and with the frost came snow. Enormous rocks came tumbling down Parnassos right at them, and cliff faces broke away and came crashing down. Not by ones and twos now, but in twenties and thirties or more, on the guard and where they slept, they perished together under the storm of rocks.

In spite of all this, the Celts did reach Delphi and looted the sacred shrine, killing the Pythia in the process. They also began to make off with much of the ancient treasure which was gathered there. Pompeius Trogus records that among the attackers were the Tectosages, undoubtedly the same tribe that were to be one of the three founding tribes of Galatia. Branches of this tribe were situated in southern Gaul with Tolosa (Toulouse) as their capital. According to Julius Caesar, however, Eratosthenes of Cyrene (c.285/280–c.194BC) knew of yet another branch of the Tectosages in Orcynia (the Hercynian forests) east of the Rhine. Caesar says that the area was 'seized and occupied by the Volcae Tectosages who remain there to this day and have a high reputation for fair dealing and gallantry'. The Tectosages who took part in the Greek invasion were, apparently, a large offshoot of this tribe. Strabo says:

> The tribe called Tectosages lives near the Pyrenees but also extends over a small part of the northern flank of the Cévennes and their land is rich in gold. It appears that they once held a dominating position and were so strong in manpower that when civil conflict arose they banished a large part of their number from their native land, who were joined by other men from other tribes; belonging to this stock are the people who settled in the part of Phrygia that borders on Cappadocia and Paphlagonia. We have as proof of this the fact that the people are still called Tectosages . . .

The tribal name means, roughly, 'they who seek to possess'. The *sages* element of the name is found in the Old Irish verb *saigid*, seeks, approaches, attacks, while *tecto* is found in the Old Irish *techtaid*, possesses.

Tolosa was later the capital of the Tolosates but these might have been a sept of the Tectosages.

However, Trogus observes that part of the great treasure from Delphi passed into the keeping of the Tectosages. The interesting point is made by Timagenes and Strabo that, when the Romans captured Tolosa in 106BC, the consul Quintilius Servilius Caepio found the treasure in a sacred Celtic lake nearby. Timagenes was certain that it was part of the Delphic treasure. This treasure is reported to have consisted of the fabulous sum of 100,000 pounds of gold and 110,000 pounds of silver. Caepio was ordered to send this treasure to Rome but it vanished *en route* with its guards. Caepio was deprived of his pro-consulship but managed to escape serious charge for being involved in the disappearance of the Tolosa gold. Timagenes, however, says that Caepio was exiled as a 'temple robber' and ended his days in misfortune, with his daughters becoming prostitutes to earn a living. That's as may be, but certainly a new phrase entered Latin – *aurum Tolosanum* (Tolosa gold) meaning ill-gotten goods. It was clear that history had condemned Caepio. According to Timagenes, Caepio suffered this bad luck because he was plotting to steal the sacred objects that belonged to the god of Delphi which the 'Tectosages' had brought back from Greece to their kinsmen in Gaul.

The acceptance of the fact that treasure was removed from Delphi would appear to contradict the Greek claims that the god Apollo had successfully intervened to protect the sacred shrine and further, according to Pausanias, that no Celt involved in the attack on the shrine escaped unpunished. However, Poseidonius actually says that most of the treasure of Delphi had already been looted by the Phocians during the Third Sacred War (356–354BC) so there was nothing to pillage. If this is so, why was the Greek world so shaken by the 'sacrilege'?

An inscription discovered on the island of Cos claims the Celts did not even pillage Delphi, although artwork and some textual evidence say otherwise. It has been argued that the Cos inscription might have been later Delphi propaganda. Dr Rankin renders the Cos inscription thus:

> Diocles Philinou prosper: whereas the barbarians [Celts] having made an expedition against the Greeks and the temple of Delphi it has been reported that some of them that attacked the temple have been given their just deserts both by the gods and at the hands of men who came to the aid of the temples in the barbarian onset and that the temple has been preserved and adorned with the captured arms of its attackers and the rest of these have been destroyed in engagements between themselves and the Greeks: in order that the people [of Cos] should be manifest in their joy at the victory that has been gained and in the making of offerings to the god for his epiphany in the crucial engagement in the environs of the temple and for the safety of Greece; it has been

resolved invoking good fortune by the people that the *architheoros* and the *theoroi* [chief *sacra* ambassador and ambassadors] who have been elected when they may come to Delphi shall sacrifice to Pythian Apollo and Zeus Saviour and Victory and let them also sacrifice to each of the other gods a fully grown animal.

It is likely that as the Celts began to withdraw from Delphi, the Greek forces who had initially been driven out used the moment to counter-attack: Pausanias says that at sunrise the Greeks attacked them on the road from the precipices of Parnassos, shooting arrows and throwing javelins down on the Celts so that they could not shoot back. He says that the Celts resisted with spirit 'though they were shot at from every direction, and suffered badly from the cold, especially the wounded. But when Brennos was wounded too and was carried out of the battle fainting, and the Celts saw Greeks in position against them all around the mountain passes, they began to retreat, killing their own wounded who were unable to follow them.'

We are told that when night came down and they made camp 'they were seized with a terror inspired by the god Pan'.

A disturbance broke out among the warriors as dusk came down. A few were driven out of their minds as they thought they could hear the sound of horses coming at them. It was not long before a madness seized the entire Celtic army. They snatched up their arms and killed one another, without recognising their own language or one another's faces or even the shape of their shields. They were out of their minds and this madness brought about by the gods created a massacre of the Celts.

Pausanias claims some 10,000 were killed in this fashion.

The Phocians increased their attacks during the next day. The figure given by Pausanias for dead in battle with the defenders of Delphi is 6000. So we are to believe that a total of 16,000 Celts were slain in the first stages of the withdrawal.

Acichorios, hearing the news from Delphi, left part of his army at Heracleia and set off to join Brennos in order to cover his withdrawal. As Acichorios marched towards Brennos, the Aetolians and Phocians attacked and managed to capture his baggage and supply wagons.

The two sections of the Celtic army finally reunited with Acichorios' fresh troops beating back the attacks.

There are several versions of what now happened to Brennos – all, however, agree in the essential that he died. One version is that he was wounded personally by Apollo and driven insane and died; another that he drank undiluted wine – neat alcohol – and thus killed himself; and finally from Diodorus we hear that he simply drank wine before committing ritual suicide, presumably aghast at having pillaged a sacred shrine. Pausanias gets in his propaganda: 'Brennos' wounds left him with no hope; it is said that out of fear of his companions because of the shame and suffering he had brought on them by invading Delphi, he died deliberately by drinking undiluted wine.'

A small bronze in the Naples museum, a replica of the original, is said to represent his suicide.

It is more likely that Brennos died of his wounds but the Greeks needed a more 'moral' ending for the leader of the invasion of their sacred shrine.

According to Pausanias:

Some Athenians went to Delphi as observers and raced home with news of what had happened to the Celts, with stories of the vengeance of Apollo. The Athenians raised an army and immediately marched out. When they reached Boeotia, the Boeotians joined them and together the Greeks marched on the Celts, ambushing them in the retreat and continually killing the stragglers.

It could well be, though it is not mentioned, that Callippos was still in command of the Athenians and, wishing to redeem himself after the defeat at Thermopylae, was determined to inflict as much punishment as possible for his embarrassment. The fact that he distinguished himself in this way would account for his heroic portrait in the council chamber of Athens in later years.

Pausanias goes on to say that after Brennos' death, Acichorios led the Celts back to Heracleia. 'The Aetolians had slowed down their march, raining javelins on them and whatever else came to hand, so that it was not many who escaped to the camp at Heracleia.' Acichorios decided to withdraw across the Spercheios 'with great difficulty under savage Aetolian attacks. When they arrived at the river the Thessalians and Malians were waiting for them, and those people so overwhelmed them that not one man of them returned safely to their homes.'

Again Pausanias bends the facts for we know that this statement is not borne out by the evidence.

The Celts began to move northward out of Greece. They did so in an orderly manner, taking much of their booty with them. The fact that there were so many Celts still moving about Macedonia during the next year or so shows that they still represented a powerful threat and had not been defeated by either the Hellenic gods or their armies. The city states were in such a turmoil that the Panathenaea, the great annual celebration of the birth of the goddess Athena held during July, had to be suspended for the year 278BC, the year after the Celtic invasion. The impact of the invasion had long-felt consequences.

According to Dr Rankin:

It is difficult to conclude that really serious damage was done to the Delphic precinct in the course of the Celtic war. This is not to diminish the magnitude of the threat posed by the Celts or the sufferings they inflicted on Greece. The Greek world was deeply stirred by the war and its outcome; epic poems called *Galatika* were composed by several poets, but only pieces of these works remain embedded like fossils in the texts of later authors. Their story must remain unclear.

As well as the outpouring of epic poems about the Celtic invasion, there were numerous memorials. We have heard from Pausanias of the portrait of Callippos at Athens and the wall painting of the battle of Thermopylae in the council chamber. Representations of the sack of Delphi were to be seen at various temples dedicated to Apollo both in Greece and in Italy, at Delos and even in Rome where one of the ivory-plated doors of the temple of the Palatine, according to Sextus Propertius (c.50BC–after 16BC), showed 'the Celts thrown down from the heights of Parnassos'. A medallion found at Capua shows a Celtic warrior with his foot placed on the severed head of the Pythia. Another from Cales shows the Celts fighting Greek warriors against a background of Delphic colonnades.

As Acichorios took the remaining Celts northward into Macedonia, he found that the armies of Bolgios and Cerethrios had both moved eastward towards Byzantium. By now, however, Antigonus Gonatus had arrived at Lysimacheia. The city of Lysimacheia, founded by Lysimachos during his kingship of Macedonia, stood on the shore of a bay, not far from Cardia, on an arm which developed into Thracian Chersonese (Gallipoli). Hieronymus of Cardia was infuriated at its construction and accused Lysimachos of uprooting Cardia to build the city for his own aggrandisement.

Antigonus had sent messengers to the Celtic leaders asking them to return ambassadors to him so they could discuss peace terms. These ambassadors were sent and duly returned to their chieftains with tales of Antigonus' wealth and simplicity of character. The Celts believed that they could overwhelm Antigonus' camp in a surprise night attack and loot his treasures. They made their attack and found the camp empty. They had no time to reorganise before they found Antigonus and his army attacking them in the rear.

The victory of Antigonus at the battle of Lysimacheia has been placed to the winter months of 278/277BC. However, there is a slight problem about the sequence of events for we find that Livy mentions two Celtic war bands led by Leonnorios and Luturios who had occupied the shores of Propontis (the Sea of Marmora). It would seem that they were part of the army of Bolgios. Poseidonius claims that these Celts had already detached themselves from the army of Brennos before the sack of Delphi but if they were part of Bolgios' army they obviously had not followed Brennos south. Livy says they had captured Lysimacheia by a ruse. He then says they were stationed in Thracian Chersonese in force. It is not certain whether this happened before or after the battle of Lysimacheia. It is more likely that it happened before and that Antigonus' victory ended their scheme to dominate the area.

According to Livy, the group commanded by Luturios broke away from Leonnorios, who had moved towards Byzantium. Luturios is said to have crossed the Hellespont in boats captured from the Macedonians and was thus the first of the Celts to arrive in Asia Minor. The historian Zosimus (4th century AD), who preserves material from Phaenno of Epiros, confirms this crossing at the time when Democles was *archon* at Athens, that is the winter of 278/7BC.

The defeat of the Celts at Lysimacheia finally deflected the Celtic invasion force from the Greek peninsula.

Indeed, in that year of 277BC, the Amphictyony, the religious association or league of Greek states which met twice a year, instituted a festival of commemoration called the Soteria, 'Salvation Festival', to celebrate Greece's deliverance from the Celts. The Soteria became the subject of much controversy in the following years when the Aetolians, who regarded themselves as the real victors over the Celts, tried to reorganise it. The Macedonians claimed that they had defeated the Celts and should have the final say over the festival organisation.

Dr Rankin observes:

Brennos may be classed as a very able and courageous general, who, if he had been leader of a more disciplined and better supplied army, could have crushed Macedonian power and established Celtic rule over Greece. Greek tradition does not underestimate his quality. The fact that the Celts were still able to expand towards Asia and the establishment of a Celtic kingdom at Tylis in Thrace provided clear indication that the force of the Celtic migrations was not spent and that the defeat in Greece, serious though it was, did not decisively reduce Celtic power.

[7]

Pyrrhos and the Celts

ntigonus Gonatus, following his victory over the Celts
at Lysimacheia, was now officially recognised as king of Macedonia. His main rival for the kingship, the ambitious Pyrrhos
of Epiros, was out of the country. Pyrrhos (319–272 BC) was a
second cousin to Alexander the Great. He had been ousted from his
throne in Epiros after the battle of Ipsus in 301 BC but had, with the
aid of Ptolemy I of Egypt, been restored in 297 BC. He was a good
organiser and an ambitious military adventurer. His ambition was
to retrieve the empire of Alexander under his rule. Plutarch says, 'As
for Pyrrhos' knowledge and mastery of military tactics and the art
of generalship, the best proof is to be found in the writings he left
on those subjects.' It is said that when Antigonus (Gonatus) was
asked who was the best general, he replied, 'Pyrrhos, if he lives to
be old enough.' Hannibal once said that Pyrrhos was the greatest of
all generals and next to him Scipio. Unfortunately the writings of
Pyrrhos on military matters have not survived.

While the Celts of Brennos were gathering on the northern borders
of the Greek peninsula, the Romans were trying to establish their
dominance over the Celts of northern Italy as well as over the Etruscans, Samnites, Lucanians and other peoples of the Italian peninsula.
In 283 BC, having defeated a combined army of Celts and Etruscans
near the Vadimonian Lake on the river Tiber, just north of Rome,
the Romans, now confident and expanding, turned their eyes to the
rich Greek city states of southern Italy. These were called Magna
Graecia (Megale Hellas), and had been colonised centuries before
from Greece.

The Greek city states had decided to combine against the inevitable
onslaught by Rome. The city of Tarentum (Taranto) was the principal organiser of this defensive movement. According to Plutarch:

The Romans were at this time at war with the people of Tarentum, who were neither strong enough to carry on the struggle, nor, because of the reckless and unprincipled nature of their demagogues, inclined to put an end to it. They therefore conceived the idea of making Pyrrhos their leader and inviting him to take part in the war, since they believed that he was the most formidable general of all the Greek rulers and also that he was more free to act than the others.

A formal invitation called upon Pyrrhos of Epiros to come to their aid and command their armies. Plutarch says that Pyrrhos saw this campaign as a first step in seeking to build a new empire. Pyrrhos sent Cineas, a Thessalian in his service, to Tarentum with 3000 soldiers as an advance guard. He then assembled a fleet containing 20,000 infantry, 3000 additional cavalry, 2000 archers, 500 slingers and twenty elephants. Elephants, as war machines, had not been used in Italy before.

Pyrrhos landed at Tarentum in 281 BC. He immediately imposed his rule on the city by closing the gymnasia and public walks, banning drinking parties and stopping the indolent life which he believed that the citizens were leading. It was not long before he heard that the Roman consul P. Laverius Laevinus was marching against the city with an army of 35,000 men. Pyrrhos sent an embassy asking if the Romans would be prepared to come to an accommodation with the Greek cities, respecting their independence, without resorting to arms. But Rome was in its first flush of success in creating its empire. Pyrrhos then advanced to a plain between Pandosia and Heracleia in Lucania.

It was the Thessalian cavalry which won the day for Pyrrhos, who was nearly killed in this battle. The Roman losses were placed, by Dionysius, and repeated by Plutarch, at 15,000 dead with Pyrrhos losing 13,000. However, the more accurate Hieronymus gives 7000 Roman dead and 2000 captured with Pyrrhos losing 4000 men.

Pyrrhos was now looking for allies against Rome and was joined by Lucanians and Samnites. To find the time to gather a new army, Pyrrhos dispatched Cineas as his ambassador to Rome to start new negotiations. Cineas laid a number of proposals before the Senate as a means of ending the conflict. Pyrrhos, through him, said that he wanted Rome's word that it would leave the Greek cities of southern Italy unmolested. It is said that the Senate was tempted but the intervention of the venerable Appius Claudius, then aged and blind, swung their votes to a resolution for a continuation of the war. Gaius Fabricius was sent by Rome to attempt to gain the release of the prisoners held by Pyrrhos; the two became good friends on a personal level but remained enemies politically. Indeed, Fabricius even warned Pyrrhos of a plot to assassinate him because he did not wish Pyrrhos' downfall to bring reproach on Rome by history stating that his end was brought about only by treachery. It is certain that Pyrrhos tried several times to make a peace with Rome but Rome refused to offer the guarantees to leave the Greek city states alone.

Fabricius became consul of Rome and Pyrrhos marched to Apulia. Here he was joined by warriors from the Insubres and Senones, the Celtic tribes of Cisalpine Gaul, in northern Italy. The Celtic territory stretched north of the Apennines, along the Po valley. Their southern-most border reached as far south as Ancona. The Cisalpine Celts did not join Pyrrhos as mercenaries. They were fighting their age-old enemy, Rome, as allies of Pyrrhos on an equal footing in order to stop the inevitable movement of Rome into their homelands. Once Rome controlled all southern Italy, it would only be a matter of time before it turned on the Celts of northern Italy.

However, it is argued that Pyrrhos also enrolled Celtic mercenaries from as far afield as what is now Picardy, the territory of the Belgae, for Daphne Nash demonstrates the use of various coins from Tarentum of the period c.334–272BC in that area; coins which returning veterans would have brought back with them having been paid for their services.

At Asculum (Ascoli Satriano) Pyrrhos was faced with a Roman army commanded by Sulpicius Saverrio. Once again, Pyrrhos pushed the Romans back but only after a fierce battle which lasted from sunrise to sundown. Pyrrhos was wounded in the arm by a javelin. Hieronymus, echoed by Plutarch, estimated Roman losses at 6000 dead compared with 3500 dead of Pyrrhos' forces. Pyrrhos is said to have commented: 'One more victory like that over the Romans will destroy us completely!' – hence the term 'pyrrhic victory'.

Most of his friends and able commanders had now been killed and there were no reinforcements which he could summon from Greece, which was in turmoil facing the Celtic invasion there. According to Plutarch: 'And from Greece messengers reported that

Ptolemy, surnamed the Thunderbolt [Ptolemy Ceraunnos] had been killed in a battle with the Celts and his army annihilated, and this was the moment for Pyrrhos to return to Macedonia, where the people needed a king.' While he pondered the problem, a delegation from Sicily offered him command of the cities of Agrugentum, Syracuse and Leontini on condition that he help free them from the Carthaginians.

Pyrrhos made what now seems to be a curious decision. Had he returned to Greece he would have undoubtedly been welcomed by all the Greek states as the saviour from the Celtic invasion. However, he decided to go to Sicily. He garrisoned Tarentum and moved into Sicily in 278BC. Carthage, having concluded a peace treaty with Rome, was now threatening the Greek trading ports in Sicily. Pyrrhos met with indifferent success while continuing to evade the pleas for help from Tarentum.

Three years later, in 275BC, Pyrrhos, frustrated that he was making no gains in Sicily, recrossed the Straits of Messina, having to fight a sea battle with the Carthaginians as he did so. Back on the Italian mainland he managed to gather a combined army of Greeks, Celts, Samnites, Lucanians and Bruttians. At the Samnium town of Beneventum, 130 miles south-east of Rome, he was met by an army commanded by consul Manlius Curius Dentatus. Pyrrhos opened the battle with a night attack but the Romans drove the advance guard off with heavy losses which included eight of Pyrrhos' war elephants. Encouraged, Dentatus launched a counter-attack on the main body. The first Roman legion crumpled against Pyrrhos' defence. A second legion, following immediately on, broke the Greek phalanxes and put an abrupt end to the battle.

Plutarch says:

This manoeuvre gave the victory to the Romans and finally established their superiority in the struggle against Pyrrhos. These battles not only steeled their courage and their fighting qualities, but also earned them the reputation of being invincible; the result was that they at once brought the rest of Italy under their sway, and soon after Sicily as well.

This Roman victory saw the end of Pyrrhos' campaign in Italy and he decided to leave Magna Graecia. In fact, he left the Greek cities to the mercy of the Romans without nominating a commander to replace him. The Greek city states fell a couple of years later and Rome was master of the Italian peninsula as far north as the Rubicon, the border with the Cisalpine Celts who would eventually become the last people on the peninsula to be conquered by Rome. Pyrrhos' withdrawal had another important effect on the Celtic world. When Rome conquered Tarentum in 272BC and formed an alliance with Syracuse, the first Greek state to use Celtic mercenaries, the two most important western Greek markets for the recruitment of Celtic mercenary soldiers were closed. As an offshoot of this, the Celtic tribes of the remoter areas, who had sent their young men to serve as mercenaries to bring back the gold and silver coins, began to concentrate on producing their own coinage.

A final aspect of these events was that the new Roman empire was brought into a collision course with Carthage over the matter of trade and involvement in Sicily. According to Plutarch, Pyrrhos had already seen the danger signs and, as he was leaving Sicily, he is said to have looked back at the island and remarked to his companions: 'My friends, what a wrestling ground we are leaving behind for the Romans and Carthaginians.' It was eight years later when the First Punic War between Rome and Carthage commenced. It was soon followed by the Second Punic War, in which the Celtic world was to be involved, including the Celts of Iberia, Gaul and Cisalpine Gaul who formed an alliance with Carthage against Rome. When Rome emerged as victors, that Celtic world would be irreparably altered and begin to rapidly shrink.

On returning to Epiros in 275BC, Pyrrhos found that much had changed. The Celts had devastated Greece, had sacked Delphi, and had, by now, mostly moved on. But in Macedonia, Antigonus Gonatus had recruited large numbers of them into his new Macedonian army under their chieftain Ceredrios. We are told that after Lysimacheia, Antigonus had recruited no fewer than 9000 Celtic warriors into his army. Antigonus watched the return of Pyrrhos with suspicion. He had compared him to a player at dice who made many good throws but did not know how to exploit them once they were made.

Pyrrhos had certainly lost none of his ambition after his defeat in Italy. He was not simply satisfied with returning to his kingdom of Epiros but he now made an attempt to reassert himself as king of

Macedonia. He had a small army of 8000 infantry and 500 cavalry, all he could save from Italy. However, in the spring of 274 BC he persuaded a number of Celts to join his force in an invasion of Macedonia. It is not clear where these Celts came from, whether they were Celts already in Greece or whether they were remnants of his army from Italy.

He started his campaign by capturing some Macedonian cities from which 2000 Macedonians decided to join him. He then clashed with the army of Antigonus Gonatus who had positioned himself at the entrance to a narrow defile. Pyrrhos' attack broke the Macedonian force, who began to retreat leaving a rearguard in the mountain pass. Plutarch says:

> A strong contingent of Celts who formed the rearguard of Antigonus' force stood their ground bravely, but after fierce fighting most of them were cut down, while the division of the army which contained the elephants was hemmed in and drivers surrendered themselves and their animals.

It seems that Pyrrhos knew many of the Macedonian commanders by name; he had, after all, been erstwhile king of Macedonia. The Macedonians defected to him without further conflict.

Antigonus Gonatus, with a small detachment of cavalry, escaped from the battlefield and found refuge in a coastal city. It seemed that once again Macedonia would change her king.

Plutarch says:

> Pyrrhos considered that of all his successes the victory over the Celts was the one which added the most to his reputation and so he dedicated the finest and richest of the spoils to the temple of Athena between Pherai and Larisa and placed an elegiac verse inscription over them.

The inscription began:

> Pyrrhos, the king, dedicates these long shields to Athena Itonis,
> Trophies he earned from his victory over the valiant Celts
> When he defeated the host of Antigonus . . .

He also went to the sanctuary of Dodona and dedicated other shields there.

After Pyrrhos captured Aegae he left his own Celtic mercenaries to garrison the city. Plutarch says:

> As a race the Celts possess an insatiable appetite for money, and they now dug up the tombs of the rulers of Macedon who are buried there, plundering the treasure and insolently scattering the bones. This outrage Pyrrhos treated with indifference: he either postponed action because he had too many urgent matters on his hands or decided not to take any because he was afraid of punishing the Celts. In any event the episode did much harm to his reputation with the Macedonians.

Pyrrhos, whose resources had been depleted by his failures in Italy, had probably allowed the Celts to plunder the tombs by way of repayment for their services in his army.

At this stage a new development occurred. Cleonymus of Sparta arrived and invited Pyrrhos to help him gain the throne of Sparta. Cleonymus was an elderly man who had a long-standing grudge against the Spartan king, Areus. Cleonymus' ambition was sharpened by a personal grievance. His young wife Chilonis had eloped with Acrotatus, a son of Areus. Pyrrhos, once again, made a wrong political decision. Instead of strengthening his position in Macedonia, he took an army of 25,000 infantry, 2000 cavalry and twenty-four elephants and marched south to the Peloponnese. His real aim was not just to conquer Sparta but to grab the entire Peloponnese for himself.

Pyrrhos' sudden descent on Sparta was unexpected. Areus was in Crete with his army helping the people of Gortyne. The Spartans, however, quickly raised an alternative army. Women and old men joined in the work of preparing fortifications outside the city of Sparta. A trench 800 feet long, 9 feet wide and 6 feet deep was excavated, protected at the flanks by wagons whose wheels and axles were embedded so that any charge by Pyrrhos' elephants would be impeded.

Pyrrhos' son, Ptolemy, led a picked force of 2000 Celts to one flank in order to break through the wagon barricade. The wagons were firmly embedded but, as Plutarch says, 'the Celts succeeded in pulling the wheels up'. Acrotatus, Chilonis' lover, saw what was happening and led 300 men around the back of Ptolemy's Celts and attacked their rear. They were forced to turn to defend themselves but were hemmed in against the wagons where they were then driven into the trenches and finally pushed back with great slaughter.

The first day of fighting ended without resolve. On the second day Pyrrhos was thrown from his horse when it was struck by a javelin and the Spartans used this moment of confusion to drive off the attack. Just as Pyrrhos was finally about to make an overwhelming attack, Areus arrived from Crete with 2000 soldiers while Ameinias of Phocis appeared from Corinth with an army of mercenaries to help out. Pyrrhos had to withdraw and Areus, using ambush techniques, managed to cut off the Celts who formed Pyrrhos' rearguard. Pyrrhos ordered his son, Ptolemy, to go to their relief and, during the skirmishing, the young man fell transfixed by a javelin cast by a Cretan named Oryssus.

Pyrrhos retired to Argos where he found Antigonus Gonatus with a new army. The city of Argos chose neutrality and tried to mediate between them. While Antigonus withdrew from the city precincts, Pyrrhos, having promised to go, marched his troops to the city gates. A traitor named Aristeas opened the Diemperes gate of the city at night and Pyrrhos sent a detachment of Celts into the city. They were able to enter and seize the market-place before the alarm was given.

The people of Argos, realising that the Celts of Pyrrhos were in the city, sent a message to Antigonus to come to their aid. He immediately dispatched a force which was reinforced by Areus and his lightly armed Spartans, who had also arrived. These forces counter-attacked the Celts. Pyrrhos, entering the city from another direction, heard that the Celts in the market-place were under attack. In the confusion of the narrow streets and the darkness of the night, Pyrrhos attempted join with them. But the attack on Argos turned into rout and confusion. At dawn Pyrrhos was able to see that Antigonus and Areus held the city and he began to withdraw.

But while fighting in the narrow defiles of the streets, Pyrrhos was wounded by a spear thrust from a poor citizen of Argos, a man trying to defend his house. The man's mother was watching from the roof of their house and saw Pyrrhos turn on her son to cut him down. The distracted mother threw a roof tile at Pyrrhos and knocked him unconscious. A man named Zopyrus, serving with Antigonus, recognised Pyrrhos, dragged him into a doorway and cut off his head with a short Celtic sword. This could imply that he was one of the Celtic mercenaries. He took the head to Alcyoneus, Antigonus' son, who immediately took the head to his father.

Pyrrhos died in his forty-seventh year. This great general, acknowledged by Hannibal as the best military commander of his age, had shown a high regard for the Celts as warriors. Antigonus Gonatus returned to the throne of Macedonia and was able to preserve his kingdom from that time until his death in 239BC. He continued to employ Celtic warriors in his army. Not only did he establish a tradition of Celtic mercenaries in the Macedonian army but he also seems to have acted as a broker in recruiting Celtic war bands and their dependants into the armies of the other Hellenic kingdoms.

Justin recounted that down to the end of the Macedonian Wars of Succession, the Celts left their dead scattered about the battlefields of Greece, martyrs to the cause of every Greek party and faction.

The Greeks, with memories of the invasion ever in their mind, always treated Celtic misdemeanours with harshness. In 265BC, for example, when a contingent of Celts, stationed in the city of Megara, mutinied over irregular and poor pay, they were all put to the sword. Megara was a Dorian city at the eastern end of the isthmus of Corinth where Eucleides of Megara (c.390BC) founded his school of philosophy.

The repulse of the Celts did not mean, of course, that there were now peaceful relations between the Macedonians and the Celts dwelling along the northern Macedonian borders. It was in the later part of the 3rd century BC that Rome, now fairly secure on the Italian peninsula, took some interest in the area of the Illyrian coast. Sending trading missions, the Romans found a mixture of Illyrian and Celtic tribes, the Celto-Illyrians of Henri Hubert. One of the main tribes had their capital at modern Kotor and was ruled by a king named Agron. Agron carried a Celtic name for it is the masculine form of a war goddess, Agrona, whose traditions still survive in Wales as 'the Washer of the Ford'. According to Polybius, Agron died from pleurisy in the autumn of 231BC. He was succeeded by his widow, Teuta.

This name presents some fascination: was it a Celtic title meaning 'the people's queen' from *teutates*, people, cognate with the Irish *tuath* and similar to the Gaulish title name Toutiorix, 'people's king'? Teuta was either a Celto-Illyrian or one of the Celtic ruling class which had established itself among the Illyrians. She ruled with an advisory council of chieftains, and certainly this was a Celtic form of government.

Polybius had little good to say about Teuta. 'She suffered from a typically feminine weakness, that of taking the short view of everything.' Teuta had apparently decided to extend her rule by an attack on the neighbouring state of Epiros, the kingdom recently ruled by Pyrrhos. In attacking Epiros her 'shock troops' were clearly identified as Celts. She sent ships to Phoenice, a town in Chaonia near modern Saranda. Here, interestingly enough, they found that the garrison of the town were some 800 Celtic mercenaries in the employ of Epiros. Teuta's men persuaded them to make common cause. According to Polybius: 'The plot was agreed, whereupon the men of Teuta landed, attacked the city and captured it and its inhabitants with the aid of the Celts, who gave help from within the walls.' Polybius obviously reserves his venom for the Celts who betrayed Phoenice. 'These were the men whom the Epirots made the protectors of the republic, whom they made guardians of their laws and to whom they entrusted their most prosperous city.'

An Epirot army marched to the rescue and found that the brother of Agron, Scordiliades, with an army of 5000 Celto-Illyrians, was marching on them through a pass near Antigoneia, about 20 miles south of modern Tepelenu in Albania. The Epirot army turned to face this new threat, taking up a position before a river whose bridges they had destroyed and where they thus felt secure. But, like Brennos and his men fifty years before at the Spercheios, Scordiliades and his warriors crossed the river in the middle of the night and at daybreak the next morning were facing the astounded Epirots. Polybius records: 'The Epirots were defeated, a large number of their men were killed, and even more taken prisoner; the remainder fled in the direction of the country of the Atintanes.'

Epiros now appealed for help to the Achaean League, which explains Polybius' tone as a former cavalry officer in the Achaean League. An army was raised. Scordiliades marched his men to Helicranum to face the Achaean forces but apparently his strength was in chariots and cavalry – as with most Celtic armies – and there was no good ground to use them to effect there. Teuta had sent messages to Scordiliades informing him that the Dardanians were taking the opportunity to raid their territory. Scordiliades marched his army back. Polybius reports:

This expedition had spread dismay and terror among the Greeks who were settled in the coastal region. They had seen the city, which was both the strongest and the best protected by nature in all Epiros, unexpectedly plundered, and henceforth they became anxious not, as in the past, for the mere fate of their crops, but for the security of their cities and their own lives.

It was at this point that Rome decided to intervene by sending two ambassadors, Gaius and Lucius Cornuncanius, to Queen Teuta. Rome not only passed on the complaints of the Greeks but apparently presented a list of wrongdoings against Roman traders in the area. 'Teuta listened to them with an arrogant and contemptuous air throughout the interview,' says Polybius. Some forthright words were exchanged.

After this plain speaking, Teuta gave way to a fit of womanish petulance, and was so furious at the ambassador's words that she cast aside the civilised convention, which governs the treatment of envoys, and as the delegation were leaving on their ship, she sent agents to assassinate the Roman who had uttered the offending speech. When the news reached Rome, public opinion was violently roused by this outrage on Teuta's part, and the authorities immediately began to enrol legions, assemble a fleet, and prepare an expedition.

The result was that a fleet of 200 ships under Gnaeus Fulvius, containing land forces commanded by Lucius Pistumius, was sent to systematically reduce Teuta's cities. Teuta herself withdrew into Kotor, which was strongly fortified. From there she finally managed to conclude a treaty with Rome agreeing to pay reparation and giving assurances of future good behaviour in that she promised not to continue her attacks against Epiros nor any other Greek states. Rome duly celebrated their victory in 228 BC. After that, no more is heard of this fascinating lady nor of her general, Scordiliades.

We do hear of continued Celtic raids deep into Macedonian

territory and it is recorded that as late as 110BC the Scordisci linked up with Thracian tribes and threatened Delphi once again.

In spite of these incursions by the restless Celtic tribes, Celtic mercenaries were still serving in the Macedonian army when the last Macedon king, Perseus, came to the throne in 179BC. There is also an intriguing reference by Livy who remarks that towards the end of the 2nd century BC there were Celtic settlers living in the area of Pella, the Macedonian capital, who were 'indefatigable tillers of the soil'. We certainly know that one thing the Greeks and Romans respected about the Celts was their farming abilities and technology. That there were Celtic farmers who had settled in Macedonia, apart from the great war bands, is intriguing information and the fact that they were numerous enough to be noticed by Livy is even more fascinating. One wonders to what extent such settlement went on and how extensive were the Celtic communities within Greece.

[8]

The Celts in Egypt

P TOLEMY II Philadelphios succeeded his father as Pharaoh of
Egypt in 283 BC. His mother was Berenice, the mistress of
Ptolemy I, whom the old king had married, thus disinheriting
his son Ptolemy Ceraunnos. Ptolemy I had been the only successor
of Alexander the Great to die in bed. The title 'Philadelphios' means
'sister lover': he married his sister Arsinoe, which was contrary to the
laws of Macedonia but acceptable to Egyptian monarchial practice.

Ptolemy II recruited a large corps of Celtic warriors for his army.
Pausanias records that some 4000 warriors and their dependants
went to Egypt following Antigonus Gonatus' victory at Lysimacheia
in 278 BC. There were troubles among the Ptolemy family. Ptolemy
II had executed his brother Argaios and his half-brother for plotting
to take over his throne. His second half-brother, Magas, who was
governor of Cyrene, the Greek colony in what is now Libya, was
not happy under his brother's rule. Finally, Magas rebelled.

Magas gathered an army against the Pharaoh but before he could
move he found that he had to deal with an uprising against his
authority by the Marmaridai of Libya. These nomadic tribesmen
threatened to destroy the prosperous trading colony which he controlled. Ptolemy II was about to take advantage of this problem when
the unexpected happened. His Celtic troops mutinied.

These events seem to have taken place in 259 BC. Therefore there
must have been a Celtic division in the Egyptian army for nearly
twenty years. The Celtic warriors tried to engineer a *coup d'état*.
Pausanias says: 'Ptolemy caught them plotting to take over Egypt.'
This gave Magas a sufficient breathing space to secure his own position in Cyrene. Pausanias also says that Ptolemy II was able to
subdue the Celts. If he was right about the Celts seeking to set up
their own rule in Egypt, then it was an ambitious and daring plan.
Callimachos, the Greek scholar (c.310/305–c.240 BC), who was from

Cyrene and who lived through the events, was at Alexandria at the time and had been commissioned by Ptolemy II to catalogue all the books in the famous Alexandrian library. During this period he produced several works, including his *Hymn to Delos* in which he celebrates the defeat of the Celts not only in Greece but also in Egypt and Pergamum. Callimachos speaks of a Celtic conspiracy to steal the treasures of Ptolemy II rather than to take over the government of Egypt. He says that the Celts used the opportunity of Ptolemy's concern over his brother Magas to make their attempt.

The Celts were defeated and treated with great severity by Ptolemy. Those that weren't killed immediately were taken to an island on the Sebennytic arm of the Nile and left to starve there. They perished, either by ritual suicide or by starvation. The suppression of the mutiny was considered of sufficient importance to be commemorated. Ptolemy struck a coin depicting a Celtic shield. A monument was also raised of which only fragments now survive; a piece shows the head of a Celt with an expression of intense pain. This is now in the Cairo Museum. There is also a younger Celtic head showing anguish and a headless body of a fallen Celtic warrior. The pieces are said to have come from one large monument which represented the scene of mass suicide and, in its original form, must have been a magnificent piece showing the epic story of these Celtic warriors. Other smaller monuments, showing the Celtic defeat, have also been discovered.

It seems that Ptolemy II was not a person to harbour grudges for we find him recruiting more Celtic mercenaries into his Egyptian army when he was developing commerce between the Nile and the Red Sea. This seems to endorse the fact that Ptolemy's policy was to keep a regular division of Celtic mercenaries within the Egyptian army whose personnel were changed periodically to ensure the best fighting men. Ptolemy reopened a canal originally excavated by Rameses II and built a road from Copto, near Thebes, to northern Berenice, named after his mother, and established trading links with Arabia, Ethiopia and India.

Ptolemy III Euergetes ascended to the throne of Egypt in 247BC and continued to recruit Celtic warriors to serve in the Egyptian armies. When he invaded Syria in 245BC and defeated Seleucus Callincos, captured Antioch and overran Mesopotamia, Babylon, Media and much of Persia, he had a strong Celtic contingent in his forces.

During the reign of Ptolemy IV Philopator (222–205 BC) there were significant numbers of Celts living in Egypt, warrior bands with their wives and dependants. According to M. Launey in his *Recherches sur les armées hellénistiques* (2 vols, 1949 and 1950), there is proof of an entire colony of Celts living near Alexandria. It could well be that they intermarried for Polybius speaks of them as the Katoikoi and their descendants as Epigovoi. Some of their graves and painted tombstones have been found in the cemetery of Hadra, south-east of Alexandria. Pottery inscribed with Celtic names has also been found, such as a vase bearing the name 'Dadórigon'. It is interesting that several of the Celtic males buried in this cemetery had Greek names, though Celtic names do appear here and there such as Adiatorix, Epossognatus and Toredorix, while their women nearly all had Celtic names such as Boudoris (which is cognate to the British Celtic Boudicca). We might assume that the move to Hellenise themselves was a purely male venture.

Ptolemy IV, on ascending the throne, had put to death his mother, Berenice, his brother, Magas, and his uncle, Lysimachos. This blood-thirstiness does not correlate with a story that is recorded about his attitude to his Celtic mercenaries. Some of the Celts in his service became demoralised because of an eclipse of the moon (c.220 BC). They would not fight because they believed the eclipse portended their defeat. We are told that Ptolemy contemplated killing them, as well as their wives and children who accompanied them, but then decided to be humane and ship them all back to the Hellespont, the place where he had recruited them.

It is recorded that 4000 of these Egyptian Celts fought at the battle of Raphia (Rafa) on the Palestine-Egyptian border. Ptolemy found himself in a war against Antiochos III of Syria, who had become monarch in 223 BC. Antiochos' Syrian kingdom had been greatly depleted. The wars with Egypt between 280 and 241 BC had left little of the western part intact and much of the east had broken away as a new kingdom of Parthia. Antiochos, in a bid to rebuild his kingdom, sent an army under his general Achaeus against Egypt.

At first Ptolemy suffered considerable losses. Antiochos' army of 20,000, which also included many Celtic mercenaries, met the Egyptian army of 25,000, including a division of 4000 Celtic cavalry, at Raphia. At first the Syrians drove back the Egyptian lines but as they began to pursue them from the battlefield, the Syrian infantry became disorganised. Ptolemy saw an opportunity and managed to regroup his men, while throwing his Celtic cavalry into the Syrian infantry. Antiochos lost 14,000 killed and 4000 captured. Only 2000 men, together with Antiochos himself, managed to escape. Polybius records that a Galatian named Lysimachos was in command of the Cardaces, a Celtic tribe, fighting for the Syrians at the battle of Raphia.

Egyptian Celtic cavalry had played a decisive role in this victory for the Pharaoh.

Another fascinating record of Celts serving in the Egyptian army of the Hellenistic Pharaohs occurs in 186/185BC when Ptolemy V Epiphanes was on the throne. Ptolemy was only five years old when his father died, aged forty years, and during his minority the affairs of Egypt were badly managed by his guardians Agathocles and Tlepolemus. Antiochos III, still thinking of revenge for his defeat at Raphia, re-established the Seleucid empire of Syria, and made an alliance with Philip V of Macedonia. The Macedonian navy provided Antiochos with much-needed sea power. However, a joint offensive against Egypt in 201BC was defeated and turned back at the island of Chios.

Undaunted by this, Antiochos launched a land attack through Palestine and his Syrian army confronted the Egyptians at Panion. The Egyptians were commanded by Scopas, on behalf of the then ten-year-old Pharaoh. They were defeated and Antiochos was able to seize all of Egypt's 'Middle East' territory. Only the threatened intervention of Rome in this war stopped Antiochos from invading Egypt itself. Peace terms between Syria and Egypt were settled in 195BC when Antiochos' daughter, Cleopatra, was betrothed to Ptolemy. The marriage took place in 193BC but it did not prevent Egypt from joining Rome in its attack on Syria in 190BC.

There was considerable unrest during Ptolemy V's reign. A revolt in Upper Egypt in 186/185BC caused Ptolemy to send an army of Celtic mercenaries along the Nile valley to quell the rebellion.

From this campaign survives one of the most intriguing testaments to the sojourn of the Celts in Egypt. In the small chapel of Horus, in the tomb of Seti I, at the great temple of Karnak, four Celtic warriors inscribed a piece of graffiti.

Τῶν Γαλατῶν
Θόας Καλλίστρατος
Ἀκάννων
Ἀπολλώνιος
ἤλθομεν
καί ἀλώπεκα
ἐλάβομεν ὧδε

'Of the Galatians,' they wrote in Greek, 'we, Thoas, Callistratos, Acannon and Apollonios, came, and a fox we caught here.' It is a fascinating inscription. Four Celts, serving Ptolemy V, had taken time off from putting down the revolt to wander into the tomb in idle curiosity. They caught a jackal, which they mistook for a European fox, and recorded what they had done, adding their names. It underlines a point. They did not write in Celtic. They wrote in straightforward Greek, so correct that Henri Hubert demonstrates that it was an acquired language and not a mother tongue. Hubert points out that Greek was the language of the mercenaries serving in the Hellenistic armies in much the same way as French was the common language of the many nationalities serving in the French Foreign Legion.

And with this piece of Celtic graffiti in the tomb of a Pharaoh who had reigned sometime prior to 1400 BC, the Celtic mercenaries of the Egyptian army disappear from historical record until the reign of Cleopatra VII (69–30 BC), the last of the Ptolemies to rule Egypt. According to the Jewish historian, Flavius Josephus (AD 37–c.100), there were still Celts serving in the Egyptian army at that time and, indeed, 400 Celtic warriors formed Cleopatra's élite bodyguard. After Octavian's victory over Antony and Cleopatra, this Celtic unit was given as a gift to Herod the Great of Judaea. Herod seems to have maintained the unit for twenty-six years afterwards. Josephus tells us that they took part in the parade at Herod's funeral in 4 BC. Obviously, these were not the same soldiers that served Cleopatra so one presumes that Herod continued to recruit either from Galatia or directly from Europe for this unit.

It would therefore seem, from these many references, that the Ptolemies of Egypt continually recruited Celtic mercenaries into their forces from the time of Ptolemy II for a period of 250 years until the end of the Ptolemaic dynasty in Egypt.

In understanding these Celtic links with Egypt, we might usefully return to insular Celtic mythology, particularly the mythology of Ireland. In the *Leabhar Gabhála* (the Book of Invasions), containing Ireland's origin myths, which survives in the *Leabhar na Nuachongh-bála* (sometimes referred to as the Book of Leinster or the Book of Glendalough) compiled in AD 1150 by Fionn Mac Gormain of Glendalough, we find the link with Egypt as part of Irish prehistory.

We find the story of a warrior named Golamh or Míl – from the Latin *miles Hispaniae*, soldier of Spain. It has been suggested that Golamh, which also appears in texts as Galamh, could be a compound of *gae* (spear) and *lamh* (hand). His story, having been written by Christian scribes from oral sources, has been regarded with great suspicion and not a little ridicule. The scribes give Golamh an ancestry through twenty-two Irish names and thirteen Hebrew names back to Adam. However, he is described as an Iberian Celt who took service with Reafloir, the king of Scythia. He eventually married the king's daughter, Seang. After Seang died, Reafloir grew fearful of Míl and plotted to kill him. Discovering the plot, Míl took his two sons, Donn and Airioch Feabhruadh, and they set off with their followers in sixty ships. Landing in Egypt, they took service with the Pharaoh Nectanebus. They fought as mercenaries in his army against the Ethiopians.

Míl is said to have married Scota, daughter of the Pharaoh, and his two sons Eber and Amairgen were born in Egypt. A third son, Ir, was born on an island off Thrace. We are told that Míl, with his wife and family, moved back to Iberia and from there he and his sons and followers went on to Ireland. Míl died on the voyage and his widow Scota was killed fighting the Dé Danaan in what is now Co. Kerry. His sons eventually established their rule in Ireland. It is from the sons of Golamh or Míl that the Gaels of Ireland claim their descent rather than from the previous mythological invasions of Ireland.

There is plenty that one might criticise in historical terms in this myth. Professor O'Rahilly dismisses it out of hand as a Christian invention. Dr Dáithí Ó hÓgáin correctly points out that the story is based on a biblical chronology and the 7th-century writings of Isidor-ius of Seville. The myth says that one of Golamh's ancestors, Fénius, helped to build the tower of Babel and that his grandson Gaedheal Glas (who, the myth states, created the Irish language) was in exile in Egypt at the same time as the Israelites. In one text we find that Gaedheal's life was saved by Moses after a snake bit him leaving a green (*glas*) mark from which he received his epithet. Moses, in curing him, promised that his descendants would dwell in a land where no such creatures existed and thus would be forever safe from them. This predates the legend about St Patrick driving all the snakes out of Ireland. The myth continues that Sru, grandson of Gaedheal, and his people were persecuted in Egypt and went to Scythia. They continued their wanderings and finally, in Iberia, Míl was said to have been born.

It is a fascinating piece of mythology. But is it purely mythology? We know enough these days to realise that myths are often based on symbolic renderings of a real history. One only has to look at Hebrew myth.

Why does the name of Nectanebus occur in Irish myth? There were two Pharaohs of the Thirtieth Dynasty called Nectanebus, one reigning in the years 380–363 BC and the second in 360–343 BC. This, of course, is just before the Ptolemaic take-over of Egypt. It was Darius III of Persia who invaded Egypt in 335 BC and took control of the Nile valley soon after the death of Nectanebus II. Only three years later, in 332 BC, Alexander and his Macedonians seized Egypt.

It is hard to believe the argument that this particular Egyptian connection is a piece of fiction to tie the ancient Irish into the history of the Israelites and that it was merely invented by biblically minded Christian scribes. The accepted dates of the Israelite bondage in Egypt are based around 1450/1400 BC, over 1000 years before either of the Nectanebus Pharaohs took the throne. If this was merely a fanciful biblical connection, why choose the name of such a late Pharaoh?

The Nectanebus period in Egypt was one of highly unsettled relations with surrounding countries – a period when mercenaries were used to fight Egypt's battles. The Persian king Cambyses (530–522 BC) had occupied the Nile valley and delta, and the Persians were eventually thrown out by Nectanebus I. Certainly by this time the Celts were serving as mercenaries in Sicily and in Sparta, at no great distance from Egypt.

The Celts were by now also settling in the areas ascribed to the Scythians so that aspect of the story is also believable. Could the story of Golamh therefore contain some elements of truth? Did such a war leader named 'spear hand' serve in the army of the Egyptian Pharaoh, Nectanebus, in his wars against the Persians and the Ethiopians? Could such a warrior, with his family, or even his entire war band, have eventually made his way to Ireland? We know that Iberian Celts had served as mercenaries in Sparta. So the fact that Golamh is also described as coming from Iberia is also believable. When they arrived in Ireland, did they carve out a kingdom for themselves and did their story lay the seeds which became the myth? Another interesting point is that many archaeologists have placed the date of the introduction of a La Tène Celtic culture in Ireland at about this very period, in the 4th/3rd centuries BC.

Perhaps the tales of mercenary soldiers, either returning home or coming as new settlers, could also account for the stories of other mythological heroes such as Partholon (Parthalán), who appears not only in the Irish *Leabhar Gabhála* but in the 9th-century *Historia Brittonum* of the Welshman Nennius. Partholon is said to have fled from Greece after the slaying of his father and mother when an attempt to take the kingship from his brother failed. He had lost his left eye in this episode and after seven years of wandering he arrived in Ireland with his wife, his three sons and their wives.

From Nennius and Geoffrey of Monmouth's *Historia regnum Brittanniae* – and I am well aware myths must be treated with a high degree of scepticism – we also find Greek links. After the Trojan war, someone called Brutus, grandson of Ascanius son of Aeneas, is said to have arrived in Britain and to have set up his rule over the Celts. Another fascinating tale is that of Brennos who sacked Rome. He appears as one of the two sons of Molmutine. He and his brother Belinus are said to have sacked Rome and while Belinus returned to Britain as king, Brennos remained in Gaul among the Allobriges and married the daughter of Seginos their chieftain.

There is also the story of the Irish Fir Bolg whose translation here, rather than O'Rahilly's 'lightning men', is given as 'bag men'. The story concerns Semeon, the grandson of Neimheadh. Neaidheadh (Nemed) was a name designating a sacred person, perhaps a Druid, coming from Nemet which we will discuss in Chapter Ten. Neimheadh led another settlement of Ireland some thirty years after Partholon. His grandson, Semeon, is said to have led a war band to Greece. They were enslaved by the Greeks and made to carry earth from one place to an area of bare rocks in order to turn it into a fertile plain; hence they became known as 'bag men' after the bags they had to carry the earth in. They eventually escaped from Greek captivity and made their way back to Ireland, arriving in three war bands. These were the Fir Bolg, the Gaileoin (*gai leoin*, spear for wounding) and the Fir Domhnann (*domhan*, deep, cognate with the Dumnonii of Britain). The interesting thing is that both the Gaileoin and the Dumnonii clearly come from the Continent. Is there an element of truth in this story? Did Semeon lead a war band to Greece, find himself enslaved after a battle, escape and join up with two other Continental Celtic war bands, and eventually return to Ireland where, we are told, he and his chieftains divided the country between them?

How well connected were the outlying parts of the Celtic world? I think they were extremely close, for the Celts of southern Gaul, in the 2nd century BC, were asked to use their influence with the Celts of Galatia. It would be easy to accept that such references were put into insular Celtic pseudo-history and myth because the scribes were intent on displaying their 'Classical' knowledge. However, the Celts of southern Germany certainly knew all about Brennos and his sack of Rome when, in the 1st century AD, they were seeking to throw off Roman influence. Cornelius Tacitus says that in AD 69 they maintained an oral historical tradition of Brennos' victory at Allia in 390 BC and subsequent sack of Rome, and that was some time before the Christian scribes started to commit their 'book learning' to paper. The stories could, therefore, be a rendering of a real oral tradition.

I believe that returning Celtic mercenaries, having served their terms in various foreign armies, came back not only with coins – for Egyptian, Greek and other Mediterranean coins have been found in Britain – but with stories of their endeavours which might well have laid the foundation for some of the insular Celtic heroic myths.

Throughout the Hellenic world, from the 3rd century BC, individuals as well as groups of Celts were to be found not only in the armies but as craftsmen, metalworkers and potters. To what extent they assimilated into the Hellenic world, or simply served the Hellenic states to make their fortunes before returning to their own homelands, is uncertain. Certainly, service in the armies of the numerous Hellenistic kings had become an important way of life for countless thousands of young Celtic men who, as was the custom of the time, took their wives and children with them in their campaigns.

Dr Mitchell observes:

> Celtic names occur at a number of city sites in Asia Minor during the Hellenistic and Roman periods, including the Asian cities of Priene, Smyrna, Ephesos, Pergamum, the country district of inland Mysia, Nicaea, Prusias ad Mare and Prusias ad Hypium in Bithynia, and in the Phrygian hinterland at Eumeneia, Philomelium, Docimeium and Apamea.

Indeed, a leading citizen at Apamea was Briccon, son of Ateuristos, whose epigram, found at Maroneia in Thrace, shows him to be the commander of a Celtic mercenary force, perhaps in the employ of Antiochos III of Syria. The reward for good and long service might well have been full citizenship of a Greek state. Another leading citizen of Docimeium, in Phrygia, south of the Celtic city of Trocnades, was a man who was in charge of the marble workshop there – Andaev.

Yet the biggest Celtic impact of all in the Hellenistic world was made by the tens of thousands of Celts who settled in the centre of Asia Minor and formed a state there which was to last, in its latter years as a Roman province, for over 800 years. It was to take its name from the more popular Greek name for the Celts, the Galateae – Galatia. And the Galatians are best remembered today in Christendom as the first non-Jewish people to accept Christianity, to whom Paul of Tarsus wrote his remarkable epistle, one of the earliest documents of the Christian Church.

[9]

The Celts in Asia Minor

WHILE Luturios and his Celts were crossing the Dardanelles into Asia Minor in the winter of 278/277BC, following the victory of Antigonus Gonatus at Lysimacheia, his fellow chieftain Leonnorios, with his tribe, was negotiating with Nicomedes, a claimant to the throne of Bithynia. Nicomedes decided to employ the Celts of Leonnorios as mercenaries. Bithynia had been allowed semi-independence in the Persian empire and when Alexander invaded Asia Minor its king was Bas. Bas was, somehow, able to survive, accepting Alexander as his overlord. When he died in 336BC his son Zipoetes became king, ruling for an incredible (for the time) forty-eight years. He exercised suzerain authority over the Greek cities of Heracleia Pontica, Astacus and Chalcedon. On his death, his kingdom was disputed between his two elder sons, Nicomedes and Zipoetes.

Nicomedes was looking for allies to help him gain the throne in that year of 278BC while Zipoetes had already secured the help of Antiochos of Syria (281–261BC), the son of Alexander's general, Seleucos. After Nicomedes made his deal with Leonnorios, getting permission for him to cross the Bosporus at Byzantium, Luturios immediately decided to rejoin him, bringing his Celts along the southern shore of the Propontis. Nicomedes sanctioned this reinforcement. Some of Nicomedes' supporters were worried by the new alliance with the Celts. Phaennis, a prophetess, born c.300BC, was the daughter of the king of the Chaonians and gave oracles at Dodona. She pointed out the consequences of admitting 'the lion' (Leonnorios) and 'the wolf' (Luturios) into the rich lands of Bithynia. Phaennis had obviously misunderstood the meaning of the Celtic name, which is 'mouse'. She is said to have foretold that the Celts would be defeated. The verses of the oracular poem are preserved by Zosimus.

Behold! the dread army of the Celts
at Hellespont, leaping the narrow strait
clamouring for battle and the booty of Asia!
The gods will bring down shame on you
who dwell along the seashore;
but Zeus shall send you a champion,
the beloved son of the god-suckled bull.
He will bring about the destruction of the Celts.

The 'god-suckled bull' is said to be a reference to Attalos of Pergamum of whom we shall speak later.

It is claimed that Nymphis, an historian of Heracleia at this time, wrote down the treaty made between Nicomedes and the Celts which is preserved in the work of Memnon of Heracleia. Stephen Mitchell, in his work *Anatolia*, believes it to have the look of authenticity, except that the Celts are referred to as *barbaroi* in the document which, if they were a party to it, would not have seen the word originally chosen.

According to this document, the Celts became allies, rather than mercenary forces, of Nicomedes and his descendants. They agreed to make no other treaties but to share the same friends and allies of Nicomedes. In this respect they would be allies to Byzantium, Tium, Heracleia, Chalcedon and Cius. In return for this alliance, Nicomedes granted them the right to plunder the lands of his enemies and provided them with weapons and support to do so.

While the names of Leonnorios and Luturios are the only personal names mentioned as leaders, Memnon speaks of a total of seventeen chieftains. The Celts were reckoned to number some 20,000 of whom 10,000 were under arms. But one would have reckoned that 10,000 warriors, bringing their wives, children and the elderly of the tribe with them, would have produced an additional population greatly in excess of this figure.

Within one campaign, presumably taking place in the spring or summer of 277 BC, Zipoetes and his supporters were defeated and driven out of Bithynia, and Nicomedes was safely installed on the throne. It is now that the tribal names of the Celts are recorded for the first time. Livy says that they were the Trocmi, Tolistoboii and Tectosages. We have already spoken of the Tectosages. Tolistoboii (often given as Tolistobogii) has the element of 'lightning' in the name but there has been no accepted etymology for the Trocmi. Livy says that Nicomedes I allowed his Celtic allies to raid Asia Minor, apart from Bithynia, as they willed and that they divided the lands on a tribal system. The Trocmi were to raid the Hellespont coast, the Tolistoboii the areas of Aeolis and Ionia and the Tectosages the eastward-lying lands.

During the following decade the Celts struck terror into the cities of Asia Minor as they moved around demanding 'protection money' from the Greek city states. On the payment of annual tribute the Celts agreed not to attack the cities. If the cities did not pay up then they would be attacked and plundered.

One of the first places to be attacked by the Tolistoboii was the shrine of Didyma, controlled by Miletus, the city near the mouth of the river Maeander. It was regarded as one of the richest shrines of the area. The Greek poet, Parthenios of Nicaea (c. 1st century BC) – interestingly, a friend of Gaius Cornelius Gallus, of a Celtic family – recounts an exotic love story connected with the sack of the shrine which, it seems, he had transcribed from an earlier source, probably from the romance by Aristodemos of Nysa.

When the Tolistoboii attacked the shrine a group of women were celebrating Thesmorphoria outside the city. This was a three-day festival held in honour of Demeter in almost every part of the Greek world. It was attended only by women and excluded virgins. Celebrated around October/November, it was a fertility ceremony to ensure good results for the cereal crops sown at this time.

A band of Celts seized these women whom they later ransomed. But one Celtic chieftain named Cauaros (a name perhaps coming from the same stem as *caur*, giant) fell in love with his captive, a lady named Erippe. Cauaros appears in the story as a man of integrity. He declared his love for his captive and took Erippe back to Gaul to be his wife. The woman's husband, Xanthos, a noble of Miletus, swore to reclaim his wife and he followed Cauaros all the way to Gaul, travelling via the Greek city states of southern Italy and landing in Massilia. Cauaros is said to be from the Gaulish tribe of the Cauari (the giants) who were settled around the modern towns of Avignon and Orange. Xanthos finally found Erippe. In the tale Erippe betrayed both her husband and her Celtic lover.

Another early record of a raid comes from Cyzicus where a relief was set up by the leading citizens to the god Heracles, showing

Heracles clubbing a Celtic warrior who is dressed in typical Celtic breeches, with large oval shield and short sword. According to Stephen Mitchell the date of this monument would be around 278/ 277 B C and its erection was doubtless in thanksgiving for the city's deliverance from the Celts.

An inscription at Delos records that a king or general named Philetaerus won a victory against the Celts about this time and we also find the same Philetaerus giving gifts of wheat and barley to the city of Cyzicus to support its citizens during the conflict. Strabo mentions that the Trocmi decided to use Ilium as a base for their raids while its population had to take refuge in nearby Petra, which was a fortified city.

The city of Pirene was the next to feel the might of the Celts. Inscriptions here show that a leader named Sotas (saviour) undertook measures to protect the place from the Celts. This was near Miletus and the area in which the Tolistoboii were active. Accounts say that the Celts desecrated temples and shrines throughout the countryside, set fire to farms and killed inhabitants. Sotas, it seems, brought all the rural population into the city, fortified it and took the step of paying able-bodied citizens to fight as infantry or cavalry.

Further north from Pirene, the city of Erythrae decided to pay the Celts to leave them alone. An inscription raised by one Polycritus, presumably the military commander of the city, indicates that the citizens had collected money and sent it to Leonnorios. This seems to indicate that Leonnorios was chieftain of the Tolistoboii. The inscription gives thanks for the lack of bloodshed. But a second memorial indicates that the Celts, presumably to ensure the payment of the money, had taken hostages and when Polycritus took the money to pay them, these hostages were released unharmed.

From Miletus came tales of the women of that city preferring to commit suicide than fall into the hands of the Celtic warriors.

Inland, to the east, where the Tectosages were now raiding, a similar story was emerging. At Thyateira, an inscription, dated to the summer of 275 B C, was raised by a grateful father, thanking the gods for the rescue of his son who had previously been captured by the Celts. In the territory of Laodicea, another inscription thanks the agents of one Achaeus for helping to ransom prisoners during the wars with the Celts. Pausanias repeats stories of how the inhabitants of towns such as Themisonium were saved through the intervention of the gods. However, Themisonium was not founded until twenty years after these events although it is possible that folklore from a previous community could have been incorporated in Pausanias' account.

The Celtic raids extended as far as the southern coast of Asia Minor to Limyra where a circular temple was erected soon afterward; one of its surviving panels shows a Celtic shield carved in relief. The fragmentary inscriptions give thanks for relief against the Celtic raids and provide the evidence that the Celtic warriors, with Nicomedes' blessing, were active over a wide field.

It was inevitable that Antiochos, the son of Seleucos and now firmly in control of Syria and much of eastern Asia Minor, would personally intervene. The city states of Asia Minor, over which he claimed suzerain control, would surely have sent emissaries asking the Syrian king to come to their aid. It is generally accepted that it was in 275BC that Antiochos marched against the Celts and won a major victory over them which earned him the title of Soter (saviour). This title Soter is not to be confused with the proper name of Sotas of Pirene. Stephen Mitchell points out that the earliest appearance of the title, on inscriptions, belongs to the period 268–261BC and that the Celts were still raiding with impunity as late as 269BC. He believes, and it seems reasonable, that the date of this major victory over the Celts should be placed around 269BC and not 275BC.

This battle was the cause of celebration among the Hellenic kingdoms and caused Simonides of Magnesia, a third-century BC epic poet, to write an account. Lucian (AD115–c.180) gives an account from earlier sources in *Zeuxis*. He says that the Celts put into the field some 240 chariots of which eighty had scythed wheels. Certainly the Celts used such chariots and we find them depicted on the reliefs commemorating the victories over the Celts by Pergamum. Caesar describes such chariots being used by their cousins, the British Celts, when he invaded Britain over 200 years later. In a chambered tomb at Mal Tepe, at Mezek, the third-century BC remains of a Celtic chariot with bronze fittings have been found together with La Tène C type artefacts, such as brooches and ornaments.

Antiochos' victory was claimed as decisive. It was achieved by the use of war elephants, creatures which the Celts do not appear to have encountered before. Four centuries later, the Roman Emperor Claudius, during the invasion of Britain, brought to an end the fighting at Camulodunum (Colchester) by the use of elephants. Antiochos, we are told, used his elephants to smash through the lines of Celtic warriors. In the necropolis of Myrina, in Aeolis, figurines showing an elephant trampling a Celtic warrior to death have been discovered, confirming the importance of what is now called the 'elephant victory'.

What precisely happened in the wake of this victory is unclear. Appian of Alexandria (*fl.* AD160) maintains, erroneously, that Antiochos drove all the Celts out of Asia Minor. Livy implies that Antiochos' victory was not as complete as other sources claim and that the Celts continued to dominate Asia Minor, imposing a levy on the Hellenic kingdoms whose kings continued to pay them 'protection money'. Livy also says it was the Celts themselves who chose an area of permanent settlement and disputes the popular theory that Antiochos forced the Celts to settle on the central plain of Turkey as a result of his 'elephant victory'. Even more importantly, Livy says that even the Seleucid kings paid the Celts the 'protection money' or tribute, down to the time of the victory of Attalos I of Pergamum over the Celts around 230BC. The term *galatika* was said to mean 'Celtic tribute' and entered the Greek vocabulary at this time. Strabo believes that the Celts were not even confined to the area of settlement, which became known as Galatia, until the time of Attalos of Pergamum.

The proposal that Antiochos was paying the Celts tribute after his 'elephant victory' is reinforced when the Seleucid king writes to the city of Erythrae to grant them autonomy and telling them they did not have to pay certain financial levies especially 'for Galatian/Celtic matters'. Importantly, Antiochos' victory did not see any change in the kingship of Bithynia. Nicomedes retained his kingdom. As he was the monarch responsible for introducing the Celts into Asia Minor and supporting and encouraging their attacks on the Greek cities of the area, Antiochos, had his victory been absolute, would have imposed some penalty on Nicomedes. As Antiochos was supporting Nicomedes' brother, Zipoetes, in the struggle for the throne of Bithynia, it is more than possible that the penalty would have been the removal of Nicomedes. It could be that Zipoetes was already dead by this time. But the evidence, I believe, points to the fact that Antiochos' 'elephant victory' was not as complete as claimed. Such a complete victory does not accord with the fact that Antiochos now lost control over the northern part of Phrygia and the north-western portion of Lydia which became Pergamum. Nor does the fact that in 261 BC Antiochos was killed in another battle against these same Celts near Ephesos bear out the theory that the Celts had been subjugated by him.

What the 'elephant victory' probably did was make an initial check to the Celtic raids on the rich cities of the western coastal region. Whether it was caused by the 'elephant victory' or not, we can be certain in saying that it was at this time that the Celts made their settlement on the central plain of Asia Minor in the area which became known as Galatia.

Both Livy and Justin support the idea that the initial strength of the Celts was 10,000 fighting men and 10,000 others. What appears in Galatia within a decade or two, however, is an entire nation. Livy and Justin believe that the population growth was merely due to the fecundity of the Celts. Livy says: 'And so great was the terror of their name, their numbers being also enlarged by great natural increase, that in the end even the King of Syria did not refuse to pay them tribute.' It is an idea echoed by Strabo, writing on the proliferation of the Celts in Gaul proper.

However, Polybius indicates that the original Celtic tribes were continually being reinforced by new waves of Celtic settlers from Europe, crossing the Bosporus. This seems the more likely reason for the expansion of the original tribes into the Galatian nation.

[10]

The State of Galatia

THE state of Galatia was established sometime during the decade of the 260s BC. That much is fact.

'What we know of the Galatian state gives us our first example of the organisation of a Celtic state,' said Henri Hubert in *The Greatness and Decline of the Celts* (1934). If, as I and others have argued, it was not the result of Antiochos' 'elephant victory' and did not emerge as a result of Antiochos' idea to solve his 'Celtic question', how and why did it come about? Primarily it was allowed to come into existence through the disunity of the petty Hellenic kingdoms of Asia Minor. I think we may believe those accounts which imply that the Celts simply settled in the territory of their own volition.

It was Hieronymus of Cardia, writing contemporaneously in the 3rd century BC, perhaps the most trustworthy historian of these events, whose death is placed between 373 and 263BC, who first used the term Galatia for the land of the Gauls or Galli – the synonym for Celts. He called it 'Koinon Galation', the Commonwealth of Galatians. This reference would mean that the existence of a Celtic state, which was not a kingdom with a single king, in Asia Minor before the end of the 260s BC, was a fact.

The area in which the Celts settled was the northern zone of the central plateau of Asia Minor, a region rising to 2000–4000 feet above sea level. The actual geographical limits of Galatian occupation have never been firmly fixed and some scholars are of the opinion that Celts continued to display nomadic habits within this territory and were not tied to any one spot. This does not quite accord with the evidence of Celtic sites and hill-forts which occur in the area as well as the towns which bear obvious Celtic names. Whatever initial arguments there might have been for the nomadic theory, by the time of the Roman invasion, one hundred years later, the Celtic tribes were well established in identifiable areas.

To make some attempt to assess the extent of this new Celtic land one could take a rough measurement from the area of Trocnades in the west – a town bearing a Celtic name – on a longitude to the area of Vanota in the east, which would be 480 kilometres. From Bolu in the north – where Celtic remains have been found – south on a point of latitude to the Celtic town of Tolostochara, is some 160 kilometres. This land area would thus give us 76,800 square kilometres. The entire country was one of few trees, bare hills, but small fertile plains, especially when watered during a good rainy season. It was, however, a land frequently affected by droughts and consequent famines. It had once been the centre of the Phrygian kingdom, famed for King Midas and Gordius of the renowned Gordian knot. The Phrygians were an Indo-European people who had lost their independence in the 6th century BC to Greek settlement. In the *Iliad* the Phrygians were represented as an heroic warrior people. It was generally thought that they were part of an early movement from Greece and therefore spoke a related form of Greek.

When the Celts settled in this area, they lived side by side with the native population for we have no records of population displacement or serious conflicts within Galatia itself. It has been argued that there was very little aboriginal population left in the area following the devastations created by Alexander's conquest and the subsequent wars of the *diadochoi*, the 'successors', those who sought by force to inherit Alexander's empire. So, apart from the urban population centres, the Celts were moving into a depopulated area.

The Celts built their traditional hill-forts and farming settlements throughout the area. They continued to grow cereal crops and changed their livestock herds mainly to sheep flocks, in keeping with the animal husbandry of the country. One notable dietary change has been noticed: they ceased to eat pork. Pigs and wild boar were one of the main meats eaten by the European Celts, and such animals often assumed a sacred standing in Celtic religious matters. In Asia Minor the Celts, for reasons of good health, quickly adopted local dietary custom.

Among the prominent sites in Galatia was the city of Pessinus, once the main religious centre of the Phrygians. A mixed population continued to live there. We know that Deiotaros I of Galatia preferred to rule from a *dun* or hill-fort to the north. We also know from the evidence that the sacred shrine of the Cybele at Pessinus and its Attis, or chief priest, bore Celtic names in the years after the settlement.

By the mid-2nd century BC the Celts had certainly adopted the local religion. One Attis of Pessinus had a brother whose name was Aiorix, obviously a Celt, proving that the Celts were involved in the organisation of the temple. While the *rix*, king, element is easy to identify, the meaning of the *aio* element, occurring in many Continental Celtic names, is still a matter for learned speculation. We also know from Diodorus that a dispute between the Galatian king, Deiotaros, and one Brogitaros (bull of the territory) over his claim to the high priesthood at Pessinus actually spread to Rome where the Senate was asked to pass judgement. Celtic names occur among the Pessinus priesthood even as late as the 1st century AD when we hear of the Attabocaoi, shadowy members of the temple hierarchy. It has been suggested that this name would signify 'the reborn ones' and is related to the Old Irish *aithgein*, rebirth.

The later eunuch priests of Cybele were actually called Galli, supposedly named after the river Gallus – which had undoubtedly been renamed by the Celts. This river flowed near the temple of Pessinus. It was said that anyone who drank the waters of the Gallus would be driven mad. The remnants of the Phrygian culture, as we know from St Jerome (Eusebius Hieronymus, c.AD 342–420) were merged into Celtic culture and not, as some maintain, the reverse.

The Cybele was a Phrygian 'Mother Earth' goddess, originally known there as Agdistis. She was later fitted awkwardly into Hellenic myth as being identified with Rhea, mother of Zeus, greatest of the gods. The myth states that Zeus was lying asleep on Mount Didymos in Phrygia and let his seed fall on the ground. From this grew a being with both male and female parts. The gods, in fear, castrated the creature and, as a female, it grew into Cybele. The male genitals, having fallen to the ground, grew into an almond tree from which an almond one day fell into the lap of the river goddess Sangarios. The fruit entered her womb and she conceived a son, Attis, who grew into a beautiful youth and with whom Cybele eventually fell in love. Attis was unaware of Cybele's passion and was about to marry the daughter of the king of Pessinus. Cybele, angry, drove Attis and the king of Pessinus insane so that they castrated themselves. Attis died and Cybele repented and obtained a promise from Zeus that his body should never decay. Thus he was buried at Pessinus, at the site of the holy shrine, where it was said his hair continued to grow and his little finger continued to move. From his body grew a sacred tree (usually identified as a pine).

There are small variations on this theme, but it explains the site of the temple and the name of the high priest, the Attis. The Galli, or priests of Cybele, were said to castrate themselves in imitation of Attis; though such an act would be contrary to what we know of Celtic culture.

But why would the Celts adopt this piece of Phrygian religion and become high priests at the temple, which also implied that generally they worshipped there? The fact was that the Phrygian myth of Cybele and Attis was not far removed from the Celtic story of Danu and Bíle; they were both Indo-European peoples and had once shared a common pantheon of gods and goddesses. The similarity of ideas would have allowed the Celts to accept the story of Attis, the sacred tree, born of the Sangarios river, along which they had now settled. The concept of the 'Mother of the Gods' and her spouse, Attis, as a sacred tree, would be at one with Celtic theology.

The Cybele of Pessinus had close links with the Delphic oracle and, later, with the Sybilla at Rome. Her cult was introduced into Rome around 205BC when it was claimed the Romans thought that they had to bring the Cybele to the city if they were to ensure victory over Carthage. Roman delegates were sent to Pessinus and returned with – interestingly enough, when thinking of Celtic symbolism – a sacred stone in which the spirit of the goddess dwelt. The story goes that the ship transporting the stone became stuck in the Tiber; a girl called Claudia Quinta, who had been unjustly accused of adultery, prayed to Cybele and, pulling on a rope, freed the ship by her own strength from the mud bank and thus proved her innocence.

The cult was found on Rhodes where, in 190BC, Roman troops commanded by Gaius Livius Salinator landed to attack Sestos. Livy says that:

The soldiers were already coming up to the walls when some mystic Galli, in their ceremonial dress, met them before they reached the gate. They told the soldiers that they were servants of the Mother of the Gods and that at the bidding of the goddess they were coming to beg the Romans to spare the walls and city. No violence was offered to them; and before long the senate (of Sestos) came out in a body, with the magistrates, to surrender the city.

The Galli also intervened when the Roman general Vulso was marching through Galatia. Livy says: 'The Galli of the Great Mother from Pessinus met them, in their peculiar accoutrements, prophesying in a mystic chant that the goddess was granting the Romans a clear road in war and giving them victory and dominion of that region.' This is confusing for, knowing that the priests of Pessinus, during this period, had Celtic names, it is hard to imagine they would give their blessing to the Roman conquest over their fellow Celts.

The Celts obviously brought their own religious practices with them. Pausanias had attacked the Celts, during the sack of Delphi, for their general impiety and for having no gods or priests. That is, of course, an understandable attitude from a Greek viewpoint. Pausanias, curiously, also attacked the Celts for not having 'the science of prophecy'. We know that the Galatians shared the same religious concepts as the rest of the Celtic world, in which prophecy played a dominant role. They were certainly 'god-fearing' and much inclined to take note of auguries. They practised divination, the interpretation of dreams and natural phenomena, astrology and other matters. Deiotaros, in his conversations with Cicero, showed the Roman consul his enthusiasm for augury. They also looked for signs in the entrails of sacrificially slaughtered animals, as was recorded before the battle at Lysimacheia in 277BC. In such matters their customs differed little from the Romans and Greeks, who also sacrificed animals in search of portents.

Unfortunately, there are few relics of the native Celtic religious practices in Galatia. Plutarch recounts the story of Camma, a wife of a Galatian chieftain named Sintaros (storm-bull). Plutarch says she was an hereditary priestess of Artemis, 'the goddess whom the Galatians revere most'. While the description by Plutarch is of a Hellenised goddess, we should bear in mind that in the western Celtic world, Artemis was equated with Brigantu (or Brigid), the goddess of fertility. Camma's husband, Sintaros, was murdered by a man called Sinorix. This name, appropriately enough, seems to mean 'king of storms' or 'ruler of the weather'. He then forced Camma to marry him, but, as the ceremony involved drinking from a common cup, Camma contrived to put poison into it. She allayed Sinorix's suspicions by drinking first and so accepted death herself. Sinorix drank and died. Dr Mitchell is inclined to dismiss the story as Hellenic in origin as there was no evidence of Artemis being worshipped in Galatia. But if Artemis, who certainly was recorded as being worshipped by the Aedui of Gaul, was no more than an equation for a Celtic goddess like Brigantu, then there is no need to dismiss the story.

As for the Celts adopting local deities, we find that one Dyteutus, son of Adiatorix, a Celtic chieftain who ruled in the city of Heracleia Pontica in the 30s BC, was high priest of the goddess Ma at Comana Pontica. He remained high priest there until AD 34/5. Even Strabo mentions him and we must conclude that he was a very influential person.

The three Celtic tribes settled, as was the tradition, in separate areas. The Tolistoboii settled in the upper valley of the Sangarios (Sakarya), by whose winding river path the tombs of the long-dead Phrygian kings lay. Pessinus, as has been said, was the main city in this area. But also in this territory stood the city of Gordium (now Polatli), once the capital of ancient Phrygia, where, in the acropolis of the temple of Zeus Basileus, there stood a pole around which was tied an intricate knot. Legend had it that Gordius, father of King Midas, had tied this knot and a prophecy was handed down that he who unravelled it would become lord of all Asia. In 333 BC Alexander of Macedonia had rested in the city and, on examining the knot, simply hacked it to pieces with his sword, claiming that the prophecy was now fulfilled. And into many languages has come the phrase 'to cut the Gordian knot', meaning to overcome a difficulty by violent measures. Gordium was renamed Vindia, 'the white place', by the Celts (*vindos*, white).

The Tolistoboii territory bordered Bithynia where the fortresses of Deiotaros have been identified, the first at Karalar, overlooking the valley of the Ova Cay, and the second at Tabanlioglu Kale, commanding the gorge of Girmir Cay. These fortresses were obviously the main strongholds of the chieftains of the Tolistoboii before Deiotaros used them. Many other Tolistoboii fortresses have been identified throughout the area but the Karalar fort is the only site to have been excavated. Near Karalar are three chamber tombs, one of which belongs to Deiotaros II, the son of Deiotaros I. It would seem that the funerals of Galatian Celtic chieftains were lavish affairs and, even after the plundering of these tombs over the centuries, many fascinating grave goods have been found there including a Celtic gold torque and pieces of purple cloth. In one grave was a gold belt buckle, with a bearded and moustached face of a Celt on it.

Further to the south-east of the Tolistoboii territory, the Tectosages claimed the land. However, we have some problems identifying its boundaries exactly. We know that the Tectosages were situated between the Tolistoboii and the Trocmi. Strabo claimed that their territory started from a point east of Pessinus with Ancyra as their stronghold. This gives the impression that the Tectosages extended between the rivers Sangarios and Halys diagonally across Galatia. We know that the Tectosages' chieftains had their main fortress some 21 miles south of Ancyra at a place called Gorbeous, a hill-fort, where in the late 40s BC a Tectosagean chieftain named Castor and his wife were murdered.

Their territory must have reached to the banks of the river Halys (now the Kizilirmak), with Ancyra (Ankara) as their chief settlement. Strabo referred to Ancyra as a Celtic *phourion*, a stronghold. This would mean that it was originally a hill-fort.

There is an interesting story connected with the foundation of Ancyra in the work of Stephanus of Byzantium (*fl.* early 7th century AD) whose *Geography* was based on early works by Polyhistor and Strabo. It is recorded that the Tectosages were fighting in alliance with Mithridates II of Pontus and Apollonorius of Aphrodisias against the forces of Ptolemy II of Egypt in the Black Sea. According to Stephanus, the Celts managed to capture the anchors of the enemy ships thereby rendering them unmanageable in the battle so that they were easily overcome. For this feat of arms the Pontic king gave them the land around Ancyra as a reward and they then named their capital after the trophies they had captured – *ancyra*, the Greek word for 'anchor', which has permeated into many modern European languages. Ancyra did not became a capital of Galatia until the Roman period. This sea battle must have occurred before 266BC when Mithridates II died. This is another indication that the date of Celtic settlement in Galatia was in the early part of the 260s BC.

The third tribe, the Trocmi, settled along the Halys to the east and their major stronghold was Tavium (Posdala).

In further confirmation, we note that when Galatia became a Roman province, the Romans issued three coins giving the tribal capitals as Pessinus for the Tolistoboii, Ancyra for the Tectosages and Tavium for the Trocmi.

If there was any friendship between the Celts and the kingdom of Pontus, it was shattered when Ariobarzanes II, who had succeeded as king in 266BC, attacked the Celts and a war broke out. The citizens of Amisus were forced to send an embassy to the Celts led by the historian Nyphis and agreed to pay them 2000 gold pieces in addition to 200 for each Celtic chieftain in order to end the conflict.

Looking at the borders of the Celtic territory, Strabo mentions a district north of the Siberis river in southern Bithynia and west of Paphlagonia, the valley of what is now the Girmir Cay, as being the country of Gaezatorix. Polybius refers to a Galatian chieftain named Gaezatorix (king of the spears) in 180BC. His tribal land places Celtic influence well in the north of Asia Minor at that period. In his area a city with a Celtic name, Souoibroga (*broga*, country), stands at the headwaters of the Siberis. There is a surviving inscription from this Kizilcahamam district showing that a cult of 'Zeus Souolibrogenos' flourished here. To the north-west of the Siberis is Bolu (Claudiupolis) where a significant Celtic tomb has been discovered.

The Celts therefore occupied the country south of Bithynia, Paphlagonia and Pontus and north of Pisidia and Cappadocia. In the west Pessinus marked one boundary while its eastern border was at Tavium (Posdala). Tavium appears as both a Celtic fortress and a settlement, rather than just an existing town subsequently occupied by the Celts. Its name seems to derive from the same stem as does the Welsh *taw*, rest. Thus Tavium would be 'place of rest'. Several new towns do appear to have sprung up in Galatia at the time of the Celtic settlement and, significantly, they all bear Celtic names – most of them in the area of the Tolistoboii: Articnus, Petobriga, Noventi, Vindia, Trocnades, Ocondiani, Tolostochoria and, of course, the fortresses of Peium (modern Yassihüyük, east of Gordium), from the stem *pau*, inhabited country, and Blucium, cognate with the Welsh *blwgh*, a box-like shape. Among these names we see many familiar elements such as *briga*, a height. In the land of the Tectosages we find a city called Orosologiaco; in that of the Trocmi we find Bussurix, Vanota and Eccobriga, as well as Tavium. This would argue against the belief that the Celtic tribes were merely nomadic.

Life among the Celts in their Asian hill-forts and settlements appeared to continue as it did among their European cousins. One particular cultural custom was noticed by the Greeks. The descriptions of Celtic feasts in Gaul and elsewhere in the western Celtic world were paralleled in the world of the Galatians. Phylarchus, an Athenian historian of the 3rd century BC, provides an example. A chieftain named Ariamnes is said to have organised a feast and invited not only his fellow Celts but visitors and other guests. All types of meat were available, served from huge bronze cauldrons. Great canopies were erected under which some 400 people could sit at a time. It was mentioned that priority was given to the king and his leading chieftains within the feasting hall.

In the *Vita S. Theodori*, the life of St Theodore of Sykeon, written in the 7th century AD, there appears a curious echo of the ancient Celtic custom of feasting which seems to indicate that it was still surviving in Galatia at the time. Theodore and two companions were returning from a pilgrimage to Jerusalem. They were staying in a monastery in southern Galatia. After eating well as guests of the Galatian abbot, one Cambolomaros – certainly a Celtic name – Theodore observed: 'Truly, my children, we have eaten like Galatians.' The point is that the Galatian Celts were still as renowned for their feasting as were their western brethren.

It is Strabo who assures us that all three Celtic tribes spoke the same dialect of Celtic (*homoglotti*).

> The three tribes used the same language and differed from one another in no other respect; they were divided each into four sections, and called *tetrarchies*, each having its own *tetrarch*, one judge and one military commander, subordinate to the *tetrarch*, and two junior commanders. The council over which the twelve *tetrarchs* presided consisted of three hundred men, and they assembled at the so-called Drynemetos. The council decided murder cases, the *tetrarchs* and the judges all others. This, therefore, was the constitution in the old days, but during my time power has passed to three, then to two and then to a single ruler, named Deiotaros, and then to Amyntas who succeeded him.

A wounded Celt. One of the many marbles and bronzes
which Greeks, especially of Pergamum, created to
mark their battles with the Celts. Most of these marbles
date from the second century BC. *Museo Nazionale,
Naples.*

A dead Celt, fallen on his shield.
Museo Archeologico, Venice.

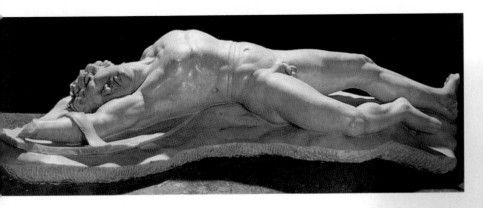

A Celtic warrior being overwhelmed and attempting to defend himself.
Museo Archeologico, Venice.

A disarmed Celt awaiting the death blow.
Museo Archeologico, Venice.

One of the most famous renderings of a Celtic warrior, known as
'The Dying Gaul'. Wounded, wearing only his golden torc, and
lying on his long shield with Celtic short sword and battle horn,
this marble is in the *Capitolino Museum, Rome.*

A detail from 'The Dying Gaul',
showing a typical Celtic moustache and torc.

Detail of Celtic warrior committing suicide (see jacket cover)
having killed his wife so she would not fall into the hands of the
Greeks. This was raised by Attalos I of Pergamum, originally as a
bronze at the Nicropolis of Athena at Pergamum. This marble
copy is in the *Museo Nazionale, Rome.*

A Celtic chieftain from Vachères, Basses Alpes, second century BC, showing his torc, chain mail and long shield. Chain mail was a Celtic invention and Polybius mentions the Celts wore it at the battle of Thermopylae. *Musée Calvet, Avignon.*

Part of the base of an altar to the god Zeus at
Pergamum, symbolising Pergamum's victories over the
Celts circa second century BC. *Staatliche Museen,
Berlin.*

A fourth century BC Celtic bronze war
helmet from Agris. *Musée de la Société
Archéologique et Historique de la
Charente.*

A selection of Celtic war helmets which were remarked on by the
Greeks. *l. to r.* fourth century BC bronze, *Museo Nazionale,
Ancona*; fourth century BC bronze, *Musée du Louvre*; second
century BC iron, *Schweizerisches Landesmuseum, Zurich*; fifth
century BC bronze, *Musée des Antiquités Nationales,
St Germaine-en-Laye*; and two fourth century BC bronzes from
the *Staatliche Museen, Berlin.*

Delphi, seen by the Greeks as the centre of the world
and the sacred site of the oracle of Apollo. This spot is
the *tholos* or sanctuary of Athena Pronaia built
circa 400 BC and was one of the buildings looted by
the Celtic army of Brennos.

The Celtic 'Father of the Gods'. Known to the Irish as The Dagda ('The Good God'), he was called Dis Pater by the Romans and likened to Jupiter. He carried a massive club or hammer and possessed a magic cauldron. He is thought to be equivalent to Gaulish and British Cernunnos. This bronze is from Prémeaux in the *Musée des Beaux-Art, Beaune.*

is inscription comes from temple of Augustus at the ital of the Trocmi Celts at cyra (Ankara). It is of ticular interest as it ntions two British Celtic gs, Dumnovellaunos and commius who ruled in th-east Britain before the man conquest.

A group of second/first century BC kitchen utensils and pots found in a Celtic grave at Goeblingen-Nospelt. *Musée de la Société Archéologique et Historique de la Charente.*

A Galatian coin of Deiotoros from the first century BC. *Schweizerisches Landesmuseum, Zurich.*

Coins of the Celtic Boii
(Czech Republic),
bearing the Celtic names
Devil, Evoivirix and
Cobrovomarus.
First century BC.
*Slovenské Národné
Múzeum.*

A Celtic coin with a
mounted warrior
carrying a spear circa
second century BC
from Hungary.
*National Museum,
Budapest.*

Coin of one of the Celts' most unrelenting enemies, Eumenes II of Pergamum, second century BC. *British Museum, London.*

Three Celtic silver coins from Transylvania dated circa fourth century BC. *Schweizerisches Landesmuseum, Zurich.*

Other sources tell us the names of the four septs into which each tribe was divided. Pliny mentions that among the Tolistoboii were septs called the Voturi and Ambitui, and among the Tectosages was a sept called the Teutobodiaci; while Plutarch refers to the *tetrarch* of the Tosiopae. There is also a mention by Stephanus of Byzantium to the Skorpioi living in Ancyra, while Pliny refers later to a tribe, not a sept, called the Rhigosages who had hired themselves as mercenaries to Seleucus of Syria in 212BC.

Each sept was ruled by a chieftain, a war chieftain, with two petty chieftains and a judge. This judge would have been one of the Celtic intellectual caste, in other words a Druid, although no writer specifically mentions that name when referring to the Galatian Celts. Certainly, while references to the Galatians avoid the term, it is clear from Clement of Alexandria (c.AD1150–1216) that there were Druids among the Galatians. Elsewhere in the Celtic world, this caste was identified by the Greeks as *druidae*. It is not to be supposed that the Galatian Celts were any different from their European cousins; their society would have been divided in the same manner: the king and his warriors, the Druids combining all the intellectual professions, the craftsmen and the labourers.

Strabo mentions that the twelve septs of the Galatian tribes sent their 300 representatives to an assembly at Drynemetos, or Drunemeton, which means 'the sacred grove of the oak'. Unfortunately, the exact site of Drunemeton is not clear. If Pessinus was, in reality, the chief city of the Celts as one Greek source claims, then perhaps it and Drunemeton were one. But this seems doubtful. *Nemeton* as a word for 'sanctuary' occurs in many Celtic place-names throughout Celtic Europe. Indeed, it is one of the most popular roots for names connected with religious sites, both pre-Christian and Christian. Nemetodurum was an early name for Nanterre. Nemetobrigia occurs as a place-name in Spanish Galicia. Vernemeton is mentioned by Fortunatus as a Celtic centre in modern Nottinghamshire in England, while the same place-name occurs three times in Gaul. Medionemeton was situated in southern Scotland. *Nemed* occurs in Old Irish, *nemet* in British Celtic and *nemeton* in Gaulish.

In describing the assembly, Strabo seems to be portraying a form of government which is paralleled by the assembly of Gaul which met at Lugdunum (Lyons), the fortress of the god Lugh. The fourfold division of the tribes is to be seen also in the four cantons of the

Helvetii in the western Alps (now Switzerland) and the four septs of the Cantii of southern Britain at the time of Caesar's invasion.

The form of government of Galatia accords with everything we know of later social and political structures among the Celts, with a system of representatives to a tribal assembly ensuring that no single despot could exert supreme sovereignty. However, this very laudable decentralised form of government and lack of a single powerful monarch, in the early years of Galatia, made the Celts anarchistic and prone to weakness when faced by their powerful, centrally governed neighbours, as we will see.

Although Strabo points out that the Galatians all spoke the same Celtic dialect, they did not bequeath any documentation in their own language, not even lengthy inscriptions using Greek characters as did their cousins in Europe. Those few inscriptions that do survive were written in Greek. According to Henri Hubert: 'Their Greek is so correct . . .' He maintains: 'Greek was the language of the Gallic troops . . .', that is, the mercenaries serving the Hellenistic kings. 'Greek was likewise the official language of the Gauls of Asia Minor. They have not left a single inscription in Celtic.' However, Professor Rankin proposes the theory that the Galatians were, in fact, anti-Greek, did not become Hellenised to any large degree and, when the area fell under Roman conquest, actually adopted Roman forms in preference to Greek. This does not quite accord with the evidence for we find that the Celts of Galatia were using Greek names from a very early period in their settlement. In fact, the Celtic use of Greek names is a problem for the historian. We find that many personages whom we believe to be Greek, because of their name, turn out to be Celts. The best example of this is the famous friend of Julius Caesar, Mithridates, with whom we shall deal later.

The Galatian Celts certainly used Greek in the early period and later Latin in their commerce with the surrounding Graeco-Roman world. Deiotaros, for example, was sufficiently learned to be able to quote from Euripides and to be the subject of a dedication to a weighty work on Greek agriculture. But the truth is also that they maintained their own Celtic language among themselves until a surprisingly late period.

According to Justin, the Celts of Galatia soon acquired the Greek language and became known as Gallograeci. But Strabo says that they were speaking Celtic in his day (c.63 BC–AD 21) and Lucan

(ADc.39–65) reiterates this. He refers to a Greek soothsayer being unable to understand questions from Galatians until an interpreter was sent for. Pausanias, in the 2nd century AD, talks of the native language of Galatia, giving words that are clearly Celtic. Pausanias speaks of a visible Celtic presence in Galatia and says of Attalos of Pergamum that 'the greatest thing he did was to force the Celts to retreat inland in Asia Minor to the country *they now still occupy* [my italics].'

Then we have the famous evidence of St Jerome. He had spent some time among the Treveri (at Trèves) of Gaul, around the northern French-German border area, and when he stayed in Ancyra for a while he was able to state categorically that not only did the Galatians speak Celtic but the language was very close to that spoken by the Treveri of Gaul. He states: '*Galatas, excepto sermone Graeco, quo omnis oriens loquitur, propriam linguam paene habere quam Treviros.*'

Celtic was therefore spoken in Galatia for seven centuries at least. The question is, how long after the 4th century AD did the language last? I think we may safely assume that it probably lasted a few centuries more. Indeed, we have a 6th-century account of a Galatian monk who was 'possessed by the devil' and was struck dumb. He was serving in the monastery of St Euthymius (the Great) about the latter half of the 6th century. It is said that he was cured of his dumbness by a posthumous miracle of Euthymius and on recovery of his speech was, at first, only able to converse with his fellow monks in his native Celtic Galatian. This could imply that it was somewhat unusual at this time to speak only Celtic.

As Dr Mitchell comments: 'Celtic remained widely spoken in Galatia, especially no doubt in the country districts, until late Antiquity.'

Sadly, however, no more than a few Celtic words are recorded in ancient texts together with several proper names for persons and places. The work of Dr Leo Weisgerber, 'Galatische Sprachreste' (1931), remains the standard work on the linguistic remains of the Celts in Asia.

Today, there is little to see of over eight centuries of Celtic occupation on the central plain of Turkey.

[11]

Pergamum Immortalises the Celts

I N spite of the petty squabbles between the Greek city states, the Syrian kings maintained their suzerain rights over all Asia Minor. In 261BC, however, only a few years after Antiochos I won his 'elephant victory' – that is, if we accept Stephen Mitchell's dating – the Syrian king made another attempt to quell the Celts. He met them near Ephesos, a major Ionian Greek city, founded by Athens, on the west coast at the mouth of the Cayster. It was a wealthy city and cultural centre which, in 133BC, Rome was to make the capital of its new province of Asia. Its famous citizens included the philosopher Heracleitus, the poet Hipponax and the painter Parrhasius. A picture of the city in the early years of the Christian epoch emerges in Acts 19. In the battle fought at Ephesos, the Celts defeated and slew Antiochos Soter and scattered the Syrian army.

The Celts made no attempt to follow up their advantage. They continued to maintain their alliance with Nicomedes I of Bithynia. When Nicomedes died, c.255/253BC, he left his kingdom to Prusias and Tiboetes, sons by a second marriage. However, Ziaelis, a son by his first marriage, then living in exile in Armenia, decided to make a grab for the kingdom. He enlisted the Tolistoboii to help him. Presumably the Tolistoboii reasoned that the death of Nicomedes now absolved them from the treaty they had signed with him. It was a good Celtic proverb which observed that 'every dead man kills his own liabilities'; this could also be interpreted to mean that all agreements became null and void after death. A civil war broke out in Bithynia. The people of the city of Heracleia Pontica sent an embassy to mediate between the two brothers. After the mediation, it was Ziaelis who emerged in a dominant position and he soon established himself as king. Ziaelis reigned in Bithynia for the next twenty years.

We are told by Greek sources that the Celts were annoyed with this settlement by mediation for it prevented them carrying off sufficient booty as the spoils of war. They blamed the people of Heracleia Pontica, who had mediated, and a Celtic army therefore invaded the territory governed by the city, as far as the river Calles. According to Memnon, the Celts were able to return home laden with plunder.

The son of Antiochos I Soter, Antiochos II Theus, succeeded to the Syrian kingdom but he was a weak and profligate ruler. During his reign several provinces, such as Bactria and Parthia, broke away from his rule and established their own monarchies. Antiochos II was similarly unsuccessful in his conflict with Ptolemy Philadelphios of Egypt and was finally murdered in 246 BC by his wife Laodice. His elderly son Seleucus II Callinicos succeeded. He made his brother Antiochos Hierax co-regent and governor of his territorial possessions in Asia Minor because he was busy trying to defend himself in what was a third major war between Syria and Egypt. Having dealt with Ptolemy of Egypt, Seleucus turned his attention to Asia Minor.

Antiochos Hierax was ambitious. Seleucus found that his brother had made alliances with the local kingdoms of Asia Minor in an attempt to seize supreme power. One of these alliances was with the Celts whom we can now safely call Galatians. Galatia was a state recognised by all the surrounding kingdoms. In attempting to reassert his rule over the petty kingdoms of Asia Minor, Seleucus seems to have singled out the Celts for special attention. His actions would appear to have been prompted by the desire to drive the Celts out of Asia Minor entirely. He marched his Syrian army, fresh from their victories over Egypt, into Galatia. The Galatians, together with Antiochos Hierax and his ally Mithridates III of Pontus, had taken up positions near Ancyra sometime during 240 BC. The Celtic cavalry and chariots outflanked Seleucus' phalanxes with considerable ease. The battle was a resounding defeat for Seleucus of Syria.

Antiochos Hierax had agreed, according to Justin, to treat the Galatians as full allies in his cause, recognising Galatia as an independent state, even though they had no central king. Likewise, the Galatians also seized the opportunity to make Mithridates III of Pontus agree an alliance with them which was advantageous to them.

It was during this unsettled period that a new Hellenic kingdom began to emerge as a power in Asia Minor. Pergamum was a city of Mysia in the valley of the Caicus in the north-west of Asia Minor, originally a fortress founded by the Greeks. It was the last of the dynastic kingdoms to emerge after Alexander's death, becoming a rich city with a library second only to that of Alexandria – indeed, it is regarded as the place where parchment was first used extensively for the production of books; it was also famous for its sculpture and art. Pergamum was regarded as the most important world cultural centre during the period of the 2nd century AD.

The city had been governed by a eunuch named Philetaerus under the suzerainty of Lysimachos of Macedonia, on whose death at Corupedion Philetaerus had set himself up as an independent king. Philetaerus ruled until 263BC. During the conflict between Seleucus II and Antiochos Hierax, Pergamum was ruled by Philetaerus' nephew Eumenes. It was Eumenes I who had secured the city's total independence. He died in 241BC and was succeeded by his second cousin, Attalos. In fact, according to Polybius, Attalos only received the title 'king' after his victories over the Celts.

Attalos I was to prove a remarkable king.

In the year following his succession, in 241BC, the Celts arrived to demand their annual *galatika*, or tribute from the city. Attalos refused to pay, met the Celtic army at the source of the Caicus, in Mysia, and defeated them in battle. Livy says that the refusal to pay the tribute provoked a decisive war between Pergamum and the Galatians.

However, it was in 233/232BC, when the Tolistoboii advanced into Pergamum territory, that Attalos met them, near the shrine of Aphrodite, not far from the city of Pergamum itself, and was able to inflict a defeat upon them. The defeat was celebrated in an inscription found in the Athena Polias Nikephoros in Pergamum, which offers thanks to Athena for having conquered the Tolistoboii.

The Galatians now called upon their ally Antiochos Hierax to help them against the Pergamum kingdom. Attalos won a victory over Antiochos Hierax and his Celtic allies at the river Harpasus in Cardia, a region in the south-west, south of the river Maeander, in which Cnidus and Halicarnassus stood. This battle is thought to have been fought as late as 228BC. There is a stone inscription, found by chance in a Turkish farmer's wall, referring to Attalos and his general Epigenes as Pergamum commanders at this defeat of Antiochos Hierax and his Celtic allies. The defeat marked the end of the Celtic raids on Bithynia and Pontus as well as on Pergamum. An agreement seems to have been drawn up to the effect that the Hellenic kingdoms would recognise Galatia as an equal kingdom provided the Celts kept within its boundaries.

The victories of Pergamum over the Celts are well 'documented' thanks to the monuments which Attalos I erected to commemorate them. The entire Hellenic world now hailed the victory in the same vein as the victories of their ancestors over the Titans in mythology. The poet Callimachos, in *Hymn to Delos*, waxes lyrical over the matter. Pausanias mentions that a great relief monument depicting the victory was set up on the south wall of the acropolis at Athens. The most famous of the monuments was the statue of The Dying Gaul, at the Capitoline Museum in Rome, which shows a Celt dying from his wounds, naked except for the torque around his neck, showing his rank, with his great shield under him, his sword and war trumpet. The Ludovisi group of carvings, depicting a Celt stabbing himself with his own sword, having killed his female companion, is in the National Roman Museum. Such statues were said by Pliny to be the work of the sculptor Epigonus, son of Charius, a Pergamum master craftsman, and set a new fashion in lifelike Hellenic art. The original bronzes were copied in marble. Certainly Epigonus thereby fixed the Classical image of the Celt for all time. According to Pliny, Epigonus also created a celebrated masterpiece depicting a dead Celtic mother being caressed by her child.

Isogonus, Pyromachus, Stratonicus and Antigonus are other artists mentioned as working on the great sculptures celebrating the victories; this work extended into the reign of Attalos' successor Eumenes II.

Such pieces were set up in the temple of Athena, in the acropolis at Pergamum, with inscriptions giving the details of the victories. Here we find mentioned the defeat of the Tolistoboii near the river Caicus and a dedication to a victory over Antiochos Hierax and his Celtic allies beside the river Harpasus in Cardia. Other victories include one at the Hellespont and another over the Tectosages and Tolistoboii at Coloe in Lydia. This obviously important victory is dated by Eusebius to 229/8 BC. Copies of these works were set up at Athens as well as frescoes which have even appeared as far afield as Naples. Medallions found at Capua also celebrated the Pergamum victories.

In all the pieces, the Celts are depicted as dying savage but noble deaths, which Greek and Roman opinion doubtless held appropriate to the Celtic character. Dr Rankin observes that the 'statues of the Celts were given ethnic attributes by which they could be recognised. The males, who predominate in number in subjects that concern warfare, are given thick, wild hair, moustaches and bodies which, though classically muscular, yet hint at the length and sinewy texture of a Nordic people. Often the cultural identifier of the torque is shown.' The faces of the Celts are all emotional and expressive of wild anger or despair, usually moulded in the agonies of death. These works immortalising the Celts are important in that they show, not so much what the Celts were, as how the Greeks perceived them, with the terror and apprehension they engendered in the Hellenic world.

From these Greek originals, Roman artists took over the theme. The Romans had as much cause to be afraid of the Celts as the Greeks had but their art is not so fearful in its style or approach. In the Roman versions we find the figures more ludicrous and always suffering at the hands of gods who drive them from the temples. From the Città della Pieve there is an interesting group of figures which include a Celtic chieftain on his knees, a bird tearing his eyes out. We are reminded of Livy's story of the single combat between M. Valerius Corvus and a Celtic chieftain. The Roman is saved when a crow (*corvo*) flies down and pecks the Celt's eyes out. This is a Celtic story motif which is found in the story of Cúchulainn in the *Táin Bó Cuailgne*.

Doubtless, the new wave of Pergamum art, which fixed the image of the Celts in the Classical world, had repercussions throughout Greece and Italy. The surviving pieces are fascinating. But, as Dr Rankin has rightly observed:

> The representations of Celts do not tell us what the Greeks and Romans actually saw when they encountered the Celts, but rather what they thought they should be seeing. They wanted them to be defeated, distant and far removed from the sphere of actuality in which they wrought such palpable harm. Nevertheless the heroic style of the Celts and their wild courage struck chords of admiration in the hearts of Greeks and Romans brought up to revere the fighter for his people as admirable above all men.

The war of Attalos I, with his victories over the Galatians, was not simply a war against the Celts. It became part of the wider war against attempted domination of the region by Antiochos Hierax. The importance of Attalos' victories over the Celts can be over-emphasised because the Galatian territory remained intact and none of the plunder previously taken from the Hellenic kingdoms was returned.

Seleucus II had died after a fall from his horse in 226BC and had been succeeded by Seleucus III Ceraunnos (225–223BC), who was determined to reconquer the whole of Asia Minor from the influence of his uncle, Antiochos Hierax, and return it to the Syrian empire. Before he could embark on such a venture he was assassinated by one of his bodyguards. Interestingly the name of the man is recorded. He was a Celt named Apotouros. It has been argued that the name might well signify a 'horse champion'. At this point we can usefully indulge in an historical speculation. Why did Apotouros assassinate the Syrian king? Through Antiochos Hierax we know that the inde-pendence of the Celts of Galatia had been recognised. We know that the Syrian kingdom saw the Celts as a problem. Seleucus III doubtless wanted to continue the policy of Seleucus II to drive them out of Asia Minor. Before Seleucos III could undertake his military expedition he had been killed by a Celt. Perhaps Apotouros' cultural allegiance overcame his financial allegiance to Seleucus?

Seleucus III was succeeded by Antiochos III (223–187BC) who became known as Antiochos the Great. He began to systematically restore the pre-eminence of Syria. Polybius says that the Syrian army now had a large number of Celtic mercenaries serving in it and that these were, in fact, recruited from Europe rather than from Galatia. Among them were the Rhigosages (kingly people) who accompanied Antiochus on his attack against Molon, the rebellious Syrian gov-ernor of Medes, the mountainous country south-west of the Caspian Sea.

Antiochos III turned his attention to Asia Minor and soon Antiochos Hierax had been driven into exile and obscurity. One would have expected that the Syrians would have accepted an ally in Attalos of Pergamum; after all, he had fought for some years against Antiochos Hierax. But Antiochos III had appointed his uncle, Achaeus, as governor of Asia Minor, and not only did Achaeus begin to deprive Attalos of all the territory he had gained in his war against

Antiochos Hierax but he set himself up in Antiochos Hierax's place. By 220BC Achaeus had shown his true allegiance. Not content with serving Antiochos III as governor, he declared himself king of Laodicea and Lycus.

Attalos of Pergamum resorted to hiring mercenaries to fight against Achaeus. In spite of the reputation he had built up as the 'hammer of the Celts', he began to recruit Celts from Europe to his army. Polybius says that a large tribe called the Aegosages came from Europe into Pergamum at his invitation. It has been suggested that as the Thracian Celtic kingdom of Tylis had begun to collapse at this time, then these Celts might have been refugees from there. Polybius places the collapse of this kingdom around 218/212BC when the last king with a Celtic name, Cauaros, was overthrown by the Thracians. Dr Hoddinott says:

> We do not know how numerous the Tylis Celts were, but their rule was harsh, probably leading many Thracians, including nobles, to become mercenaries. Some served with Antiochos II in his siege of Kypsela, while others were among the defenders. Polyaenus (Strat. IV, 16) relates that Antiochos provided his Thracian mercenaries with fine weapons and gold and silver ornaments; seeing these the Thracians on the other side came over to him. The last statesmen like king Kavaros (Cauaros) whose coins were found in the Silven district and perhaps minted at Kabyle (Gerasimov, 1959), was overthrown in 218 by a Thracian rising and the Celtic kingdom eliminated.

According to Polybius, this king Cauaros was 'a man of magnanimity and regal character' who had been of assistance to Byzantium. He had mediated for that city against an alliance of Prusias of Bithynia and the kingdom of Rhodes.

It could well be that Attalos' Celtic mercenaries came from Tylis. Attalos used them to make a series of raids into Aeolis and across Lydia into northern Phrygia, presumably against their fellow Celts of Galatia. The aim of the campaign, presumably, was to ensure that the victories of Achaeus did not persuade other Pergamum lands to revolt and join his new kingdom. If that was his purpose then Attalos certainly succeeded.

The Aegosages had been promised booty which was not forthcoming. The Celts were disgruntled. It is claimed that it was an eclipse of the moon (dated to 1 September 218BC) which caused the Aegosages to rise in revolt against Attalos and start to plunder the surrounding countryside. As the Aegosages had their wives, children, elderly and baggage with them, they were not really equipped for any campaign that involved the rapid movement of the whole tribe. Therefore Attalos negotiated with the chieftains and decided to settle them on some land in the Hellespont region.

However, within a short time, the Aegosages, still not having received the promised payment from Attalos, rose up and laid siege to Ilium which was saved only when a force of 4000 men from Alexandria Troas arrived under Themistes, a Pergamum general. The Aegosages withdrew from Pergamum into the kingdom of Bithynia. Bithynia was now ruled by Prusias I (228–180BC) and he was not happy about the arrival of a large band of Celts in his kingdom. He raised an army, met the Celts at Arisba in 217BC, defeated and killed the warriors in battle and then marched on the Celtic encampment. There, observes Polybius, he killed not only the elderly men but the women and children.

Attalos had now formed an alliance with Antiochos III of Syria and forced Prusias of Bithynia to accept him as suzerain during a campaign in 207/206BC. While Attalos was busy reinforcing the borders of Pergamum, the Syrian king was anxiously looking westward into Europe. He had observed that a Roman victory over the Macedonians at Cynoscephalae in 197BC had left the Greek states powerless. Would Rome follow up this advantage and take control of all Greece or should he make a grab for Greece first?

Antiochos believed that he was heir to Alexander's empire which had emanated from Greece. He decided that he would try to fill the vacuum left by the Roman victory over Macedonia. Greece was looking for a saviour. Certainly, the Aetolians were. Antiochos therefore took his Syrian army to Detrias, a city in the Gulf of Pagasae, in 192BC. Only the Aetolians, among the Greeks, welcomed and joined him. The rest of Greece united to demand Rome's help against him and an army of 40,000 men, under M. Acilius Glabrio and Marcus Porcius Cato, was sent by Rome to Greece, landing in Epiros in 191BC. Antiochos, like others before him, fell back to Thermopylae where, like Leonidas of Sparta and Callippos of Athens, he was outflanked by Romans crossing behind him on the mountain path. The Syrian king fled with only 500 survivors and established himself at Ephesos.

Antiochos thereby became a resolute enemy of Rome. The Carthaginian general Hannibal, the implacable adversary of Rome who had been defeated at the battle of Zama in 202BC by Publius Cornelius Scipio, sought sanctuary at Ephesos after discovering that Rome was plotting his assassination. Antiochos granted him that sanctuary at his court. This gave the Romans the excuse they needed to send their armies into Asia Minor. A Roman army was already marching towards Byzantium and preparing to cross the Bosporus. It was commanded by Lucius Cornelius Scipio, the younger brother of the famous Publius Cornelius Scipio now named 'Africanus' in honour of his defeat of Hannibal at Zama in Africa. Lucius was, in fact, consul in 190BC. But his elder brother, who was accompanying him, was effectively in command although designated as his legate.

Before these events, in 197BC, Attalos I of Pergamum had died and been succeeded by his eldest son, Eumenes II (197–159BC). Attalos had already shown a preference for Rome and had offered an alliance with Rome against Antiochos. Eumenes II carried on that pro-Roman policy.

It is now that we hear of the Galatian Celts raiding the kingdom of Pontus. Perhaps this was in an attempt to gain an outlet to the sea, in order to establish direct contact with the Celtic tribes of the Lower Danube. The Celtic kingdom of Tylis on the Black Sea was breaking up at this time and the Celtic tribal kingdoms in this area of the Danube were also under threat. Did the Celts of Galatia want a port to use as a means of going to their aid or to bring them, as reinforcements, into Asia Minor? They attacked the city of Heracleia Pontica, on the shore of the Black Sea. Memnon says the Celts lost two-thirds of their force in this attack. It was certainly unsuccessful.

There had been little activity, however, reported from the Galatian Celts after the defeat of Antiochos Hierax and the victories of Attalos of Pergamum. The reassertion of power by Achaeus and Antiochos III over Asia Minor had not provoked them in any way. But we learn that in 197/196BC the people of Lampsacos, a Phocian colony, contacted their kinsmen in Massilia, asking them to request their Gaulish Celtic neighbours to mediate with the Galatian Celts, specifically with the Tolistoboii. In this reference we have one of the earliest examples of a recognition of the solidarity that existed between all the Celtic peoples even when of different tribes living at great distances from each other. The thought behind the senate of Lampsacos asking the senate of Massilia to intervene is that Massilia was seen as the Greek city most closely linked with the Celtic homeland in the west and that that homeland would have some influence with their eastern cousins.

The Massiliots did so and, being pro-Roman, sent to the Tolistoboii, asking them not to fight or supply Antiochos the Great against Rome. They pointed out that the surrounding Celtic tribes enjoyed good relations with them and the Romans. Some years earlier, of course, the same pro-Roman Massiliots had asked the Volcae Tectosages, situated around Toulouse, to be neutral when Hannibal and the Carthaginian army were passing through their territory.

As Hannibal's army had been primarily a Celtiberian one, the appeal had fallen on deaf ears. Similarly the Tolistoboii of Galatia now decided to throw their lot in with Antiochos the Great against Rome. They also persuaded the Tectosages and the Trocmi to join them. It was to be a momentous decision.

[12]

Roman Conquest of Galatia

THE Roman conquest of Asia Minor began in 190BC when the Roman navy defeated the Syrian ships off the coast of Crete. The land invasion was then launched with 40,000 troops under the Scipio brothers. They arrived at Magnesia (ad Sipylum) and were joined by the forces of Eumenes II of Pergamum. Antiochos the Great was able to put into the field a considerable army of 72,000 men, backed by elephant detachments. Livy estimates that the Syrian army consisted of 60,000 infantry and 12,000 cavalry. Among their numbers were large Galatian cavalry, chariot and infantry divisions.

Antiochos III attempted to negotiate with the Scipios at first, conceding all the points which had already been agreed in previous negotiations with Rome. He accepted to pay a third of Rome's military costs in mounting the expedition. This offer was declined by the Romans.

The younger Scipio heard that Antiochos' army was near Thyatire and set out after him. His elder brother, 'Africanus', was ill and unable to help, remaining in bed in Magnesia. The younger Scipio found that Antiochos and his army had left Thyatire. He began to follow along the river Phrygius and encamped 4 miles from Antiochos' new position. Livy reports that about 1000 cavalry, a Celtic division, attacked the Roman outposts throwing them into confusion.

There followed two days of quiet but then the Romans, on the third day, crossed the river and came to within 2 miles of Antiochos' camp. Livy says that Antiochos had fortified his encampment.

To prevent the Romans from an attempt on his fortifications, in case he should wish to play for time, he dug a ditch nine feet deep and eighteen feet wide; and on the outside of it he built a double palisade round the trench; and on the inner lips he erected a wall with numerous towers, from which the enemy could easily be stopped from crossing the ditch.

For several more days the two armies manoeuvred but did not engage in battle. 'No enemy was ever regarded by the Romans with such contempt,' observes Livy.

He gives the battle order of Antiochos by saying that the centre was formed by 10,000 infantry armed in Macedonian fashion called *phalangitae*. In front of them were ten sections in each of which were two elephants.

This was the chief strength of Antiochos' army, and it presented a very terrifying appearance in general, but especially because of the elephants who stood out so conspicuously among the soldiers. These elephants were of immense size; and they were made more impressive by their frontlets and crests and by the towers on their backs, with four soldiers standing in each tower, besides the driver.

On the right flank were 1500 Celtic infantry and 3000 cavalry. Livy calls them *cataphraci* because of their breastplates. A further squadron of 1000 cavalry of mixed nationality plus sixteen elephants stood in support behind them. On this flank also were Antiochos' royal bodyguard, the Argyraspides (silver shields), together with some 3000 light infantry from Crete and Tralles, 2500 Thysian archers and then 4000 Cyrtian slingers and Elymaean archers.

On the left flank the Celts were in the forefront, consisting of 1500 infantry. Backing them were 2000 Cappadocians, 2700 mixed auxiliaries, 3000 *cataphraci* and 1000 other cavalry. There was a cavalry squadron of the royal bodyguard, mostly Syrians, with Phrygians and Lydians. There were scythed chariots and camels (dromedaries) with mounted Arab archers. Then behind this right flank, came another division with 2500 Celtic cavalry, 1000 Cretans, 1500 Carians and Cilicians and Trallians, 4000 from Pisidia and Paphlagonia, and contingents from Lucua and Cyrtia and Elymaea with a further sixteen elephants.

Antiochos himself took personal command on the right flank with his son Seleucus and his nephew Antipater commanding the left, while the centre was commanded by his generals Minnio and Zeuxis with Philippus as master of the elephants.

Against this formidable army, the Roman centre had four legions of 5400 men each. The right flank consisted of the Pergamum troops of Eumenes, 3000 Achaean targeteers and 3000 cavalry, together with the Roman cavalry. Behind them were Trallians and Cretans consisting of 1000 men with an additional 2000 Macedonians and Thracians. The Romans also had sixteen elephants as against the fifty-four elephants of Antiochos. These were African elephants and Livy says, 'African elephants cannot stand up to Indian even when numbers are equal, either because the latter outmatch them in size – they are in fact much larger – or because they are superior in fighting spirit.'

The day of the battle began with a morning mist, like a soft drizzle, blown by a west wind, soaking everything. Antiochos struck first at the Roman left flank. There was a problem with his scythed chariots which seemed to be doing more harm in his own lines than with the enemy. Livy describes them:

These chariots were generally armed as follows: they had sharp blades on either side of the pole, sticking out like horns three feet from the yoke, with which to pierce everything they met, and at each end of the yoke two scythes projected, one level with the yoke, the other pointing downwards towards the ground, the former to cut up whatever came in its way at the side, the latter to reach men who had fallen and came under the chariot; also from the axle of the wheels at both ends two scythes were fastened in a similar manner, one level, the other pointing downwards.

Antiochos, from the Syrian right, had pushed the Romans back to their camp site. The camp commander was Marcus Aemilius, a tribune. 'When he saw the flight of his comrades he met them with his whole guard and ordered them first to halt and then to fight, reproaching them for their panic and shameful flight.' The Roman soldiers did not heed him until he ordered his own men to cut down the leading fugitives and he drove the deserters back to face the enemy. Aemilius and his 2000 men turned the rout into a stand.

Eumenes' brother, Attalos, had just arrived to join him with 200 horse and he immediately used them to reinforce Marcus Aemilius.

Antiochos had banked everything on this massed cavalry charge, which he led in person, panicking the Romans. Now he was held up and he had let the cavalry charge carry him too far forward and had lost contact with the rest of his army.

On the Roman right, Eumenes of Pergamum personally commanded an assault on the left flank of Antiochos' army, driving it back. But the centre of the Syrian army was standing firm and the overall situation was still in contention. At this point an officer named Gnaeus Domitius Ahenobarbus, who was to be an ancestor of the Emperor Nero, launched an attack of slingers on the Syrian chariot lines. The charioteers were unable to keep their lines steady. Not only did the scythes of their chariots create problems, causing those infantry men near them to panic, scattering in all directions to get out of the way of their own chariots, but the war elephants stampeded and smashed into the centre phalanxes throwing them into utter disarray.

Lucius Scipio, taking advantage of the broken lines in front of him, unleashed his legions and smashed through the confused masses. Retreat became a rout.

Livy records:

Thus the Romans were victorious on both wings; and they made their way over piles of corpses which they had heaped up, especially in the centre, where the strength of the bravest of the soldiers and the weight of their arms had held up their flight, and proceeded to sack the camp. The horsemen pursued the enemy all over the plain, the cavalry of Eumenes leading the way, followed by the rest of the cavalry, and they cut down the hindmost as they came upon them. But a greater cause of disaster to the fugitives, intermingled as they were with chariots, elephants, and camels, was their own disorganised men. With their ranks broken, they tumbled over one another like blind men, or were trampled down by the charging animals. In the camp also great slaughter was done, greater, perhaps, than the slaughter on the field of battle. For the first troops to flee had mostly made off to the camp, and the garrison there, gaining confidence from the accession to their numbers, fought with greater stubbornness in defence of the rampart. The Romans had supposed that they would take the defences at the first assault, but they found themselves checked at the gates and at the rampart; and when they finally forced their way in, their rage caused them to deal heavier slaughter.

Livy says that some 50,000 of Antiochos' infantry were slain and 3000 cavalry. Some 1400 prisoners were taken with fifteen elephants and their drivers. He also claims that Roman casualties amounted only to 300 infantry and twenty-four cavalry, and twenty-five of Eumenes' men. While we must make allowances for Livy boosting the Roman victory, we may be sure that the battle of Magnesia was a singular disaster for Antiochos. He fled to Sardis while his son Seleucus went on to Apamea. The cities of Asia Minor were now beginning to offer their submission to the Scipio brothers. And soon the Romans were able to march on Sardis.

Antiochos, however, had left to join his son at Apamea. He sent emissaries back to Sardis to meet with the Scipio brothers and attempt negotiations. These emissaries were Antiochos' nephew Antipater and his general Zeuxis. They met with Eumenes first and then with the Scipio brothers. They are reported to have said:

'It is not so much that we have anything to say for ourselves, rather we are asking what expiation we can make to atone for the king's error, and to obtain peace and pardon from the victors. With your great magnanimity you have always pardoned conquered kings and peoples. And now, in your hour of victory, a victory that has made you masters of the world, how much greater the magnanimity that should govern your actions, how much readier the spirit of reconciliation it would become you to display! You should now put aside any quarrels with mortals; like the gods you should extend consideration and clemency to the whole human race.'

Scipio Africanus replied for Rome:

'The terms are these; keep out of Europe; withdraw from the whole of Asia on this side of the Taurus range. And then, as an indemnity for the war, you will pay 15,000 Euboean talents, 500 now, 2500 when the Senate and the people of Rome approve the peace, and thereafter 1000 talents annually for twelve years. Eumenes too must be compensated; and it is our decision that 400 talents be paid to him together with the remainder of the corn owed to his father.'

Certain hostages were named and asked for by Rome. Antiochos agreed to the terms and sent the hostages to Ephesos, where delegates were also gathered to go to Rome with Eumenes.

Internal Roman politics now dictated the next step in Galatia's fortunes. The political rivals of the Scipios in Rome were in the ascendant. Rumours were rife that the Scipio brothers had actually joined forces with Antiochos or that the Roman forces had been wiped out by the Syrians. However, one of Scipio's officers, Marcus Aurelius Cotta, arrived in Rome at the height of the rumour-mongering, with Eumenes, Antiochos' delegates and the hostages, plus the news of the victory at Magnesia. The Senate appointed ten commissioners to go to Asia Minor to arbitrate in border settlements and other matters connected with the victories. But the rumours had coloured the Senate's attitude to the Scipio brothers, who were now recalled home.

A new consul was sent out to continue the 'pacification' of Asia Minor – Gnaeus Manlius Vulso. Vulso's orders were to impose harsher terms on Antiochos than those the Scipio brothers had agreed to. These were for Antiochos to surrender also all his fleet, except ten ships, and all his war elephants. The other conditions still stood. As his second-in-command, Vulso took his brother Lucius Manlius Vulso.

Vulso reached Ephesos at the beginning of the spring of 189 BC where he officially took over the troops from Lucius Scipio and reviewed them. Vulso had come to believe that the Celts of Galatia presented the most immediate military problem to Roman influence in the area. They, of all the Asia Minor kingdoms, had not sent emissaries to surrender to Rome. According to Livy, Vulso told his troops, at the review at Ephesos, that the Celts were ungovernable. 'The removal of Antiochos beyond the Taurus mountains would be in vain unless the power of the Celts were broken.'

In fact, Vulso had made this decision without reference to the Roman Senate. While the military aim was to bring the Celts to heel, Livy is inclined to believe that Vulso had a personal ambition to pick up a century of booty collected by the Celts in their raids which was rumoured to be in Galatia. Livy seems correct in this assumption for when Manlius Vulso returned to Rome he was accused of conducting a '*privatum latrocinium*' (personal robbery) against Galatia and had to defend himself before the Senate.

There is one other aspect that seems to be overlooked. Gnaeus Manlius Vulso was a member of an ancient Roman *gens*, or clan, whose members, as Vulso later reminded his troops, had always been in the forefront of Rome's fight against the Celts. It was Marcus Manlius Capitolinus who, in 390BC, had held the Capitol in Rome against the Celtic attack, and this was the only part of the city which did not fall. It was Titus Manlius Imperiosus Torquatus who, in 361BC, had killed a Celtic chieftain in single combat. Did Manlius Vulso believe that he had some sort of mission against the Celts? It seems likely.

Eumenes II of Pergamum, had he not been in Rome, would have agreed with Vulso's ambition to conquer the Galatians once and for all. When Vulso asked Eumenes' brother, Attalos, if he would take part in a campaign against Galatia, he received an enthusiastic affirmative. Attalos promised Pergamum's support on his brother's behalf and when Vulso and the Roman legions left Ephesos for Magnesia again, he joined them with 1000 infantry and 500 cavalry. His younger brother, Athenaeus, was ordered to follow with reinforcements later. The kingdom of Pergamum was entrusted to those loyal counsellors of Eumenes II.

Vulso and his army moved during late spring, 189BC, and crossed the Maeander, arriving at Hiera Comê, a place where there was a shrine and oracle of Apollo. From here they continued to march for two days to the river Harpasus. They came to a fortified town called Alabanda and it was at this point that Athenaeus, Attalos' young brother, arrived with a further 1000 infantry and 300 cavalry. Vulso detached a small force to subdue Alabanda while continuing to move directly on to the city of Antioch on the Maeander.

The Maeander's source was at Celaenae, a city that was at one time the capital of Phrygia, and not far away was Apamea, named after the wife of Seleucus I of Syria. It was at Celaenae, according to the myth, that Marsyas, after whom the nearby river was named, a Phrygian satyr, had his pipe-playing contest with Apollo. Both could play the flute well but Apollo challenged Marsyas to play upside down, which he found impossible. Marsyas lost and Apollo flayed him alive, hanging him on a pine tree. His blood then formed the river. He became a local deity.

The army of Vulso reached Antioch where Seleucus, the son of Antiochos III, came to supply corn to the army under the terms of the treaty. A disagreement arose over the exact terms of the treaty. Seleucus said that he was to supply only the Roman army and not the troops of Pergamum. There was no love lost between the Syrians and those who supported Eumenes. Vulso dealt with the matter firmly, ensuring that his allies received their fair share of supplies.

From Antioch, Vulso moved on to Gordiotichi and then to Tabae, a city within Pisidian territory, facing the Pamphylian sea. Cavalry from Tabae launched an attack on the Romans not realising the strength of the Roman army. When they understood their mistake, they surrendered immediately and asked terms for the city. Vulso demanded 25 silver talents and 10,000 *medimni* of wheat. A *medimnus* was a Greek measure of capacity containing six Roman *modii* – each of the *modii* being equivalent to one peck (or 9.087 litres). The wheat therefore amounted to something like 15,000 bushels.

Vulso's army continued through Pisidia as far as the border of Pamphylia before turning due north into Phrygia and then into Galatia proper. According to Polybius, with Livy using Polybius as a source, Vulso reached the border of Galatia at Abbassium, north of modern Emirdag, and just south of Pessinus. 'He kept his camp at Abbassium for a considerable time, because they had now arrived at the frontier of the Tolistoboii,' says Livy. A day or so before this, Seleucus had arrived again with more supplies and guides for the journey. Vulso had sent his sick back to Apamea with his surplus baggage, including the booty he had collected so far.

Abbassium is the site identified as Göme.

It is here, Livy says, that the Roman consul decided to brief his troops about the enemy whose country they were about to enter. It must be remembered that at this time Rome had had little success in its wars against the Celts. Even the Celts of Italy, in Cisalpine Gaul, had not fallen under Roman rule and most Roman soldiers still had folkloric remembrances of the Celtic sack of Rome and the various defeats suffered by the Roman forces during the previous 150 years. Perhaps this was why such a speech was necessary.

It is worth examining Vulso's speech, as given by Livy, carefully:

'Soldiers, I am well aware of the fact that of all peoples dwelling in Asia Minor, the Celts have a formidable reputation as warriors.

This fierce people have travelled and fought many races of mankind and have taken almost the whole world as their abode. Their tall stature, their long, flowing red hair, their great oval shields and enormous swords, together with their songs which they sing as they march into battle, their howlings and leapings and the fearful din of their spears and swords as they pound their shields – following their ancestral custom – all are carefully designed to strike terror into their enemies. The Greeks have come to dread these things, which to them are unusual and unfamiliar; but to us Romans, the Celts are quite familiar, and their absurd demonstrations are well known.

'It is true that on one occasion our ancestors fled before the Celts but that was long ago, it was when we first encountered them at Allia. [A reference to the Celtic victory over Rome and Etruria at Allia in 390BC.] Since then, however, we Romans have been routing and killing them like the terrified animals they are! We have had more triumphs to celebrate over the Celts than over the rest of the world. [Vulso is certainly giving a rather biased view of history.]

'It has been discovered, through our experience in battle with the Celts, that if you sustain their first charge, into which they hurl themselves with blazing passion and blind rage, then their limbs will quickly tire, they grow slack with sweat and weariness, their muscles will not sustain their weapons and they drop from their hands. They are flabby in body and irresolute after their initial passion subsides. They are rendered prostrate by sun, dust and thirst, so much so that you don't even have to kill them to subdue them.

'Not only have we met them army to army but we have been victorious against them in single combat. Titus Manlius and Marcus Valerius have demonstrated how easily our Roman valour prevails over Celtic frenzy. Marcus Manlius was one man against a Celtic army and threw them down from the Capitol.'

Here Vulso refers to Titus Manlius Imperiosus Torquatus, Marcus Valerius Corvus and Marcus Manlius Capitolinus, three Roman heroes who had fought the Celts in Italy. As I have mentioned before, two of these heroes seem to be ancestors of Vulso. Titus Manlius killed a Celt during a campaign in 361BC, fighting in single combat and earning his cognomen 'Torquatus' by taking the ornamental neck chain, the torque, from his opponent's body. Valerius Corvus earned his name in a campaign in 349BC having fought a Celt in single combat and been saved from being killed when a crow (*corvus*) flew down and pecked out the eyes of his Celtic opponent. Livy, growing up in a Celtic area, seems to have revised this tale from Celtic heroic traditions, the crow being the Celtic personification of the goddess of death and battles. Finally Manlius Capitolinus, according to Roman tradition, defended the Capitol, in 390BC. Vulso neglects to mention that some time afterwards his illustrious ancestor was thrown to his death by his fellow Roman citizens from the Tarpeian rock after being accused of trying to make himself dictator.

Vulso continued his speech:

'The Macedonians who control Alexandria in Egypt, and who also dwell in Syria and Babylonia and in other Greek colonies scattered throughout the world, have degenerated into Syrians, Parthians and Egyptians. Even the Greeks of Massilia, situated among the Celts, have acquired some characteristics from their neighbours. And what remains of that once formidable Spartan discipline in Laconia?

'Anything which grows in its own proper habitat develops specific excellence. Transplant it to an alien soil, its nature changes, it degenerates towards that in which it is reared. These aren't Celts but Phrygians, accoutred with Celtic arms, and you will slay them as victors cutting down the vanquished just as you cut them down at Magnesia. I do not fear that there will be too much fighting in this campaign. My fear is that there will be too little so that you will not reap enough glory! King Attalos has often scattered these people.

'Do not suppose that it is only wild animals who grow tame when they are caught and removed from the savagery of the forests and are fed by human hand. Do not imagine that nature does not show herself in the same way when savage men are taken and placed in more civilised environments.

'Do you really believe that these Celts are the same men that our fathers and forefathers fought? They were driven from their native land by the poverty of the soil, they travelled through Illyria, that inclement land, making their way through Paenonia and

Thrace and fighting with the fiercest tribes, and they finally seized these lands. They were both hardened and made savage by their misfortunes. Here they were received by a country which could supply them with plenty. This was a rich countryside, with a mild climate and whose inhabitants were kindly and considerate to them. They have tamed the savage out of these Celts.

'You legionnaries, you are men of war. Mark my words, you must be on your guard and escape from this land as soon as possible. Otherwise you will find yourself weakened by the delights of Asia, just as these Celts have been. That is what contact with the habits of these foreigners has done to the Celts we face. If circumstances are lucky for us, their strength will be as grass before the wind! If we are victorious, remember that these people still enjoy the same reputation among the Greeks as their fathers did when they invaded and sacked Delphi. When you destroy them, you, as victors, will have the same military glory as if you had defeated the same Celts who still preserve their ancient bravery against the world.'

It was at Abbassium that Vulso met a chieftain named Eposognatus of the Tolistoboii. Livy claims he was of the Tectosages but Polybius, who probably relied on first-hand descriptions, is the more creditable source in identifying the man. Here we encounter one of those situations that often bedevilled the Celtic peoples when faced with an outside invader. Eposognatus had been thrown out of office under the tribal system whereby a chieftain could be deposed if he did not pursue the commonwealth of his people. Eposognatus, like other Celtic leaders before and since in the same position, nursing a grudge, offered his services to the Romans if they would reinstate him. Eposognatus was sent off to the Tolistoboii to arrange their submission, unsuccessfully as it turned out. While this was being done, Vulso took his army on a five-day march through an area called Axylon, the treeless country. Livy says that 'this gets its name from the fact that it produces no wood at all, not even thorns or any other fuel; the people use cow dung as a substitute for wood.' This area would appear to lie in the southern Galatian country of the Tectosages.

Near Cuballum, a Celtic stronghold, Tectosagean cavalry made a sudden attack on the Roman vanguard, throwing them into confusion and inflicting heavy casualties. Perhaps the Roman soldiers began to wonder if Vulso had spoken too soon in denigrating the abilities of the Celtic warriors of Galatia. However, reinforcements racing up from the main body of the Roman legions saved the day. Livy says:

> The Consul [Vulso] realised that he was now in contact with the enemy, and thereafter he went forward more cautiously, with his army in close column, after previous reconnaissance. He next arrived at the River Sangarios, after continuous marches, where he set about building a bridge, since there was no place where it could be crossed by fording. The Sangarios rises in Mount Adoreus and flows through Phrygia near Bithynia where it is joined by the Tymbris; and thus enlarged by the doubling of its waters, it runs through Bithynia and discharges itself into the Propontus.

It seems odd that Vulso would have to build a bridge across the Sangarios at this point, near Pessinus, and most likely this was because the Celts had destroyed the bridges already there. It was while Vulso was building his bridge, according to Livy, that the Galli arrived, the priests of the Great Mother, who foretold the Roman victory over the Celts of Galatia and blessed the Roman army. If the Galli were Celtic priests, as we have previously discussed, this does appear a curious event. It could be that they were native Phrygian priests who were hostile to the Celts but, at this time, most of the priests at Pessinus were Celts – they even used the name Galli. As we have seen, the Attis, the chief priest, had a brother who bore a distinctive Celtic name. Perhaps, as the Cybele was an important oracle in the area, Livy felt it important to encourage his readers to believe the local deities were on the side of the Romans.

The Romans crossed the Sangarios river and came along its valley to Gordium.

The renegade chieftain, Eposognatus, also met Vulso there and reported that he had not been successful in getting his tribe to surrender. In fact, the Tolistoboii 'were moving in large numbers from the villages on the plains and from the countryside and were making for Olympus mountain, taking with them their wives and children, and driving and carting off all the property that they could remove, and they hoped to preserve themselves by armed resistance in that naturally defended mountain region.'

The Tolistoboii had been reinforced by their neighbours, the Trocmi led by Ortiagon. It is now that we learn the names of the three chieftains who were leading the resistance to the Roman invasion. They were Ortiagon, the name is sometimes given as Ortagion and Orgiago, of the Trocmi, and Comboiomarus (Combolomarus) and Gaulotus (Gaudotus) of the Tolistoboii and Tectosages. It is Ortiagon who emerges as the dominant force in the Celtic hierarchy of chieftains. If we follow Sir John Rhŷs' analysis, the first part of the names, *org*, would mean 'kills'. The name would imply 'he who kills', comparable to the Gaulish name Orgetorix, 'king of killers'. Comboiomarus could be interpreted as 'big lightning stroke' while Gaulotus might mean simply 'descendant of the Gauls'.

Vulso received intelligence, perhaps from the rebel, Eposognatus, that the Tolistoboii were now occupying Olympus, while, to the east, the Tectosages had fortified Mount Magaba. The Trocmi had left their women and children among the Tectosages and marched to reinforce the Tolistoboii positions where, it was thought, the Romans would strike first.

The Celtic army's main position was on Mount Olympus, less than 20 miles from Gordium. There was a hill-fort there but the Celts had built more ditches and ramparts to impede any attack. The plan of campaign, from the Celtic viewpoint, so it appears, was to take to these higher mountains where they had transported sufficient supplies for an indefinite siege. The thinking was that they would hold out in their strongholds until the Roman army tired itself out. Livy concurs.

> For they felt sure that the Romans would not venture to climb up where the ascent was so steep and the going so difficult; and, if they did attempt the climb, they could be stopped or hurled back by a small force. They were equally convinced that the enemy would not sit inactive at the foot of the chilly mountains and endure cold and shortage of supplies. Moreover, although they were protected by the very height of their position, the Celts surrounded the summits they had occupied with a ditch and other defensive works. They made very little provision for the supply of missiles because they were confident that the rugged terrain would itself furnish stones in abundance.

It was not the first time that the Celtic war chieftains had under-estimated the discipline of a Roman army. Whereas the Celtic battle strategy was usually to throw its lines of warriors forward in one massed charge, hoping to carry everything before it, they found the Roman battle tactics, feints, strategic withdrawals and engineering work, incomprehensible. These were a people who still saw warfare as individual tests of courage, the honour of single combat and trials of strength, and not as some cold-blooded science.

The Celts, being renowned horsemen, had as usual placed a con-siderable part of their army on horseback. Livy says that 10,000 Celts were on horseback and only 1500 were infantry. But, of course, the mountain terrain made cavalry tactics impossible. The Celtic cavalry would have dismounted to fight on foot in the broken terrain around the fortifications.

Vulso marched the Romans towards Olympus and made camp about 5 miles away. On the next day he and Attalos with 400 cavalry set off on a reconnaissance to view the Celtic position. This was a slightly arrogant action and they nearly paid for it. Celtic cavalry ambushed them and put Vulso to flight with many casualties.

Three days later, having recovered, Vulso ordered a reconnaissance in force. During this examination, Vulso noted that the southern hills of Olympus sloped gently and were covered in soil whereas the northern slopes were steeply inclined and very rocky. This decided his plan of attack.

Vulso decided to split up his army into three divisions. His brother, Lucius Manlius, would command one division and advance on the south-east. He was ordered not to get involved in any battle if the terrain was difficult or to attempt to climb any precipitous places. Moving around the foothills, he was to eventually link up again with the main column for his task would be simply a feint to distract the Celts so that they would have to divide their forces to watch whether Lucius was going to attack.

A second column was given to another senior officer, Gaius Hel-vius, who was ordered to move slowly around the foot of the moun-tain and make an attempt on the north-west face. This would also be a feint. The main attack would be led by Vulso himself, command-ing a third division which would assault the Celtic position up the easiest slopes in the southern hills. The Pergamum soldiers of Attalos and his young brother, Athenaeus, were divided between the three divisions. All the cavalry, being useless in the mountains, were left on the level ground; it appears that Vulso also had elephants and these were left with the cavalry. However, it was agreed that these troops would act as reinforcements if or when the need arose.

Livy says:

> The Celts, being quite confident that their position was inaccessible on the two flanks, determined to employ an armed force to block the access on the south-facing side of the mountain, and to do this they sent a force of 4000 men to occupy a hill overlooking the roadway less than a mile from the main camp. The Romans observed this move.

Vulso's leading centuries began to march in good order up the incline towards the Celtic position. Vulso then halted his main legionary force and let his 'artillery' move in first: slingers, archers, javelin throwers and so on. The battle started with a discharge of missiles at long range. The Celts held the advantage of position. But Livy believed that the Celts had inefficient protection from their shields which were not wide enough for their bodies. They were also armed only with swords. They had some stones to throw down on the Roman troops below but did not have the skill to use them strategically, whereas the Romans were using arrows and missiles from slings and javelins.

Vulso's forces stormed the defences at the southern approach to the mountain. According to Livy, the Celts were enraged that they could not get to close quarters with their assailants so that they could fight in the traditional way, 'man to man' with their short swords. He comments:

> In close combat, where they can deal blow for blow and wound for wound, the excitement of anger gives them courage; correspondingly, when they are wounded by light weapons coming from unseen and distant sources, and when they have no objective at which they can charge with mindless violence, they rush blindly at their fellows like wounded animals. Their wounds were plain to see because they fight naked and their bodies are plump and white since they are never exposed except in battle; in consequence, there was a greater flow of blood from the excess of flesh, the

gashes were more horribly visible, and the stains of the dark blood stood out more conspicuously against the whiteness of their skin. But they are not worried about such open gashes; sometimes indeed they cut further into the skin, when the wound is broad rather than deep, and imagine that thus they are fighting with greater glory. On the other hand, when the point of an arrow or sling shot has buried itself in the flesh, leaving a wound slight in appearance but causing acute pain, and when it does not come out as they search for a way to extract the missile, these same men become maddened and ashamed at being destroyed by so small an affliction, and they throw themselves prostrate on the ground.

There are many points with which one can argue in Livy's piece of propaganda. It suits the Roman view of the Celts as 'savage animals' to have them, when wounded but unable to fight their attackers, turn on each other and attack their friends. This is sheer nonsense. The references to the whiteness of the Celtic bodies is interesting: a people who had lived for many generations in this climate would surely have been tanned from birth. And not all Celts, as we have discussed, were members of the religio-military élites who traditionally fought naked. As for their plumpness, this is an odd comment. The Celtic warriors were, as we observe from Pergamum statues as well as Greek descriptions, tough, muscular fighting men. Strabo comments: 'They try not to become stout and pot-bellied and any young man who exceeds the standard length of a girdle (or belt) is fined.' Is Livy confusing his description with the Celts of the west? However, he is correct, I believe, in stating that the Celtic warriors, armed only with their short swords and shields, would be unhappy about standing under a long-range barrage of missiles from the Roman lines without being able to hit back.

The Celts were sustaining heavy casualties under the barrage and were demoralised. Then the Roman skirmishers closed in. The Celts now observed the heavy legionary infantry beginning to press forward. The southern outpost began to fall back towards the main camp on Olympus.

Lucius Manlius and Gaius Helvius had now marched around the hills, in accordance with Vulso's directions, and rejoined him. The main attack was to begin on the Celtic fortifications. The Celtic women and children were sheltering in the main camp, around which the Celtic warriors took up defensive positions. Nevertheless, Vulso ordered his 'artillery' to be used directly at the camp and missiles were showered down indiscriminately. He continued the barrage in spite of the cries of the wounded and dying women and children. This enraged the Celtic defenders further. The advance guard of the legions discharged their javelins at the Celtic warriors who were protecting the gates. Armed with swords only, the Celts were no match for the javelins.

The gates were stormed and opened and the Celtic warriors attempted to take the women and children to safety. Livy says they fled along the trackless hillside which resulted in many of them falling to their deaths or dropping from sheer exhaustion as they ran panic-stricken before the pursuing Romans.

Vulso found himself having to restrain his soldiers from pillage and plunder and tried to reassert discipline in them so that they could go in an orderly pursuit of the retreating Celtic warriors. The column commanded by his brother, Lucius Manlius, marched up and were told to push on in pursuit of the enemy. Gaius Helvius and his column also arrived but Helvius found it impossible to restrain his men from pillaging. Vulso sent word to his cavalry, waiting impatiently on the plain below, to set off in pursuit of the retreating Celts. Livy records that the pursuit was carried out with great slaughter, Vulso 'feeling sure that the campaign could be finished if as many Celts as possible were killed or captured in that panic flight'. Livy stresses that it is difficult to assess the number of casualties. Whereas Claudius Antipater reckons that 40,000 Celtic women and children were made captive and subsequently sold as slaves, Valerius Antias makes this only 10,000. Livy observes:

No doubt the number of prisoners brought the total losses to 40,000 because the Celts had brought with them their whole horde, of all classes and ages, more in the manner of a migrating people than like a host going out to war. The Consul first burned up the weapons of the enemy in one heap, and then ordered all his men to bring in the rest of the spoil; he sold that part of the booty which had to be paid to the treasury, and the remainder he distributed among the soldiers, taking care to divide it as fairly as possible. Moreover, at an assembly of the troops, praise was given to all soldiers, and rewards were bestowed on individuals according to their merits: Attalos was honoured before all the rest, with universal approval, for that young man, besides showing exemplary courage and energy in all the hardships and dangers, had been remarkable for the modesty of his bearing.

This battle seems to have broken the spirit of the Tolistoboii for the time being but Ortiagon of the Trocmi led survivors of the Tolistoboii in a withdrawal towards Ancyra. The Trocmi and Tectosages had established another defensive position at Mount Magaba, a hill-fortress 10 miles south-east of Ancyra. We find that, as well as Ortiagon, Comboiomarus and Gaulotus were there. So, indeed, the Celtic leadership appear to have escaped the carnage at Mount Olympus. The Celts now fortified themselves at Magaba.

Vulso and his men arrived at Ancyra. It was here that we have a rather exciting story concerning Ortiagon's wife Chiomara. Chiomara, recounting the story to Polybius, says she was captured by a Roman centurion who raped her. Livy, repeating the tale, says that 'the wife of the chieftain Ortiagon was held in custody with a large number of prisoners. She was an exceedingly beautiful woman; and the guard was commanded by a centurion as lustful and greedy as the average soldier.' Livy tries to put the best 'gloss' on the tale by saying that the centurion attempted to seduce her and, 'fate having made him a slave to her body', he then raped her. Afterwards, to soothe her indignation, he offered to help her return to her own people. He had discovered that she was the wife of a chieftain and therefore of high rank, so he made a bargain for a quantity of gold. To avoid letting his own men into the deal, he allowed Chiomara to choose a fellow prisoner to use as a messenger to her own people.

The Celt entrusted with the task was escorted by the centurion past the sentries and sent on his way to Ortiagon. The plan was that two of Chiomara's relatives would come to the river bank, at an appointed place, on the following night to pay the centurion the gold and receive the person of Chiomara. The Celt arrived at Mount Magaba and told his story. Ortiagon immediately sent two kinsmen of his wife's to the assigned place – probably on the banks of the river Halys itself. Livy says:

On the next night the two kinsmen of the woman and the centurion with the prisoner arrived at the appointed spot. When her people were producing the gold, which was to amount to an Attic talent – that was the sum bargained for – the woman, in her own language, ordered them to draw their swords and kill the centurion as he was weighing the money.

Polybius, who later met Chiomara and had the story from her, says that while the centurion was busy counting the gold, Chiomara turned, grabbed a sword and decapitated him, taking his head, in Celtic fashion, back to her husband with the ransom money. Livy agrees with the end result.

'When the head was severed, the woman wrapped it in her garment and, taking it with her, she returned to her husband Ortiagon, and threw the head of the centurion at his feet. When he asked in amazement whose head this was and what was the meaning of this far from womanly act, she revealed to her husband the outrage done to her body and the vengeance exacted for the forcible violation of her chastity. The story,' says Livy, clearly not understanding the Celtic cultural values involved, 'goes on to tell how, by the purity and nobility of her whole life thereafter, she retained to the end the glory of a deed so worthy of the name of gentlewoman.'

The Greek report of their conversation, according to Dr Rankin, 'preserves genuine, gnomic, Celtic idiom'.

'Woman a fine thing [is] good faith.'
'[A] better thing, only one man be alive who had intercourse with me.'

It is an echo of an Irish triad implying that the marital fidelity of a chieftain's spouse was highly regarded. '*Cid as dech do mnáib? Ní hannsa; ben maith ad fitir fer romat ríam.*' 'What is the best sort of wife? Not hard: a good woman whom a man has never known before you.'

Livy, in observing the act was 'unwomanly', clearly does not understand the role of women in Celtic society whereby they could be, and were, leaders of their people in war and could, and did, take part in warfare as warriors in their own right.

The Celtic chieftains, having witnessed the carnage at Olympus, decided to send emissaries to Vulso at Ancyra. To save the lives of the women, children and elderly of their people, the Celts wished to discuss peace terms, for peace was preferable to the Roman concept of total war. A council was arranged for the following day and the place for the meeting was fixed half-way between Ancyra and Magaba. Vulso arrived with 500 cavalry. The Celts did not turn up. The next day the same emissaries arrived at Ancyra and explained that the chieftains could not come at the appointed hour because of a religious obstacle. They would, however, send a deputy to negotiate. Vulso said he, too, would appoint a deputy to discuss matters. In fact, he sent Attalos with a guard of 300 cavalry. This time both sides arrived for the conference.

The terms of a peace were discussed but, as neither the commander of the Romans nor the chieftains of the Celts were there, each side had to return to their principals, agreeing to meet in the same place on the following day.

From the Celtic viewpoint, the negotiations appeared to give them a breathing space for, having seen what the Romans had done to the women and children at Mount Olympus, they were anxious to find time to get the surviving women and children across the river Halys, together with their valuable possessions, in case the Romans attacked. The Celts strongly suspected the Romans of perfidy and the chieftains had selected some 1000 cavalry of tested courage to cover the next day's conference. The Romans, too, it appears, had sent some 600 cavalry to a spot near the conference camp to attack if necessary.

Which side betrayed the 'ceasefire' is a question of dispute.

We know that when the meeting broke up Vulso, Attalos and their bodyguard left the camp. Livy, of course, says that the Celtic cavalry attacked first. According to his account, Vulso and his bodyguard turned and drew their weapons, but were forced to retire against 'overwhelming odds'. It was by chance that the Roman cavalry were in the area. What were the Roman cavalry doing so near to the peace conference? Livy claims that they were merely a foraging party who just happened to be there. An odd coincidence. Why would a cavalry cohort be 'collecting wood' so many miles away from the Roman encampment at Ancyra and just by chance near the place where the peace negotiations were being conducted? Wood cutting and collecting for the legionary camp was usually the job of foot soldiers near the camp, not 5 or 6 miles away. There is a good reason to suppose that Vulso had planned to capture the chieftains, snatching them by use of a cohort of cavalry, and that his 'surprise' was countered by the arrival of the Celtic cavalry. Livy gives his version of what happened:

Then the Celts began to chase and cut down the members of the bodyguard [of Vulso], and a great part of them would have been overwhelmed had not the outposts of the foragers, the 600 cavalry, come to their aid. They had heard from afar the terrified shouting of their comrades, and, making their weapons and horses ready, they took over as fresh forces, the battle which had become a rout. And so, in a moment, fortune changed and terror changed over from the vanquished to the victors. The Celts were routed at the first charge, the foragers rushed into the fight from the fields, and the Celts were met by foes on every side, so that not even flight was safe or easy for them, since the Romans with fresh horses were pursuing the exhausted enemy. Consequently there were but few Celts who escaped, no prisoners were taken, and by far the greater part paid the death penalty for breach of faith in respect of a conference. The Romans with their hearts blazing with anger, reached the enemy next day with all their forces.

In fact, the Celtic chieftains had managed to escape back to Magaba. With the breakdown of the peace talks, for which Vulso blamed the Celts, the Romans now had the excuse to attack and 'finish the job'. But it was not, as Livy says, the next day that they attacked. Vulso spent two days reconnoitring Mount Magaba; on the third day, after taking great care about the auspices and offering sacrifices to the gods, he divided his army into four columns. Two columns were to attack the centre ranks of the Celtic defenders while the other two were to attack the flanks. It seems that Ortiagon, having learnt the lessons of Mount Olympus, decided on a 'set battle piece' whereby his men could actually get to grips with the Roman soldiers.

Livy says the Tectosages and Trocmi held the centre with 50,000 men; the cavalry were dismounted because of the terrain and 10,000 of them were stationed on the right flank. It appears that two of the neighbouring kingdoms had now sent allies to the Celts of Galatia.

Ariarathes of Cappodocia and Morzius of Gangra, a Paphlagonian sub-kingdom, were personally leading their men on the left flank. These allies totalled 4000 men.

Vulso launched his attack directly on the centre. Livy says the battle was more or less a repeat performance of Mount Olympus.

The discharge of something like a cloud of light missiles overwhelmed the Celtic lines. Not one of the Celtic warriors dared to charge forward from their ranks for fear of exposing his body to shots from all sides, and as they stood immobile, they received all the more wounds for being so closely packed. They offered a fixed target for their enemies to aim at. The Celts were now in utter confusion in their own ranks, and the Consul thought that if he showed them the standards of the legions when they were in this state they would all turn to flight straightaway. Accordingly, he took into his formation the skirmishers and the rest of the auxiliaries and then advanced his battle line.

The Celtic warriors were able to withstand only the first assault of the heavy legionary troops. With the second assault, they broke and fled for their camp. The Romans pursued them into the camp, cutting them down. Some 8000 were said to have been killed in this attack while others escaped eastward across the river Halys.

The Celts and men from Cappadocia and Gangra, on both the flanks, held their ground longer than the centre because they had not been put under the same barrage of arrows, sling shots and javelins. Now the Romans turned on them and they, too, were put to flight. Vulso's men felt free to loot the nearby Galatian settlements, making off with a great deal of booty. A large part of the Roman army remained that night in the camp at Magaba. The next day Vulso interrogated some of the prisoners and looked over the plunder that had been taken.

The retreating Celts eventually halted and reformed again east of the river Halys. Many were wounded and dying. Most had lost their weapons. There was also concern for the large numbers of elderly, women and children. The chieftains decided to send emissaries again to Vulso in the hope that they could delay any attacks or that, this time, Vulso would keep his word as to terms of peace. The Celts now had one weapon working for them. Winter was closing in. Vulso and his army wanted to get back to a winter encampment near the coastal cities. Indeed, Vulso did not want to be tied down in a winter campaign. As consul and commander in Asia Minor he was also concerned about the more important matter of finalising the treaty with Antiochos of Syria. He could not be delayed either by fighting or by protracted negotiations.

Having received the emissaries from the Celtic chieftains, Livy says, 'Manlius Vulso bade them come to Ephesos, for he was in a hurry – since it was now the middle of autumn – to get away from a district which was rendered chilly by the proximity of the Taurus mountains; and he took his victorious army back to winter quarters on the coast.'

Livy actually suggests a reason why the Romans used extreme severity in the conquest of Galatia. He says that the Romans had inherited a fear of the Celts, as demonstrated by Vulso's speech to his soldiers. By smashing the power of Galatia in Asia Minor, says Livy, the Romans had secured the eastern world from potential Celtic conquest and dominance. We are told, significantly, by Livy that 'the defeat of the Celts occasioned more rejoicing among the Romans and their allies than the defeat of Antiochos'.

It was during this winter of 189/188BC that peace talks for the entire region were conducted at Apamea. These were attended by Vulso and his ten-man Senate commission while his army was quartered at Ephesos. At Apamea, the representatives of Antiochos the Great had to accept Rome's peace terms as dictated by Vulso. We are told that the Celts sent their emissaries, who arrived at Apamea only to be told that they were a 'special case' and that they would be informed of the terms of peace when Eumenes II arrived back at Ephesos from Rome. Meanwhile Ariarathes of Cappadocia was ordered to pay 600 silver talents as a fine for his alliance with the Celts.

As for Antiochos, he would pay the money and corn demanded in the original agreement but would agree never to attack Rome or her allies and, when needed, to supply and help any Roman army, allowing it to pass through the territories of his kingdom. He would have no right to make war on the islands off the mainland nor cross into Europe. He would withdraw to the east of the Taurus mountain range. He would hand over all slaves and prisoners from western Asia Minor. He would hand over all his war elephants and not acquire others. He would surrender his warships and only retain ten ships of thirty oars for his own use and not sail beyond the promontories of Calycadnus and Sarpedon. Antiochos would have no right to hire mercenary soldiers from any peoples within Roman imperial territory. He would agree to preserve the property of any of Roman's allies in his territories, particularly the people of Rhodes. He would also give twenty hostages to Rome, all between the ages of eighteen and forty-five, and must change them every three years. Finally, Antiochos was to hand over certain persons, namely Hannibal of Carthage, Thoas of Aetolia, Mnasilochus of Acarnania and Eubulidas and Philo of Chalcis. These were deemed to be Rome's greatest enemies of the time.

Hannibal, no longer safe under Antiochos' protection, fled to the court of Prusias of Bithynia who was able to guarantee his safety for the next five years.

Under Rome's militant paternalism, Asia Minor was divided between the kingdom of Rhodes and that of Pergamum while Armenia and Bactria took the opportunity to once more break away from the weakened Syrian empire.

Vulso and his commissioners, with his army, now marched for the Hellespont *en route* back to Rome. It was at Lampsacos that he finally met with the Celtic ambassadors. Perhaps this was because there was a strong Celtic presence in this city which caused it to be chosen by the Galatians as a more 'friendly' place for such a peace conference between the Roman general and the Celtic embassy. Vulso is said by Livy to have made several stipulations. Firstly they had to keep the peace with Eumenes of Pergamum, under whose suzerain power they now came. They were to stop their habitual raids and keep within their own territory. Thus Rome actually recognised the state of Galatia. One remarkable fact is that Vulso did not demand the usual payment of indemnity. This has been explained by the fact that Vulso knew well his army had already stripped Galatia of most of its wealth.

Perhaps the most important point that came out of this peace conference was that Rome gave Pergamum power over Galatia but left it up to Pergamum to contain Galatia. It was soon obvious that Vulso's conquest had no lasting effect for the Galatian Celts formed alliances with Prusias of Bithynia and Pharnaces of Pontus against their Roman-imposed overlord, Eumenes of Pergamum. Pompeius

Trogus points out, perhaps with some pride as he was a Celt himself, that the Galatians remained a formidable people in spite of Vulso's conquest.

Vulso then crossed with his army from Asia Minor into Europe, encamping his army outside Lysimacheia. Things did not go well for him. A few days after leaving the city, his army was ambushed by some 10,000 Thracians in a narrow mountain pass. The attack was well planned and it focused on the baggage train which was loaded with the booty from Asia Minor. In fact, over the next several days, Vulso had to fight a running battle with the Thracians. He lost one prominent officer named Quintus Minucius Thermus. He managed to march the survivors of his army through Macedonia into Thessaly and cross the Epiros where, at Apollonia, he encamped for the winter months.

Vulso arrived back in Rome in the spring of 187BC and found himself under criticism by the ten commissioners, particularly Lucius Furius Purpurio and Lucius Aemilius Paulus. There were serious charges: that he did not deserve recognition as a victor, he was no more than a bandit, he had made war on Galatia without the permission of the Roman Senate and his incompetence in Thrace had been disastrous. Vulso, in turn, argued that his conquests should be recognised and he should be allowed to ride through Rome at the head of his troops in triumph. The praetor, Servius Sulpicius, granted Vulso leave to appear before the Senate to defend himself.

The ten commissioners put their case first, stating that they had been appointed to conclude the peace with Antiochos, simply to put the finishing touches to the terms of the treaty which had been drafted by Lucius Scipio. Vulso had tried every means to destabilise the situation and provoke a new war. Vulso had been eager to cross the Taurus mountains and provoke Antiochos, they said.

The commissioners claimed that when Vulso had found no excuse for war against Antiochos, he had led his army in an unprovoked attack on the Celts of Galatia – the Gallogrecians, as they were called. Yet the Senate of Rome had not declared any war against these people. How had Vulso dared to take such a step without the authority of the Senate? In all recent wars it was the Senate who had passed a resolution on whether to go to war or not, the Roman people who had given sanction, and Rome's ambassadors who had made clear the terms to the potential adversaries before there was a declaration of war and an attack. No such actions had been employed before Vulso had marched into Galatia.

The commissioners continued their accusations by saying that Vulso could not be regarded as conducting a public war on Rome's behalf but rather a private act of brigandage. If Vulso had thought that he was officially at war with the Celts of Galatia why did he not march by a direct route against the enemy? Why had he traversed every nook and corner of Pisidia, of Lycaonia and Phrygia, demanding tribute from the peoples of out-of-the-way towns who were unoffensive to Rome?

As to the conduct of the actual war against the Celts, for which Vulso was now demanding recognition in a triumph, the commissioners were quick to criticise Vulso's brutal methods. Lucius Aemilius Paulus sneered:

'You are certainly right that honour should be given to the immortal gods for your victories. They must have refrained from giving natural and moral right to the Celts against the foolhardiness of the Roman general who waged a war with no sanction of the law of the nations.'

Livy, recording the events, now returns to his old theme about 'degenerate Celts' for he puts these words into the speech of the commissioners in criticising Vulso before the Senate:

'Do not imagine that it is only the name of the Gallogrecian that is a hybrid; for a long time before this the physique of this people has deteriorated through intermixing, and so has their character. Indeed, had they been Celts from Gaul or Cisalpine Gaul, the Celts with whom we have fought a thousand times here in Italy with varying success, would even a messenger have returned from that country, the country of the Galatians? Certainly not, if the result had relied solely on the ability of our general, Vulso. Twice he fought a battle with them, twice he approached them on unfavourable ground, placing his line of battle in a valley practically below the feet of the enemy. They could have overwhelmed us simply by hurling their naked bodies upon us, without discharging a weapon from their higher positions. So what happened?

'Great is the luck of the Roman people; great and inspiring dread is the name of Rome. The recent downfall of Hannibal, of Philip and of Antiochos, caused the Celts to be thunderstruck, in fear and dread at the sight of the Roman eagles. Armies of great size were thrown into confused flight by the sling shots and arrows alone; no swords were bloodied in battle in this war against the Celts of Galatia. The enemy simply flew away like flocks of birds at the onslaught of our missiles.'

Lucius Aemilius Paulus then pointed out the fact that *en route* to Rome they had been attacked by Thracians who put to flight the Romans and captured their baggage. He mentions the death of Quintus Minucius Thermus and many others, adding that if Vulso had been killed instead it would have been no greater loss. The army bringing back the spoils of the war with Antiochos had been dispersed. Was it for this Manlius Vulso now sought a triumph?

Vulso was then allowed to present his defence. The main charge against Vulso was that he had waged war on the Galatians without the authority of the Senate of Rome. Livy puts these words into his mouth:

'The charge is twofold: they argue that I ought not to have made war on the Celts of Galatia and that my conduct of the campaign was rash and ill-advised. "The Celts," they argued, "were not enemies; you did violence to them when they were at peace and were carrying out our orders." I am not going to demand, members of the Senate, that you should form your picture of the Celts who live in Asia from what you know in general about the savagery of the Celtic people and their most bitter hatred of the name of Rome; set aside the ill-fame of the race as a whole and the repugnance they evoke, and judge these Celts by themselves.

'How I wish that Eumenes of Pergamum were here, indeed; that all the cities of Asia were present that you might hear their complaints against the Celts of Galatia instead of hearing my accusations. Why not send agents to those same cities and ask them whether they felt more free from oppression when Antiochos was defeated or when the Celts of Galatia were crushed. Find out their descriptions of how their countries and cities were ravaged, how often they were plundered, their women carried off, when they had scarcely resources to ransom their captives, and when they kept hearing of the slaughter inflicted by these Celts.

'Let us make no mistake about this, your allies in Asia have been paying tribute to the Celts for a century and more. If I had not invaded their country, the people of Asia would still be paying tribute to them.

'I would argue further. The removal of Antiochos as a power in that area would have allowed the Celts of Galatia to dominate Asia Minor. They would have been unrestrained. All the territory of Asia Minor this side of the Taurus range would have been added to the dominions of the Galatian Celts.'

Vulso taunted that he heard someone saying that, whether it was true or not, why make war on them? Even when the Celts sacked Delphi, when the oracle was the common property of mankind, the navel of the world, Rome was not bothered to declare war on the Celts. Why should she declare war on them now?

'For my part, I believe that there is a small difference between that time, when Greece and Asia were not yet under the jurisdiction of Rome and therefore Rome was not concerned in what was happening. But at this point in time, Rome's jurisdiction now ranges to the Taurus mountains and in incorporating that territory, Rome had to assume the responsibility of ensuring peace on land and sea. How could Rome ask Antiochos to withdraw his troops and regard Asia liberated if the Celts were still free to dominate uncontrolled?'

Vulso rhetorically asked why he was even bothering to answer the charges as if he had made enemies of the Celts when they had been friends of Rome – in reality they were already determined enemies. He turned to both Lucius Scipio and Publius Scipio, who were attending the hearing, and asked them to inform the Senate whether, at the battle of Magnesia, there were Celtic troops in the army of Antiochos – Celts who were fighting for the Syrian king. In his judgement, the Senate had declared war on all those within the forces of Antiochos, on all who were his allies. Scipio had concluded a peace with Antiochos but not with his allies.

Vulso went on: 'I also tested the attitude of the Celts to see whether their natural savagery could be softened and only when I realised that they were intractable and unappeasable did I decide that they had to be restrained by force of arms.'

Unfortunately, history presents us with no evidence as to when and how Vulso made this assessment. If he is claiming that he sent emissaries to the Galatian assembly then the historians, even one as detailed on the campaign as Livy, are silent. Vulso's accusers deny that any warning was given to the Galatians before the invasion.

Vulso now turned from the accusation that he started the war without justification to the charge that he was incompetent in his conduct of the campaign. As to the accusation that he fought on unfavourable ground, he demanded to know what more favourable ground could he have fought on? As the enemy had occupied a mountain and fortified it, surely he had to attack the enemy where the enemy was if he wanted to defeat them? If the enemy had been inside a city, surely he would have had to attack that city? And as for his losses in Thrace on the return to Rome, he told the Senate that those bringing such charges had neglected to mention that when the Thracians had surrounded the baggage train, his vanguard and rearguard had counter-attacked, killing and capturing many thousands. He had also won another battle a few days later with the Thracians. 'If my opponents keep silence about this, do they realise that the Senate is bound to learn about it since my whole army is the witness to the truth of the matter?'

When the Senate adjourned that day there was, Livy says, a general feeling that Vulso's triumph would be refused and Vulso condemned. However, Vulso's supporters in the Senate started lobbying support immediately. They pointed out that Vulso had completed his term of command successfully, brought home his army and crushed his enemies, and that under those conditions no Roman commander had ever been denied a triumph. Surely precedent, they argued, must prevail over any personal dislike of Vulso?

After some debate during the next day, the Senate decided to grant Vulso a triumphal entry into the city and a procession in honour of his victory over the Celts of Galatia.

[13]

Galatian Recovery

IN that year of 187 BC Seleucus IV succeeded his father Antiochos the Great and reigned for eleven peaceful years before being assassinated. His uncle Antiochos VI became king and began an unsuccessful war with Egypt before turning his attention to 'improving' his rule over Judaea. He sought to Hellenise the Jews, destroying one of the walls of Jerusalem, looting the temple and erecting an altar to Zeus there. This provoked a Jewish revolt against the Syrian empire, led by Mattathias of the Hasmoneans and his five sons. The history of this struggle for independence is told in detail in the two books of the Maccabees, which are part of the Apocrypha of the Old Testament.

Judas, the third son, defeated a Syrian army in a battle at Modin. The story is told by Jason of Cyrene, whose five books on the history of Judas Maccabaeus and his brothers are epitomised into Maccabees 2. Verses 19/20 tell us how, before the battle, Judas sought to encourage his men. There were 6000 in the Jewish army, which was outnumbered by the Syrians under Nicanor. But Judas appeals to them not to panic.

> He went on to recount to them the occasions when God had helped their ancestors; how, in Sennacherib's time, one hundred and eighty-five thousand of the enemy had perished, and also how on the occasion of the battle against the Galatians [Celts] in Babylonia, all the Jews engaged in the combat had numbered no more than eight thousand, with four thousand Macedonians, yet, when the Macedonians were hard pressed, the eight thousand, through heaven's aid, had destroyed one hundred and twenty thousand and taken much booty.

This obscure reference is exciting. The translator has, probably remembering Paul's later epistle to the Galatians, rendered Jason's

'Galatae' as 'Galatians'. But if the Syrians were recruiting European Celts to their army, the term 'Gaul' or 'Celt' would be more precise. When did this battle occur? Certainly not in Sennacherib's time. Sennacherib was king of Assyria in 705BC and made Nineveh his capital. He is mentioned in Kings 2, xviii, 13. Why would the Macedonians be fighting with the Jews? This presents a tantalising clue and would seem to suggest a period when the Macedonians united with the people of Judaea against the Seleucid Syrian kings. Stephanus of Byzantium confirms that there were Celtic mercenaries fighting for the Syrian kings against the Maccabees and he actually names the Senones. The only Senones were the Senones of northern Italy (Cisalpine Gaul), who gave their name to Senigalia (Senones Gallia). The name comes from the root *sen* (old, still seen in the Irish *sean* and in the Welsh *hen*) and appears to mean 'venerable ones'. It seems highly unlikely that they would be selling their mercenary services at a time when every warrior was needed against Rome's continuing incursions into their territory. Rome claimed, at this time, overlordship of these Celts, whose territory was not far away from Rome itself – just north of Ancona. Under the treaty with Antiochos, the Syrian kings would also have been forbidden to recruit mercenaries from among the Senones.

In the wake of his victory at Modin over Nicanor, Judas was named Maccabaeus, the Hammerer; he reconstructed the temple in 165BC, commemorating the event by a Feast of Dedication, Hanukkah. The war went on, however, and in 160BC Judas was killed at the battle of Eleasa. His brothers continued the war but it was not until 141BC that his brother Symeon was able to establish a troubled independence from Syria which lasted only seventy-five years.

As we have seen, Polybius and Livy identified the Galatian chieftain Ortiagon as one of the leaders of the resistance against the Roman invasion and also record the story of his wife Chiomara. In the period following the invasion, Ortiagon re-emerges as a Celtic leader with some vision. Ortiagon realised that there was only one path available to the Celts of Galatia if they were to withstand conquest, whether it came from Rome or from Pergamum. The Galatians would have to reorganise the power structure of their state so that the loose confederation of tribes would be united under one leader. In other words, the Commonwealth of Galatia must become a centralised kingdom, under a single monarch, in order to retain its security.

Ortiagon was to be the most intriguing figure in the difficult period of Galatian reconstruction following the devastation by Vulso. Polybius, who was born c.200BC at Megalopolis, in Arcadia, had been an officer in the Achaean Confederacy. After the defeat of Perseus of Macedon at Pydna, Polybius was sent to Rome, spending sixteen years there without trial. He was fortunate to become tutor to the sons of a highly placed Greek family, one of whom was adopted by Publius Scipio. He acquired powerful Roman friends and began to achieve a reputation for his histories. Polybius made a journey to Sardis, the old capital of Lydia, in Asia Minor, where we know that he met the wife of Ortiagon, Chiomara, who had spent some time in captivity in the city.

Lydia was now part of the Pergamum territory and it would appear that Chiomara was a captive of Eumenes or his brother, Attalos. Chiomara, who was, like Ortiagon himself, much disposed to Hellenic culture, was able to tell Polybius about her husband. Plutarch mentions a lost book of Polybius from which it appears that Polybius might even have met Ortiagon himself. The Celtic chieftain is described by Polybius as full of charm and highly intelligent.

He records that Ortiagon and Chiomara had a son whom they named Paidopolites, a Greek name meaning 'son-citizen'.

Ortiagon had been successful in bringing together the shattered pieces of the Galatian commonwealth under his rule. Polybius is inclined to call him 'king of Galatia'. Pompeius Trogus was able to verify this, mentioning that Ortiagon also became an ally of Prusias of Bithynia; indeed, an inscription from Telemessus in Lycia commemorates Eumenes of Pergamum's victory over Prusias and Ortiagon about 184BC for which Eumenes was acknowledged with the title of Soter. It is significant that this inscription places the Bithynians and Galatian Celts as coequal allies.

The war continued and Rome sent Titus Quinctius Flaminius, its leading authority on Greek affairs, to head a peace conference. Flaminius had been consul for 198BC and in 197BC had defeated Philip V of Macedonia. It was Flaminius who, having become a philhellene, suggested to the Roman Senate that they establish a protectorate over autonomous Greek states rather than extending direct rule. He was able to announce the 'liberation of Greece' to the crowds gathered at Corinth for the Isthmian games of 196BC.

Flaminius began his meeting with Prusias of Bithynia by an attack. He told Prusias that he was harbouring one of the most dangerous enemies of Rome – Hannibal of Carthage. Prusias sent soldiers ostensibly to guard Hannibal's house. It seems, however, that Flaminius had suggested that the only way Prusias could make peace with Rome was to get rid of Hannibal. What pressures caused the subsequent event are not clear. Hannibal, realising he was no longer safe, committed suicide, saying:

> Let us now put an end to the life which has caused the Romans so much anxiety, seeing that they find it tedious to wait for an old man's death. It is no magnificent or memorable victory that Flaminius will win over a man unarmed and betrayed. This day will surely prove how far the moral standards of the Romans have changed. The fathers of these Romans sent a warning to King Pyrrhos, bidding him beware of poison – and he was an enemy in arms with an army in Italy; these Romans themselves have sent an envoy of consular rank to suggest to Prusias the crime of murdering his guest.

The sixty-five-year-old victor of Trebbia, Trasimene and Cannae, as well as many other battles, who had crossed the Alps and for sixteen years held his Celto-Carthaginian army together undefeated by Rome, now took poison. Yet for four centuries after Hannibal's death, Roman mothers would still quiet their fractious children by whispering, 'Hannibal ad portas!', 'Hannibal is at the gates!'

While the war between Prusias, Ortiagon and Eumenes was brought to an end by Flaminius' peace negotiations in 183BC, no mention is made of the involvement of the Celts. By 181BC Ortiagon has vanished from the historical scene. From this year there survives a list of Celtic chieftains who have clearly refused to depart from an adherence to the traditional Celtic tribal form of government. The Celts of Galatia seem to have gone back to their faction fighting and alliances for the individual tribal chieftains, while still holding together in a loose federation under the twelve *tetrarchs* from the three tribes.

No sooner had the war between Eumenes and Prusias ended than a new war erupted, this time between Eumenes and the kingdom of Pontus. Pharnaces I of Pontus (*c.* 190–160BC) was organising an alliance with some Galatian chieftains and with Mithridates II of Armenia, to exert the power of Pontus in Asia Minor. Eumenes moved immediately on to the offensive. He marched an army into Pontus, capturing Sinope, a seaport dominating the Black Sea. At the same time, Eumenes sent his brother Attalos to Rome to ask for help against Pharnaces. Attalos returned with assurances that Rome would send an embassy to sort things out.

Pharnaces I made a tactical error. He sent his general, Leocritus, into Galatia, which was ravaged, while he himself attacked Ariarathes III in Cappadocia. Two Celtic chieftains, Gaezatorix and Cassignatus, who had previously been considering the proposed alliance with Pharnaces, now offered their services to Eumenes. This time Eumenes made the tactical error by ordering his brother Attalos to march into Galatia, arrogantly rejecting the help of the Galatians against Pontus. Attalos marched his army across their territory to Cappadocia. Here he joined forces with Ariarathes, crossing the Halys into Camisene. Instead of allies, Attalos, by rejecting the offer of friendship from Gaezatorix and Cassignatus, had merely found new enemies.

It was then that Rome's ambassadors arrived at Ephesos. Eumenes had put another army into the field to help his brother, who was bogged down in warfare against the Celts. The Roman attempt at mediation was ignored until the end of the year. It was in 179BC that Eumenes defeated Pharnaces I. A treaty of friendship was agreed between Prusias of Bithynia, Ariarathes of Cappadocia and Eumenes. Eumenes had gone out of his way to provoke the Galatian chieftains and this created bitter feelings.

In spite of Ortiagon's ambition to see a united Galatia, this decade saw the Galatians divided, with their chieftains pursuing difference policies. What emerged from the peace established by Eumenes was that the king of Pergamum considered Galatia to be under his control.

Indeed, we find the chieftain Cassignatus as commander of Eumenes' cavalry during the war against Perseus of Macedonia (179–168BC). Perseus, the son of Philip V of Macedon, was the last Macedonian monarch. He fell because he procrastinated when he should have acted. He knew that Rome was going to move against him and he spent some time organising alliances, including one with the Celtic Scordisci on his northern borders. However, he allowed many of his allies to be invaded and defeated without lifting a finger to help. When his turn came, he found that Aemilius Paulus in 168 BC completely overwhelmed his army. Paulus' army was helped by an alliance with Pergamum.

When the Third Macedonian War started in 178 BC we find that the Bastarnae were invited by Philip V to leave their homelands and cross the Danube with a large body of infantry and cavalry. Cotto was the Macedonian leader who negotiated this alliance. It had been Philip's intention to reward the Bastarnae for their services by allowing them to settle in the lands occupied by the Dardani, and Philip wanted to use them to attack Rome itself. Livy seems to support the contention that the Bastarnae were Celto-Germanic rather than Germans for he says:

> There was a route [to Rome] as Philip knew through the country of the Celtic Scordisci to the Adriatic and on to Italy; an army could not be brought across by any other way. The Scordisci would readily offer a passage to the Bastarnae for they were not widely different in language or culture; in fact they were likely to join forces with the Bastarnae once they realised they were on their way to plunder a people of great wealth.

The entry of the Bastarnae into Thrace and Philip V's death were badly timed. In fact, the Thracians were able to stand up to the Bastarnae. At a mountain range called Donuca the Thracians met them in battle. Livy says:

> When the Bastarnae tried to reach the Thracian position they were caught as they vainly attempted to get to the crest of the range, by a storm like that which, as the story goes, annihilated the Celts when they were plundering Delphi. Not only were they overwhelmed with torrential rain, followed by incessant hail storms, accompanied by tremendous crashes in the sky, by claps of thunder, and blinding flashes of lightning; thunderbolts also flashed all round them, so they seemed aimed at their bodies, and not just the soldiers but even the chieftains were smitten and fell to the ground.

Livy says that one chieftain, whom he later identifies as a Celt, with 30,000 men, did arrive at the destination which they had been making for while the rest of the Bastarnae retraced their steps back to the northern territories. These moved back during the winter and when they were crossing the Danube the ice of the frozen river cracked and many perished in the icy waters.

Having succeeded his father to the kingdom of Macedonia, Perseus prepared for the Roman onslaught on his kingdom. Livy mentions that in his army were 2000 Celts under the command of Asclepiodotus from Heracleia in Sinitica. At the start of 168BC Perseus, however, refused the offer of assistance against Rome by a confederation of Celtic tribes. These were scattered throughout Illyria and together they could supply the Macedonian king with an army of 10,000 cavalry and 10,000 infantry. Livy says that the infantry were so strong that they could keep up with the cavalry, running by the side of the horses, and take the place of a fallen cavalryman by seizing the riderless mount and carrying on the fight. These Celts agreed to a payment of ten gold pieces, cash down, to each cavalryman, and five to each foot soldier, and 1000 pieces to their commander.

Perseus met them on the Elpeus and presented some horses and cloaks to the chieftains together with a small amount of gold and a supply of corn, wine and cattle. He believed that he could buy the Celtic army with vague promises that the agreed money would be paid at a later date. He returned to the city of Almana, encamping on the bank of the river Axius. The Celtic army halted near Desudabain Maedica, and said they would await the payment agreed.

Perseus sent one of his nobles, Antigonus, to instruct the Celts to move their camp to Bylazora, in Paeonia, while inviting their chieftains to meet him again to discuss matter. The Celts were in no mood to bargain. While Antigonus made promises, Clondicus, who appears to be the supreme leader of the Celtic army, demanded to know whether the king had brought the gold that he had agreed for payment with him. Antigonus knew that Perseus did not have the gold and was silent. Clondicus then rose and said: 'Go back and tell your king that the Celts will not move a step further unless they receive the payment which has been promised.'

When Antigonus reported to Perseus, the Macedonian king summoned his council. His council suggested that he fulfil his promise to the Celts and pay them. It was now a matter of urgency for the Roman army would soon be upon them. Perseus, we are told, was a cautious and mean man. He gave his council a discourse on the supposed treachery and savagery of the Celts and reminded them that, long before, they had caused many disasters in Macedonia. This was obviously a reference to the invasion and the defeat of Ptolemy Ceraunnos. It was, he said, dangerous to receive the Celtic army into Macedonia for the people might find them even more troublesome as allies than they did the Romans as enemies. He thought that they could hire a force of 5000 cavalry and dispense with the rest.

Livy says that Perseus, being a mean man, was worried only about the money he had to pay the Celts. Antigonus was sent back to Clondicus and the Celtic chieftains to announce that Macedonia would employ only 5000 of them as cavalry. There was instant uproar. Clondicus asked whether Perseus was prepared to pay the ten gold pieces to each of the 5000 cavalry immediately, and seeing that the reply was evasive, the Celtic leader gave orders for the Celts to return towards the Danube – Livy adds, 'without doing any harm to the messenger who had tried to trick them (he could scarcely have hoped for such good luck) although they ravaged that part of Thrace which lay on their route.'

Livy admits that if the Macedonians had used this 20,000-strong Celtic army, then the Romans might have been put in a difficult situation. As it was, Perseus had brought the Macedonians into disrepute for his meanness. Perseus went on to meet his fate at Pydna, on the Gulf of Salonika, on 22 June 168BC, when he confronted the Roman army of Lucius Aemilius Paulus. According to Livy, 20,000 Macedonians were slaughtered, 6000 were captured immediately and 5000 more fugitives were rounded up over the next few days. Macedonia was no more. A year later Perseus was taken as a captive to Rome and administratively Macedonia was divided into four small republics governed by Rome. An uprising in 149BC by Andriscos, claiming to be king, came to nothing and Macedonia was made into a Roman province.

While Pergamum's main army was away in Macedonia, fighting for the Romans, and including some Galatian Celtic elements in it, the other Galatian chieftains rose up against Eumenes' overlordship and inflicted a serious defeat on Pergamum. In fact, Eumenes' person was actually threatened, according to Polybius. Unfortunately, we do not know the details but the inference is that Eumenes was personally attacked by the Celts and came close to losing his life. We are told that the Celtic chieftain responsible for this defeat of Eumenes in 167/6BC gathered together his prisoners from the battle, selected the most handsome, had them garlanded and then sacrificed. There seemed religious implications in this for the other prisoners were said to have been slaughtered without ceremony. Sopater of Paphos (*fl.c.*270BC), an Alexandrian writer of burlesque, had already convinced the Greek world that the Celts always sacrificed their prisoners to the gods after a victory.

Eumenes was forced to send his brother Attalos off to Rome once again to ask for help. Attalos was certainly a diplomat. According to Livy, he told the Senate that he first congratulated them on their victory over Perseus of Macedonia, a victory in which Pergamum's army had played no small part, and implied that it was as a result of this army being sent to Macedonia that the Galatians had been able to devastate Pergamum. By this time, however, Rome had begun to get fed up with Eumenes' pleas for help every time he was in trouble. He was mistrusted by the Roman Senate, although they personally liked his brother. Attalos made a passionate plea for help. 'Attalos left the Senate house,' Livy says.

> Rarely has anyone, whether king or private citizen, been listened to with so much favour and with so much general approval; Attalos was courted with every mark of honour and with all manner of gifts while he was there in Rome, and the citizens escorted him on his departure.

But Attalos, acting as ambassador, failed to get more than a vague promise of a diplomatic mission to look into the matter. Meanwhile, Eumenes managed to gather a large force at Sardis, according to Polybius, to defend Pergamum against the Galatians. At this point, Publius Licinius Crassus, a former consul, arrived to mediate on behalf of Rome. He met the Celts at Synnada in the spring of 167BC. Their chieftain here was Soloventios, according to Livy. Nothing else is known about this Celtic chieftain, although a silver coin was found in Pisidia bearing the name 'Solovettou', which appears to be the same name. This would indicate that Soloventios was a tribal chieftain, one of the 'big three', rather than just a *tetrarch*.

We do not know what Licinius Crassus said to Soloventios. Whatever it was, it angered the Celts and further increased their warlike attitudes. Eumenes had placed his headquarters at Apamea, to counter the Celtic army at Synnada. Eumenes was also worried about Licinius' equivocation in the negotiations. Then news came of a surprise development: Prusias II of Bithynia had arrived in Rome, with his son Nicomedes, claiming overlordship of Galatia.

Prusias was not such a good diplomat as Attalos. He entered the city with a large retinue and proceeded straight to the forum, to the office of Quintus Cassius, the praetor, the executive officer of government. He announced that he had come to offer salutations to the gods of Rome and congratulations on the Roman victory over Macedonia. Quintus Cassius said he would arrange a meeting with the Senate as soon as he could and ordered Lucius Cornelius Scipio, one of the quaestors (the magistrates), to find lodgings for the king.

Prusias came before the Senate on the third day after his arrival in Rome and started off by recalling his services to Rome in the war with Macedonia. He then said that the territory captured from Antiochos, which had not been given to anyone by the Roman people and which was being occupied by the Celts, i.e. Galatia, should be given to him. He would, as token of his good faith and friendship, entrust his son Nicomedes to the protection of the Senate.

In this matter Prusias was supported by those Romans who had held commands in Macedonia. All the claims that he had made to the Senate were granted except the territorial claim. The Senate said they would look into this matter; while they held that Prusias would be a worthy recipient of the territory, it might not be Rome's property to give away. If it proved that Galatia had not belonged to Antiochos the Great in the first place then it was, consequently, not legally in the remit of Rome. Even if it had belonged to Antiochos' ancestors, it may subsequently have been assigned to the Celts; in which case Prusias would have to excuse the Senate if they refused to make him any present which involved injustice to anyone else.

Eumenes of Pergamum had dropped his plans for war on the Celts and left for Rome in person immediately he realised what his rival, Prusias of Bithynia, was up to. He arrived demanding a Roman army to help him bring the Galatians to heel, pointing out that Manlius Vulso had given him to understand that the Galatians were under his authority.

The Senate, demonstrating how fed up with Eumenes they were, promptly passed a law forbidding the presence of any foreign kings within the confines of the city of Rome.

Eumenes returned home outraged and decided to chance a full-scale battle with the Celts on his own account near Synnada. He and his brother Attalos were able to secure a victory and statues were set up in honour of Eumenes, who promptly instituted a five-yearly festival in celebration.

Now the Celtic chieftains of Galatia decided to play the diplomatic game and, following Eumenes' example, they sent off a diplomatic mission to Rome to appeal against the treatment they were receiving from Pergamum.

The Senate, considering the claims put to them by both Eumenes and Prusias, as well as taking into account the arguments of the Galatian chieftains themselves, came to a surprising judgement – surprising, that is, in view of their avowed racial antagonism to the Celts typified by Manlius Vulso's speeches. They decreed that Galatia should be regarded as an independent state, but only so long as the Galatians remained within their own borders. In effect, the instructions of Vulso were to be adhered to. For nowhere had it been part of the peace agreement that Galatia was to be simply a province of the Pergamum kingdom.

The judgement was not regarded as binding among the Greek kingdoms. Polybius says that Prusias of Bithynia was still accusing Eumenes in 164BC of interfering in Galatian affairs and if Eumenes was doing so why shouldn't he? The Roman Senate reiterated their judgement that year that Galatia was autonomous. Prusias made the same complaint a few years later.

In the meantime the Galatian chieftains, whatever skirmishes they were having with Eumenes and Prusias, were certainly answerable to no neighbouring kingdom. The Trocmi, apparently with Rome looking the other way, attempted to annex some territory from Ariarathes V of Cappadocia (162–131BC). Appeals were made to the Senate of Rome and some money passed hands before they finally found in favour of Cappadocia. But the Celts continued to expand southwards until 123BC, when they added parts of Lycaonia to their territory.

The border disputes continued; Eumenes of Pergamum's clear policy was to attempt to exert his authority over Galatia whenever he could – either by diplomacy or by war, whichever method was successful. Eumenes and his brother Attalos wrote several letters to the Attis of the temple at Pessinus (it is from these letters that we find that the Attis bore Celtic names). The letters were put on public display in the late 1st century BC for political reasons. They showed, as Stephen Mitchell suggests, 'a conspiratorial preoccupation [by Pergamum] with political control over the region'. In one of the letters there are references to the possible capture of a place called Pessongi by treachery. The Attis' brother, one Aiorix, is also claimed to have insulted the priests of the Hellenic sanctuary there. The letters are full of possible plots and plans to take over parts of Galatia and in the last letter Attalos II, who succeeded his brother in 158BC, is only dissuaded by an adviser telling him that he would incur Roman wrath if he invaded Galatia.

Eumenes II had reigned in Pergamum for nearly forty years. He had continued his father's policy of patronage of the arts, and the great library of Pergamene was said to rival Alexandria's. The scribes of Pergamum had invented a material prepared from the skins of sheep and goats which was called *charta Pergamina*, from which the word 'parchment' entered the world's vocabulary. When Eumenes died, his son Attalos was too young and so his brother, who had served him so long and loyally, became Attalos II. Attalos was to be king for twenty-one years but it was a time of change. As the fortunes of Pergamum began to fall into decline a new power was emerging in Asia Minor – and that power was the kingdom of Pontus.

[14]

The Rise of Deiotaros

THROUGHOUT the rest of the 2nd century BC, affairs in Asia Minor were dominated by fluctuations in power between Pergamum and the rising empire of Pontus. Around 160BC Mithridates V Euergetes became king of Pontus and started his reign with an alliance with the new king of Pergamum, Attalos II, against Prusias II of Bithynia. Rome favoured Attalos II, who had many good friends in the Senate and contacts among the patrician class. When Prusias attacked Pergamum, Rome swiftly intervened and forced him to pay compensation to Attalos of 500 talents. Mithridates also declared himself an ally of Rome.

In 138BC Attalos II died. The son of Attalos' brother, Eumenes II, became Attalos III Philopater of Pergamum. Attalos, still a young man, became increasingly insane. He started his reign by putting to death all his uncle's trusted counsellors, including his surviving uncle, Athenaeus, who had taken part in Manlius Vulso's campaign in Galatia. He also put to death all their relatives. In fact, every person who had held office during the reigns of Eumenes II and Attalos II was systematically assassinated. Finally, Attalos killed his own mother. He ignored affairs of state and devoted himself to painting, sculpture and gardening. When he died in 133BC he left a will giving the kingdom of Pergamum to Rome. Aristonicos, an illegitimate son of Eumenes II, claimed the throne but the Roman Senate, accepting Attalos' legacy even though the dead king had been clearly insane and the validity of the will was questionable, sent armies to fight Aristonicos and three years later he had to surrender all claims to the kingdom. Mithridates V of Pontus took the opportunity to declare war on Aristonicos on Rome's behalf, both to ingratiate himself with Rome and to claim a share of the spoils. In fact, he also claimed control over Phrygia and Galatia.

Yet another scion of the Manlius clan, Manlius Aquilius, the

Roman consul who had been appointed governor in Pergamum with the brief to sort out affairs there, approved Mithridates' claims. In 126BC, however, the Roman Senate officially overturned Manlius Aquilius' approval. This did not prevent Mithridates from continuing to make claims on Galatia. In 120BC while at Sinope, on the coast of Pontus, Mithridates V was assassinated. He had, by the time of his death, raised Pontus to be the predominant kingdom in Asia Minor, taking over the role that Pergamum had once exercised.

His kingdom became a regency with his widow controlling it on behalf of his two young sons. One of them was an ambitious eight-year-old named Mithridates. The family claimed descent from Persian royalty, in fact from Darius III, the last Persian emperor, himself. The boy fell to studying and preparing for his role as king. It is said that he learned to speak twenty-five languages including the Celtic of neighbouring Galatia. Still in his teens, he imprisoned his mother, murdered his brother and married his sister, Laodice; at the age of twenty he embarked on a career of conquest. Cautiously, he chose those territories where Rome would not interfere, extending his territory around the Black Sea. In the space of seven years he had annexed Lesser Armenia, Colchis, the entire eastern coast of the Black Sea, the Crimea and all the northern coast as far as the Dniester river. At the same time, he made alliances with the Getae and the Sarmatae on the Danube. He was now being hailed as Mithridates VI Eupator or Mithridates the Great.

Mithridates felt confident enough to turn his attention to Asia Minor while Rome was busy meeting the menace of the German tribes who threatened the Italian peninsula at this time. In 102BC he had made an alliance with Nicomedes II of Bithynia and partitioned Paphlagonia with him. He decided to give his sister, Laodice, in marriage to Ariarathes VII, the new young king of Cappadocia. In spite of this relationship, within a few years he launched an attack on Cappadocia and placed his nephew on the throne as Ariarathes VIII. But Ariarathes showed too much independence of spirit so Mithridates had him murdered and then set up his own eight-year-old son as king while exercising power as regent. Cappadocia finally revolted in 93BC and reasserted independence. In 96BC Mithridates married his daughter Cleopatra to Tigranes of Armenia.

It was inevitable that Mithridates should turn his full attention towards Galatia. He had made one unsuccessful attempt to occupy it in 104BC.

So far as history is concerned, the period between 160BC and 88BC was generally one of peace for Galatia. There are no references to disturbances within or coming out of Galatia. The evidence shows that the Celts were leading a fairly settled life, improving their farmsteads and developing their townships. Rome was obviously worried about the rise of Mithridates' power in the area and suspicious of his designs in Asia Minor.

The ageing Roman general Gaius Marius (157–86BC), who had reorganised the Roman army and its tactics into the legionary force with which we are familiar today, visited Galatia in 99–98BC. His stated reason was for religious purposes. He claimed that he had undertaken a vow to Cybele at Pessinus, in Celtic territory, and went there to perform the rituals. Marius had served against the Celts in the west and was at the famous siege of the Celtic hill-fort of Numantia in Spain. It was Marius who had been in the unprecedented position of being elected consul for four years running and who, after his military reorganisation, had defeated the Teutones and the Cimbri to save Rome. In spite of his age, Marius was still ambitious and wanted command of the Roman army in the inevitable war against Mithridates. Indeed, Plutarch implies that his real reason for visiting Galatia was to reconnoitre military possibilities. He did have a private audience with Mithridates in Pontus at which he is claimed to have admonished the monarch.

The attack on the Celts of Galatia opened Mithridates' defiance of Rome. In 88BC, according to Appian and Justin, three Roman armies had been defending Rome's interests in Pergamum under the command of Manlius Aquilius, the governor, Publius Cassius and Quintus Oppius. There were few veteran Roman legionaries among the soldiers, who consisted largely of Phrygian and Celtic mercenaries. Presumably these Celts were from Galatia. Manlius Aquilius, who had been ordered to counter Mithridates' border attacks on Galatia, had planned to march his army into Galatia and attack Pontus across the Galatian border. Mithridates, however, pre-empted the attack by swinging his army into Bithynia and attacking both Aquilius and Nicomedes III. Nicomedes II had died in c.94BC. The army of Pontus drove through Bithynia and into the territory of

Pergamum. In a whirlwind campaign, Mithridates drove the Romans almost entirely out of Asia Minor.

Mithridates gave orders for a massacre, on one particular day, of all the Romans living in the territories under his control – some 80,000 persons according to Valerius Maximus, although Plutarch puts the number of victims as high as 150,000. After the defeat and the murder of the Romans and their supporters, one would have expected the Galatians to have been cautious about dealing with Mithridates. He had, after all, attacked their borders and even invaded, albeit unsuccessfully, twenty years before.

Mithridates, however, declared his friendship for his Celtic neighbours and invited some sixty leading Celtic chieftains from Galatia to his court, ostensibly to dine and discuss his intentions towards the kingdoms of Asia Minor. In the events that now occurred, Mithridates displayed a knowledge of Celtic social customs. He knew that the rules of hospitality were sacred to the Celts and that no warrior went into his host's feasting hall with his weapons. Mithridates waited until the feast was well under way and then he had his soldiers kill the chieftains.

Two chieftains escaped from this mass murder. One remains unnamed while the other was Deiotaros, son of Sinorix (king of the storms, or the weather) of the Tolistoboii. In one source the name of his father is given as Dumnorix (king of the world).

Three more Galatian chieftains had, perhaps being forewarned, either refused to attend the feast or not been able to attend. Mithridates sent assassins to the fortresses of these three chieftains and they entered on the pretext of seeking hospitality as travellers. When the moment arose, they were to kill the chieftains. They succeeded in two of the cases but a third chieftain managed to escape. There were now only three chieftains left in Galatia. It was not the first time, nor would it be the last, that the sacred Celtic laws of hospitality were cynically exploited by their enemies.

Mithridates' plan was a simple one. He decided to destroy the Celtic government in Galatia so that he could move in, exploiting the ensuing power vacuum. Indeed, he had not omitted to kill many of the supporters and friends of the Galatians within his own camp. However, while he had used his knowledge of Celtic social customs to good effect, he does not appear to have considered the inherent democracy of the Celtic system, which allowed for the immediate election of new chieftains by the three generations of each ruling family.

Mithridates dispatched his army under the command of Eumachos, according to Appian, to take over control of Galatia. Deiotaros, 'the divine bull', who had survived the massacre, was now able to do what Ortiagon had failed to do a hundred years before. He united the Celts of Galatia into one central kingdom, then evicted Eumachos and the army of Pontus. The Galatian victory was, of course, helped by the fact that Mithridates had become preoccupied by Rome.

Asia Minor had become too small for Mithridates' growing ambitions. Under the pretext of liberating Greece from Roman rule, the king of Pontus had, in 87 BC, sent his armies across the Hellespont into Europe. First he had sent an agent, Aristion, to argue his cause and Athens responded by rising in revolt against Rome. All the Roman residents of Piraeus were put to death. Most of southern and central Greece joined Mithridates, who was represented by his general Archelaus. Here we encounter a curious anomaly. We find large numbers of Celts in the employ of Mithridates' army. These are certainly not Galatians, who were now fighting against Mithridates for their independence. Yet Memnon mentions a Celtic chieftain named Connacorix (perhaps 'king of hounds') commanding 4000 Celtic troops, of the garrison of Heracleia Pontica, and Appian and Justin also mention the considerable numbers of Celtic mercenaries in the army of Archelaus. Where did these Celts come from if not from Galatia? It seems that they may well have come from other parts of Mithridates' expanding empire, perhaps from along the Dneister, where we know Celtic tribes had settled, or from the Danube. Or perhaps these Celts were from the Illyrian and Pannonian areas. We know that the Scordisci had been actively fighting the Romans under C. Metellus Caprarius along the lower Save shortly before this period.

In 87 BC the Roman consul Lucius Cornelius Sulla had landed in Greece with five legions, about 30,000 men. It was not until early 86 BC that he broke into Athens and forced Archelaus to evacuate Piraeus. But Archelaus kept Sulla pinned down in Attica while a second Pontic army crossed the Hellespont and marched through Thrace and Macedonia. Finally at Chaeroneia, between spurs of the Boeotian mountains, Sulla and Archelaus clashed in a set battle. For a long time the battle was in contention. There is no doubt that Archelaus was an exceptional general. His cavalry pushed back the

Roman flanks but Sulla, using a reserve corps, counter-attacked. A well-timed Roman cavalry charge converted the battle into a rout.

Archelaus' army was nearly destroyed but reinforcements arrived from Mithridates, landing by sea, and engaged Sulla at neighbouring Orchomenus. Archelaus was able to use his chariots and cavalry but Sulla eventually won the day when he managed to force Archelaus' scythed chariots back on their own lines causing confusion reminiscent of Antiochos' defeat at Magnesia. It was an end of Mithridates' expeditionary force.

Through 86 BC Sulla followed the road through Macedonia, Thrace and into Asia Minor. In Bithynia, the new commander of Asia sent by Rome, L. Licinius Flaccus, was killed in a mutiny instigated by his second-in-command C. Flavius Fimbria, who assumed command and began sacking the Greek Asian cities. He defeated a Pontic army at Rhyndacus and Mithridates had to flee from his new palace in Pergamum. Fimbria came close to capturing the king but he escaped by sea. He now sued for peace and Sulla, who had arrived in Asia Minor, set up a peace conference at Dardanus. Mithridates came off lightly, having to surrender his western conquests, evacuate his conquered territory in Asia Minor, pay a fine of 2000 talents and deliver to Rome his Aegean fleet of seventy ships. In return Rome would officially recognise him as king of Pontus and their ally. Fimbria, having organised the mutiny and killed Flaccus, his commander, now took his own life. Sulla left, placing Lucius Licinius Murena in command of Asia Minor.

Murena treated Pontus harshly, which provoked a further conflict the year after the peace had been agreed. Deiotaros, who was now firmly in control in Galatia, allowed the pro-consul Murena to launch his punitive attacks on Pontus from Galatian territory. Another peace was made with Mithridates in 82 BC.

There followed eight years of peace and comparative tranquillity; time enough to rebuild. The Roman orator and statesman, Marcus Tullius Cicero (106–43 BC), who was to be made governor of Cilicia on the southern coast of Asia Minor, and thereby became a friend of Deiotaros, was fulsome in his praise of the Galatian king, as Deiotaros was now called. Although there is little reference to Galatia at this time we know that the survivor of Mithridates' infamous massacre of the chieftains was able to re-establish the Drunemeton assembly of chieftains and secure his position as supreme leader.

Mithridates of Pontus was not, however, curbed in his ambitions. He began making plans in private to re-establish his power in Asia Minor. In anticipation of the coming conflict the Pontus king had employed Roman dissidents to retrain his army in Roman battle tactics and drill.

The excuse came when Nicomedes III of Bithynia died and left his kingdom to Rome, as had Attalos with Pergamum. Pontus, as the neighbour of Bithynia, saw this as a threat to its security. In 74BC Mithridates overran Bithynia without opposition. There were only two Roman legions stationed in Asia Minor and the Pontus attack came as a total surprise. In fact, these legions, commanded by P. Isauricus Servilius, between 78BC and 75BC, had been supplied with provisions by the Galatians. Mithridates sent a fleet of a hundred ships through the Dardanelles into the Aegean to foment rebellion in Greece again. At the same time, Mithridates sent another army into Galatia commanded by Zeumachos, whom he designated 'governor'. Mithridates had also secured an alliance with his son-in-law, Tigranes of Armenia.

Rome reacted quickly. The new commander, Lucius Licinius Lucullus, was able to collect the scattered Roman forces throughout Asia Minor and, with allied forces, such as those of Deiotaros, he marched an army of 30,000 to Bithynia. During a winter campaign he forced Mithridates to draw back his men and his ships. In spring 73BC Rome won a naval victory over the Pontic fleet. The fleet withdrew into the Black Sea where, as fate would have it, it was crippled by a storm.

In Galatia, Mithridates' army under Zeumachos had been reinforced by the old Pontic commander Eumachos, whose policy seemed simply to be to kill as many Celts as well as Romans as he could. Deiotaros was able to push Eumachos back into Pontus during the summer of 73BC. That autumn, obviously at the invitation of Deiotaros, Lucullus and his army marched through Galatia into the valley of the Lycus. But the Romans could not capture the Pontic fortress nor bring the king into a decisive battle. Lucullus went into a winter camp.

The reconstituted Roman army consisted of five legions which were, according to Plutarch, supplied during this winter period by some 30,000 Galatian Celts, who carried grain for them as they advanced from Bithynia into the territory of Amisus. When, in 71BC,

Lucullus fought an action at Cabeira with Mithridates' army, the Galatian Celtic cavalry, personally led by Deiotaros, won distinction; according to Memnon they were also in action at Tigranocerta.

Mithridates fled into Armenia in the face of Lucullus' successful advance. It would seem that a troop of Celtic cavalry came within a whisker of capturing Mithridates himself but, according to Plutarch, they had paused to seize some pack mules laden with Pontic gold and silver. One can almost hear the Romans saying 'Typical Celts!' and one wonders just how true this was. Even so, Mithridates became virtually a prisoner in Armenia and even his own son, Machares, governor of his European dominions, declared against him.

By 70BC all Asia Minor was under the control of Rome. Yet Mithridates had managed to reach the protection of his son-in-law Tigranes of Armenia. Rome demanded his surrender from Armenia. Armenia had hardly been noticed in world history before Tigranes came to the throne in c.100BC. Tigranes had overrun Cappadocia in 78BC, taken the western territory of Mesopotamia from the Parthians and extended his southern frontiers to Mount Lebanon. Tigranes rejected the demand to hand over his father-in-law to Rome.

In 69BC Lucullus crossed the Euphrates and invaded Armenia. He took with him an army of 16,000, including 3000 Celtic cavalry. The plan was to make a direct assault on Tigranocerta, the Armenian king's fortress. Tigranes is said to have jeered, on viewing the Roman army, 'Too few for an army, too many for an embassy.' But Lucullus' assault was immediate and successful. Tigranes' empire was brought down like a house of cards and Tigranocerta became Lucullus' winter quarters. But Mithridates eluded Rome. Throughout 68BC Lucullus was still tracking a retreating Armenian army, marching across the highlands in the face of the first blizzards of the Armenian autumn. A mutiny broke out and the Roman army swung to Mesopotamia where they wintered at Nisibis. Here Lucullus suffered guerrilla attacks. No reinforcements appeared from Rome.

In the spring of 67BC Lucullus' army was in tatters. Rome had censured him for attacking Armenia without the Senate's approval. Lucullus' second-in-command, C. Triarius, sustained a defeat by Mithridates who had reappeared at the head of an army near Zela, and Lucullus began to move back towards Galatia. In a valley of the upper Halys, Lucullus made a stand with the remnants of his army. Mithridates and Tigranes joined forces but could not destroy him, but neither could he prevent them regaining their territorial possessions.

A new commander-in-chief arrived to take over from Lucullus. It seems that the Celtic country was chosen for the place where Lucullus was to hand over his command to his successor, Gnaeus Magnus Pompeius (Pompey the Great, 104–48BC), who had been helping Marcus Licinius Crassus put down Spartacus' slave revolt in Italy. Having been elected consul he was sent to continue the war against Mithridates and his conclusion of that war became his greatest military achievement.

It is of interest to make an historical aside here and remark that when Spartacus led his band of gladiators in a revolt against Rome in 73BC, the slave army appeared to be a predominantly Celtic one. We are told that Spartacus was a Thracian who had gained military experience in the auxiliary forces of Rome and led his men out of their barracks at Capua. It has been suggested that he might even have been a Celt from Tylis. A large part of Spartacus' army was certainly Celtic and Spartacus' two close friends and generals had obviously Celtic names – Crixos and Onomarus. Crixos seems to be 'curly-haired' while Onomarus could be 'big ash-tree'. When Crixos was killed in 71BC, Spartacus is said to have put to death 300 Roman captives as a 'sacrifice'. Spartacus was finally defeated in Apulia in 71BC.

It is fascinating that the hand-over to Pompey was made at a fortress of the Trocmi in east Galatia, at Tavium (Posdala). Deiotaros was doubtless present at the ceremony for he became a firm friend of the new Roman general. Deiotaros had been moving Celtic Galatia firmly into the Roman orbit. Perhaps he could see which way the fortunes of Rome's eastern empire were moving. The Romans, at this time, were doing their best to court the Celts, finding the Celtic culture of Galatia a potential advantage to them in a sea of Hellenistic states simmering with rebellion. With an independent Galatia as Rome's friend, the state would be a check to any further rise of a major Hellenistic power in the area.

Pompey's campaign against Mithridates lasted until 63BC. In 66BC Tigranes withdrew his support from his father-in-law. Mithridates found himself outmatched by 50,000 veteran Roman legionaries. At Nicopolis Pompey defeated Mithridates' army. As usual, the wily king broke through the Roman cordon and escaped to the

Crimea. He defeated and killed his son, Machares, but another of his sons, Pharnaces, raised a rebellion and Mithridates was surrounded in his fortress of Panticapaeum. He took his own life. This was in 63BC. Ironically, he had to be helped in this act by a Celtic officer in his army – one Bituitis.

Pompey went on to take possession not only of the former territories of Mithridates but also of Armenia. Tigranes had promptly made peace but he had to make reparation. Pompey also marched through the former Syrian territories and went on to take Jerusalem, which he captured after a siege of three months, even entering the 'Holy of Holies'. He deprived Hyrcanyus of all royal titles there except that of High Priest.

Pompey drew up his plans for Asia Minor before returning to Rome. Syria, Bithynia and Pontus became provinces of Rome; Pharnaces, son of Mithridates of Pontus, who had revolted against his father in 63BC, was rewarded with the kingdom of the Bosporos and allowed to retain the Crimea. Tigranes was left in possession of Armenia. Cappadocia went to Ariobarzanes I.

For the Celts of the area, the important settlement was Galatia. Once more the Romans decided, in keeping with their previous policy of sustaining the Celts in the Hellenistic world, that Galatia should be an independent state. However, now that the war against Mithridates was over, the central kingship of Deiotaros was brought into question, perhaps by the Galatian chieftains themselves.

Before 86BC Strabo had indicated that Galatia was ruled by a council of twelve chieftains (or *tetrarchs*) and their assembly. Pompey decreed that henceforth Galatia should be ruled by the surviving chieftains. These were Deiotaros of the Tolistoboii, of course, Brogitaros of the Trocmi and an unnamed chieftain of the Tectosages. Presumably this unnamed chieftain was Deiotaros' son-in-law Castor Tarcondarius. However, according to Strabo, Pompey gave Deiotaros control over the eastern territories of Pontus as a reward for his services. Deiotaros also held control of Gazelonitis, a fertile area on the east bank of the Halys, as well as territories in Pharnaceia and Trapezus as far as Colchis and south to Armenia Minor. More importantly, Pompey describes Deiotaros as 'king of Galatia' and this title was ratified by the Roman Senate in 58BC on the proposal of P. Clodius Pulcher (c.92–52BC).

There has been some argument among scholars as to the exact

areas of Deiotaros' new territory and some have suggested that Armenia Minor was actually given to the Trocmi chieftain, Brogitaros. Brogitaros certainly received lands derived from a section of Mithridates' old kingdom including the fortress of Mithridates, in an eastward extension of Galatia.

Deiotaros' main fortress was at Blucium and he had another fortress at Peium. Both were fortified positions, built to a high standard of comfort. Julius Caesar stayed at both fortresses in 47BC. Deiotaros was now an elderly man; he had married a lady called Stratonice (sometimes Hellenised to Berenice) and had a son who was now probably middle-aged, as well as two daughters. There is some confusion about his lineage as the same names appear to be used for different people. His son was also called Deiotaros. He had an unnamed daughter who married Tarcondarius, sometimes given as Castor Tarcondarius, who had a son named Castor. This Castor married and had two sons, one Deiotaros Philadelphus, who became king of Paphlagonia, and the other Deiotaros Philopater. King Deiotaros' other daughter was named Adobogiona and she married Brogitaros but Brogitaros had a sister also named Adobogiona, who married a Pergamene and had a son named Mithridates. Cicero was to observe of the old king in 44BC that it took more than one man to help the ageing Deiotaros on to his horse.

Having the title 'king of Galatia' recognised by Rome, but only being one of the ruling chieftains of Galatia, did not suit Deiotaros. He had been sole military ruler and king during the wars with Mithridates. The marriage of his daughter to Brogitaros brought the Trocmi under his control. The marriage of his second daughter to Castor Tarcondarius, the chieftain of the Tectosages, allowed him to exert an influence with that tribe. By this method he soon emerged as undisputed 'king of Galatia'. He became known as Deiotaros I Philoromaeus ('the Roman lover').

He introduced Roman methods of military training, organisation and tactics among the Galatians. However, Cicero noted that he had forbidden the use of slaves in his army. He was interested in the Roman art of estate management and became respected by the Romans for his political ability, forming successful relationships with powerful Romans of varying temperaments, including Sulla, Pompey, Marcus Calpurnius Bibulus, Gaius Julius Caesar and Cicero. It was recorded that Deiotaros never undertook an important decision without first consulting the auguries in traditional Celtic fashion.

There emerged a period of relative peace and prosperity for Galatia. The decisions of Pompey in the settlement of the area were confirmed by plebiscite in 59BC. Brogitaros had, through the intervention of P. Clodius Pulcher, demanded the privilege of nominating the Attis at Pessinus. But this matter was clearly in Deiotaros' sphere of influence: the coins of Deiotaros were minted in Pessinus during this period. Nonetheless, Clodius Pulcher put Brogitaros' case to the Roman Senate and caused Cicero to remark: 'Plena res numorum.' Basically, a matter connected with money, implying that Brogitaros had paid Clodius Pulcher to raise the point. Deiotaros took matters into his own hands and threw Brogitaros out of Pessinus.

Marcus Tullius Cicero was sent to govern Cilicia in southern Asia Minor, south of Galatia, in the summer of 51BC. He remained there until the summer of 50BC. It was during this period that Cicero came to know the Celtic king well and, as he was to admit later, 'public life brought us together as friends. The ties of hospitality have been strengthened by mutual regard. Our association has developed into intimacy.'

Deiotaros emerges in Cicero's correspondence from Cilicia as a far-sighted and able Celtic leader. Cicero was able to entrust the lives of his son and nephew to Deiotaros' son, Deiotaros junior, while he was away on business. Deiotaros appears as charitable, helping people in need and pursuing friendly relationships with leading Romans. When Cicero and Marcus Calpurnius Bibulus, the governor of Syria, were concerned about a possible Parthian invasion of the area, Deiotaros offered to place two Galatian legions of 12,000 men, with 2000 cavalry, at the disposal of Cicero.

Even Decimus Junius Brutus, distantly related to Marcus Junius Brutus who was to lead the assassination of Caesar, made an impassioned plea on Deiotaros' behalf to Caesar after Caesar's victory over Pompey. Deiotaros received from a Bithynian friend, Diphanes, a six-volume treatise by Mago of Carthage on agriculture. He was able to quote Greek verse and was certainly knowledgeable about Hellenic culture. Deiotaros had, single-handed, raised Galatia from near-catastrophe to be the only fully independent kingdom in Asia Minor recognised by Rome.

Perhaps there is an irony in the fact that a statue of this great Celtic king was erected in Athens as well as in Greek cities such as

Nicaea, Laodicea and Ephesos. The Celts had somehow become rehabilitated in the Graeco-Roman world . . . or, at least, the Celts of Galatia.

[15]

Galatia's Roman Policy

ONCE Galatia had moved into the Roman orbit it was inevitable that Roman politics would set its future course. The Roman republic had been cracking up due to frictions between various powerful patrician personalities. The process had begun concurrently with the wars against Mithridates of Pontus. Julius Caesar and Marcus Licinius Crassus had become leaders of the 'popular party' and plotted together in Rome against the return of Pompey, after his victories over Mithridates. Cicero himself had foiled an attempt at revolution in 63 BC. Three years later it was decided that Caesar, Crassus and Pompey would form a tenuous 'alliance', which became known as the First Triumvirate. They assigned themselves spheres of influence, with Caesar being allowed to carve a new empire for Rome in Gaul, the Celtic heartland, while Pompey took Spain and Crassus was sent to Syria and the eastern empire.

A dynastic quarrel arose among the Parthians. At Carrhae (Haran) in northern Mesopotamia, Crassus' army encountered an army commanded by Orodes, an anti-Roman claimant to the throne. Orodes annihilated the Roman army. Out of 6000 Roman troops, some 5500 were killed. Crassus was captured and publicly executed in much the same way he had captured and executed the troops of Spartacus' slave army a decade before.

The death of Crassus brought the rivalry between Caesar and Pompey into a new focus, leading eventually to open warfare when Caesar, ignoring an agreement, crossed the Rubicon and marched on Rome with his legions. Eleven battles later, Pompey and his allies were defeated and Caesar had become virtual dictator.

It was inevitable that Deiotaros would declare his support for his friend Pompey. After all, Pompey had been good to Deiotaros and Galatia while nothing was known about Caesar except that he had been conducting a ruthless campaign which had brought the Celtic heartland of Gaul under the control of Rome. Cicero, who also supported Pompey, noted that in 51 BC he could count on 12,000 Galatian infantry, divided into thirty cohorts, with 2000 cavalry under the personal command of Deiotaros.

As Caesar and Pompey fought out their civil war, the battlefields moved slowly and inexorably towards the east. Caesar landed in Epiros and marched on Dyrrachium, a harbour on the coast of Illyricum (modern Durazzo). He had some twelve legions at his command of which nine were veteran units. However, shipping was scarce and he had been able to move only a small part of the army across the Adriatic. Even so, he had detached Gnaeus Domitius Calvinus with the XI and XII Legions to Macedonia to deal with Pompey's garrisons there. But Pompey was deploying his troops towards Dyrrachium and, finding Caesar there, entrenched his army on a height called Petra.

Pompey's army in Greece contained a unit of 600 Celtic Galatian cavalry commanded, we are told by one source, by Deiotaros in person. But, as Cicero observed, Deiotaros was 'in the evening of his years', so it is highly doubtful that this Deiotaros was the Galatian king. Evidence points to it being his son. We are told that a further 300 Tectosages had been sent by Castor Tarcondarius and Domnilaus. Caesar's *The Civil War* says that Castor Tarcondarius had come in person while Domnilaus had sent his son. This also needs to be treated with caution: Cicero, who was commanding two of Pompey's legions, said it was Castor Tarcondarius' son Castor who was in charge of a squadron of the Tectosages' cavalry under Cicero's command.

At Dyrrachium an incident took place which apparently greatly angered Caesar. Within his own cavalry units he had Celts recruited from Gaul, not only Cisalpine Gaul but Narbonesis Gaul and Gaul proper. Among them were units from the Allobriges ('those from a foreign land') whose territory was around the shores of Lake Geneva. They were commanded by Roucillus and Egus, the sons of the chieftain of the tribe, Adbucillus. The Allobriges had, after the conquest of Gaul by Rome, decided to throw in their lot with Caesar. Caesar describes Roucillus and Egus as 'men of outstanding courage, of whose excellent and stalwart service Caesar had availed himself in all his campaigns in Gaul. For these reasons he had assigned to them the highest magistracies among their own people, and had them exceptionally enrolled in the senate.' Now it is generally supposed by most commentators that this meant a tribal senate or assembly, the senate of the Allobriges. But why would it be 'exceptional' for the sons of the chieftain to be allowed to sit in their own tribal assembly? They would have had the right to do so without Caesar's intervention. In Caesar's rearrangement of the Roman Senate – he had extended it to 900 senators from all parts of the empire – he could well have allotted places to the two Allobriges and this would, indeed, have been 'exceptional'. Caesar had allotted them lands in Gaul and given them monetary rewards. He also admits that they were very popular commanders in the cavalry.

It was at Dyrrachium that the two Allobriges deserted, taking a large number of horses and men over to Pompey's army. Caesar is not generous in his praise now. He says they were 'carried away by stupid, barbarian vanity' and 'began to look down on their own people, to cheat the cavalry of their pay, and to appropriate all the plunder for themselves'. He says they embezzled pay and, further-more, plotted to kill the cavalry general, the tribune Gaius Volusenus Quadratus.

Pompey led them all around his army and showed them to his men for they were of noble birth, richly apparelled and had come *with a large retinue and with many horses* [my italics]. They also had a reputation for bravery which had been held in esteem by Caesar. More importantly, their desertion from Caesar was a new and unusual action. Until then, no one, either from the infantry or the cavalry, had ever deserted Caesar for Pompey . . .

Why had Roucillus and Egus taken their Celts across to Pompey? Surely if they, as Caesar claims, had merely done so to escape disci-plinary punishment for embezzling their own men's pay, then their own men would not have followed them. Roucillus and Egus would have been left to their own devices. Could it be that the Allobriges encountered the Galatian Celts serving with Pompey and were per-suaded to join their distant compatriots? Alas, we do not know exactly what happened to Roucillus and Egus and the Allobroges except that one of the two brothers was subsequently killed before Pharsalus. Caesar says: 'During those days Caesar fought a successful

cavalry battle and killed several men, including one of the two Allobriges who, as related above, had deserted to Pompey.'

Pompey, although he outnumbered Caesar, held off attacking his
adversary for several months. It was not until reinforcements arrived
for Caesar commanded by Marcus Antonius, Mark Antony (c.82–
30BC), that a major battle took place. Pompey was able to destroy
the left flank of Caesar's army and Caesar lost 1000 veteran troops.
However, he retired in fairly good order and made his way into
Thessaly. After this defeat, Caesar moved southward with his 20,000
loyal troops, marching 200 miles towards Pharsalus. Pompey pursued him with an army twice as large. Both armies were exhausted
by this rapid movement.

On 9 August 48BC, on the plain of Pharsalus, the opposing forces
prepared for battle. Pompey placed on his left wing the veteran I and
III Legions, which Caesar had once commanded, and also positioned
himself there. In the centre was Metellus Pius Scipio, Pompey's father-
in-law, with legions from Syria as well as Cicero's two veteran legions
from Cilicia. If we accept Cicero's evidence, it was here that the
Galatian Celts were stationed. On the right flank were legions from
Iberia. Just beyond the left wing was a cavalry division led by Titus
Labienus, Caesar's former friend and staff officer who had accompanied him in Gaul and Britain. The estimation was that Pompey
had 45,000 troops to face Caesar's 22,000.

Caesar stationed his X Legion on his right and the IX Legion on
his left, even though the IX had been seriously mauled at Dyrrachium,
a matter for which Caesar, significantly, blamed the Allobriges. Mark
Antony was on the left, Publius Cornelius Sulla (a nephew of Sulla
who had defeated Mithridates) on the right, with Gnaeus Domitius
Calvinus in the centre.

The battle began with Titus Labienus making a cavalry sweep
around Caesar's right wing. A counter-attack stopped this movement
and then Mark Antony led an assault which, after some prolonged
and tough fighting, shattered Pompey's right. By the end of the day
Caesar reckoned some 15,000 of Pompey's army had been killed
and 24,000 had surrendered; some nine legionary eagles and 180
military standards were brought to Caesar. As for his own army, he
claimed no more than 200 troops were killed but admitted that thirty
leading centurions had been slain, therefore casualties were doubtless
much higher.

Pompey managed to escape to the coast, escorted, according to some authorities, by Deiotaros and his Celts in person. However, if a Deiotaros did accompany him, this, as we have already suggested, would have been Deiotaros' son. Pompey left by ship for Mytilene (Lesbos) but Caesar had decided that he must end the civil war as soon as possible and this meant pursuing and destroying Pompey. Hearing that Caesar was in pursuit, Pompey, having been delayed at Lesbos for two days, proceeded to Cilicia. It was here, presumably, that the Galatians left him to return to their own country just to the north. Pompey moved restlessly on to Cyprus. His aim was to get to Antioch and raise a new army in Syria but he learnt that Antioch had turned against him.

He moved on to Pelusium, the gateway to Egypt, where he found the Pharaoh Ptolemy XIV Dionysius, who was aged fourteen. He was waging war against his sister Cleopatra VII. Their father, Ptolemy XIII, had been killed in 57 BC and been succeeded by his son. According to the Egyptian Pharaoh tradition he had 'married' his sister Cleopatra in 51 BC. Pompey, who had helped Ptolemy's father in his time of trouble, appealed to the boy king to allow him to be received in Alexandria 'for the sake of the hospitality and friendship he had shown his father, and to receive protection in his trouble from the Pharaoh's resources'. The commander of the Pharaoh's army, Achillas, together with a military tribune named Lucius Septimius, were sent to invite Pompey to come ashore at Alexandria. It was a plot. Pompey boarded a small boat with a few of his companions and no sooner had he set foot on Egyptian soil than Achillas and Septimius killed him and cut off his head. His murder brought to an end the first stage of Rome's civil war.

If Deiotaros junior had escorted Pompey on his flight, he and his Celts only accompanied him as far as Cilicia for we know that Deiotaros junior, as well as his father, was back in Galatia at this time. We also know that Castor and his Tectosages had returned safely. Caesar had made Calvinus his legate in Asia Minor while he set off in pursuit of Pompey.

Pharnaces, the son of Mithridates the Great, seized this time of confusion to begin to move an army into Asia Minor, claiming that he had been invited by Pompey's followers. Deiotaros sent immediately to Calvinus and pointed out that unless Pharnaces was blocked in his aim to reclaim Pontus, the area would fall under a government hostile to Rome and Caesar. Deiotaros made no excuse about having supported Pompey but maintained that his only friendship was to Roman interests in the area. Those interests were now in danger from Pharnaces, who seemed intent on rebuilding his father's empire. The author of *The Alexandrian War* (who has been identified as Aulus Hirtius, one of Caesar's lieutenants who had served him in Gaul) says that Calvinus sent messengers to Pharnaces ordering him to withdraw. To back up his order, Calvinus took the XXXVI Legion but sent his two other legions to reinforce Caesar in Egypt as Caesar was in considerable trouble.

Caesar, in his pursuit of Pompey, had encountered problems with the Egyptians. He had followed Pompey's trail to Alexandria, taking only 3200 legionaries and 800 cavalry. His disembarkation caused riots among the Alexandrians, in which many of his troops were killed. He ordered Pompey's former legions, which were stationed in Egypt, to join him and then barricaded himself in one of the quarters of Alexandria around the royal palace. It was at this time that he met Cleopatra, the striking descendant of the Ptolemy dynasty. She openly espoused his cause, seeing him, at first, as an ally against her brother. But then she began a relationship with Caesar. To add to his worries, the etesian winds, the annual trade winds which blow for about forty days every year around the time of the dog-days, kept him hemmed in the port of Alexandria. In spite of his few troops, he demanded that Ptolemy and Cleopatra dismiss their armies and resolve their differences by negotiation.

Ptolemy's main adviser was a eunuch named Pothinus who, in answer to Caesar, summoned the young Pharaoh's army from Pelusium to Alexandria. Achillas was put in command. Caesar now found himself besieged in his quarter of the city by 20,000 men of Ptolemy's army.

Having dispatched two legions to help Caesar, Calvinus found himself outnumbered by the army of Pharnaces. Deiotaros sent his two Galatian legions, plus a hundred cavalry, to reinforce Calvinus' army. In spite of his age, Deiotaros took personal command of his troops. Calvinus was also able to raise additional troops from Ariobarzanes of Cappadocia, a legion of troops levied in Pontus and auxiliary troops from Cilicia. The army gathered at Comana. News came from Pharnaces that he was willing to withdraw from Cappadocia but that he would retain Armenia Minor by ancestral right.

Calvinus repeated his order for Pharnaces to withdraw from Asia Minor but the son of Mithridates prevaricated.

Calvinus' army marched on Nicopolis, the town on the Armenia Minor plain, identified as Purk, where the Romans had defeated the army of Mithridates. The author of *The Alexandrian War* comments:

> ... he had to go through a very narrow and difficult defile. Pharnaces posted in ambush a picked body of infantry and the whole of his cavalry; he also gave orders for a large herd of cattle to be spread about in this pass and country folk and townsfolk to be about in the area, so that, if Domitius [Calvinus] came through the pass as a friend, he would have no suspicions of an ambush seeing men and animals going about in the fields as if friends were arriving, while if he came as an enemy, his soldiers would scatter to seize the booty and could be cut down while they were dispersed.

Calvinus marched on. Pharnaces had now intercepted messengers who bore the news that Caesar was in extreme danger in Alexandria. Pharnaces was delighted. He expected Calvinus to withdraw and probably thought he would gain a victory by attacking during the withdrawal.

> Domitius [Calvinus] was more alarmed at Caesar's danger than his own; but he thought he could not safely depart if he were either to try to secure the terms which he had already rejected or were to leave after being refused terms. Accordingly, he formed his men up for battle not far from the camp. He stationed the XXXVI legion on the right wing, the Pontic on the left and Deiotaros' legions in the centre, forming up the latter on a very narrow front and posting the remaining cohorts as reserves.

Both sides began the battle simultaneously. The XXXVI Legion found themselves marching against Pharnaces' cavalry. The author of *The Alexandrian War* is, as most Roman historians usually are, critical of the Celts as allies – especially when speaking of battles lost by the Romans. Indeed, only the Romans of the XXXVI Legion behaved bravely according to the account.

As for Deiotaros' legions, they scarcely withstood the enemy charge. And so the king's [Pharnaces] forces, being victorious on the right wing and in the centre, all turned against the XXXVI Legion. The latter bore the onset of the winning forces bravely ... Almost the whole of the Pontic legion was lost and the greater part of Deiotaros' troops killed. The XXXVI Legion, however, withdrew to the high ground with the loss of no more than 250.

Pharnaces moved his full force back into Cappadocia and into Pontus and was acclaimed as Pharnaces II.

There he behaved as a conqueror and a cruel despot; promising himself his father's fortune but with a happier outcome, he stormed many towns, plundered the property both of Roman citizens and of Pontic subjects, and inflicted on those men whose beauty or youth at all recommended them a punishment more wretched than death itself [i.e. castration]. So meeting with no resistance, he took possession of Pontus, congratulating himself on the recovery of his hereditary kingdom.

Still besieged in Alexandria, Caesar was continuing his affair with Cleopatra. The details of his sojourn in Egypt are minutely given by the author of *The Civil War* (also thought to be Aulus Hirtius).

To add to Caesar's problems in Egypt, there was more faction fighting among the Ptolemaic family. Arsinoe, Cleopatra's younger sister, had raised an Egyptian army against the Romans and her brother Ptolemy on her own account, wishing to succeed her brother and Cleopatra as sole ruler of Egypt. She had persuaded Achillas, the Egyptian general who had been adviser to her brother Ptolemy and arranged Pompey's murder, to command her forces. However, a quarrel soon arose between Achillas and Arsinoe. With the help of her tutor, a eunuch named Ganymede, she had Achillas killed. 'After his murder,' says the author of *The Civil War*, 'she herself without colleague and no guardian, held the supreme command; the army was put in the charge of Ganymede, who on taking over increased the bounties to the troops and varied out the rest of his duties with an invariable thoroughness.'

The news of Pharnaces' defeat of Calvinus was obviously a blow for Caesar. He had to break the stalemate in Egypt immediately and get back to Asia Minor to deal with Pharnaces. We now hear that he had sent Mithridates 'of Pergamum' to raise fresh troops. Alas, there is no mention of how or where Caesar had met Mithridates or how Caesar came to place such faith in his military expertise. Mithridates was the son of a Celtic mother, the nephew of Brogitaros, chieftain of the Trocmi.

An inscription in honour of Adobogiona, the sister of Brogitaros, was found in the eastern part of the island of Lesbos. Adobogiona's portrait has also been found at Pergamum where she married a man called Mendotus. Their son was Mithridates. He is described in *The Alexandrian War* as 'Mithridates of Pergamum, a man of high standing at home, skilled and courageous in war, and a loyal and esteemed friend of Caesar's.' The 'of Pergamum' would indicate that his mother, Adobogiona, had settled in the country of her husband and the child had been brought up there. Some textual critics, however, have tried to make him into a son of Mithridates of Pontus but his parentage is not in question and his links with the Trocmi are clear. There is certainly a possibility that, for a time, he was a hostage at the court of Mithridates of Pontus. According to *The Alexandrian War*: 'Mithridates was of royal descent and had received a royal upbringing for Mithridates the Great had, on account of his noble origin, taken him when he was a boy, and brought him up in his own court.' But the more intriguing problem is, how did he became an 'esteemed friend' of Caesar? That he was a commander of troops serving with Caesar against Pompey is fairly clear and it may have been because of this link that the friendship developed.

Caesar sent Mithridates to raise reinforcements in Asia Minor. This can only mean that Mithridates was accompanying Caesar in Alexandria. Mithridates raised a mercenary force in Cilicia, and one might suspect that the Celts of Galatia would have constituted a large part of the army. He reinforced them from troops raised in Syria as he marched overland down towards the Nile. 'He arrived at Pelusium, by the overland route between Egypt and Syria, with the large forces which he had been able to collect quickly thanks both to his own conscientious efforts and to the extreme good will of the states.'

Pelusium was held by a garrison loyal to the Egyptian Pharaoh. Mithridates stormed the city in the spring of 47BC. The Egyptian general Achillas had garrisoned Pelusium in strength due to its strategic position, for it protected the entrance to Egypt from the landward side. 'The substantial garrison put up a stubborn resistance,' says *The Alexandrian War*, 'but thanks to the large numbers of fresh troops which he kept sending in to relieve the wounded or tired, and thanks to his persistence and determination in attack, he reduced the town on the same day as he first attacked it, and installed a garrison of his own. After this success he pressed on towards Caesar in Alexandria . . .'

A division of the Egyptian army, accompanied by the young Pharaoh Ptolemy XIV in person, was now facing Mithridates on the Egyptian bank of the Nile in the Delta. *The Alexandrian War* says:

When the Pharaoh learned that Mithridates was approaching this place, knowing that he would have to cross the river, he sent against him a large force which he thought could certainly overpower and annihilate Mithridates, or at the least hold him back. While he hoped that Mithridates would be defeated, he would be satisfied to hold him back and cut him off from Caesar.

The Gallograeco was obviously an astute commander for instead of trying to cross the defended river, he paused and built a fortified encampment. Some Egyptian troops crossed the river, according to *The Alexandrian War*, 'to get sole credit for the victory'.

When Mithridates 'saw the enemy, rashly and boldly coming right up to the defence works, he made sally all around the camp and killed a large number of them. If the rest had not taken advantage of their knowledge of the district to find cover, and some of them withdrawn to the ships in which they had crossed the river, they would have been utterly destroyed.'

Meanwhile, Mithridates sent word to Caesar as to his situation. Caesar knew that the young Pharaoh's commanders had a large fleet ready on the Nile which he would have to do battle with if he marched from Alexandria overland towards Mithridates' position. So Caesar embarked his legions in ships and sailed directly to Pelusium. Landing there he disembarked and marched up behind Mithridates to join him on the Nile. Together, Caesar and his Gallograeco friend forced a crossing over the great river.

The Celtic cavalry scattered, looking for fords in the river, and some of them swam across, where the banks were less high; and meanwhile the legionaries cut down great trees, long enough to reach from one bank to the other, threw these across, and hastily pitching earth on the top they crossed over. The enemy were so frightened by their attack that they put all their hopes of safety in flight; but this was in vain for very few came back from the rout to the Pharaoh and almost all the rest were killed.

Caesar is given the sole praise for the campaign now and, at this stage, we hear no more of Mithridates' generalship. Caesar, it is said, attacked the Pharaoh's camp, a fortress in a nearby village, connected to his main camp by trenches and tunnels. The Romans stormed the camp and the fortress. It was not easy, however.

A very large, specially picked force of Alexandrians were defending the side where the approach was easiest; but those who were defending on the side of the river Nile were the most successful in repelling and wounding our men, for the latter were being hit by missiles from two directions, in front of the ramparts of the camp, and in the rear from the river, in which a large number of ships were drawn up, harassing our troops with fire from slingers and archers.

An officer called Carbulnos (it has more a Celtic ring to it than Greek or Roman), 'a man of outstanding courage and military skill', led an attack on a weak point of the Pharaoh's encampment and managed to break it. The Alexandrians began to panic. Then one of the fortified walls collapsed, burying many fleeing Egyptian soldiers. At this point the Pharaoh Ptolemy XIV himself fled to his ship. 'It is known that the Pharaoh himself fled from the camp and was taken on board a ship but the vessel was capsized by the crowds of men swimming for the nearest ships and he perished.'

Having crossed the Nile, Caesar put himself at the head of his cavalry and rode post-haste on to Alexandria where he found that the forces loyal to Ptolemy XIV and to his young sister Arsinoe had either fled or were prepared to surrender.

'The entire population of the town threw down their weapons and abandoned the fortifications.'

Caesar, thanks to Mithridates the Gallograeco, who has temporarily disappeared from the historian's pages, took possession of Alexandria and Egypt. Ptolemy XIV having drowned, Caesar appointed his young brother Ptolemy XV Neoteros as Pharaoh with Cleopatra VII as co-regent. Cleopatra was to give birth to Caesar's son Ptolemy, nicknamed Caesarion. She was soon to be sole ruler for Neoteros died soon after, the rumour being that she had poisoned him. Other members of the Ptolemaic family, such as Arsinoe, were sent as hostages to Rome. Ganymede had apparently been captured and was also taken to Rome to take part in Caesar's triumphal parade in Rome before being ritually executed.

In the summer of 47 BC Caesar left the XXVII and XXVIII Legions in Alexandria and set out with the VI Legion and, presumably, Mithridates' army, to march by land for Syria and on to Asia Minor to deal with the problem presented by Pharnaces. In Syria, he appointed his relative Sextus Caesar as governor and commander and went on to the port of Cilicia by ship.

Caesar landed in Cilicia and held a council of war at Tarsus. He took personal command of all forces opposing Pharnaces. He marched first to Cappadocia, spent two days at Mazaca, then went on to Comana and the ancient shrine of Bellona. He confirmed Lucomedes as priest of the shrine and also confirmed Ariarathes as ruler of Lesser Armenia under the suzerainty of his brother, Ariobarzanes III of Cappadocia (52–42 BC).

He marched into Galatia where a suitably contrite Deiotaros met him. According to *The Alexandrian War*, 'He was at this time *tetrarch* [*sic*] of almost the whole of Gallograecia [Galatia], though the other *tetrarchs* insisted that he had no right to it, either in law or by custom. Deiotaros had been styled king of Lesser Armenia by the Roman Senate.'

In this, Aulus Hirtius – if, indeed, he be the author – gets various points incorrect. We have already seen that each of the three Galatian tribes had, at one time, been divided into four septs, each ruled by a petty chieftain. The Greeks had called these petty chieftains *tetrarcha*, indicating their fourth division. Above the four *tetrarcha* was the tribal chieftain. It can be shown that Deiotaros was not a *tetrarch* but initially a tribal chieftain, the son of Sinorix of the Tolistoboii. Deiotaros had then exerted power over the other two tribal chieftains as a single ruler. Pompey and the Senate had recognised him as 'king of Galatia'. Thus he was not a 'ruler of a fourth part of Galatia' or even a 'twelfth part' which must apply if he had been merely one of the Galatian *tetrarchs*. Hirtius also confuses his title, implying that it meant 'king of Lesser Armenia' because Pompey had ceded Lesser Armenia and other territories to the Galatian kingship.

However, the other chieftains of Galatia did have a point: Deiotaros' unification of the three tribal chieftainships under a central kingship was not according to Celtic custom and presumably Celtic law. Of course, had it not been for Deiotaros, the Galatian kingdom would have been submerged by Mithridates the Great of Pontus, and Rome would not have found a friend and ally in their wars against Mithridates.

We are told by Hirtius in *The Alexandrian War* that Deiotaros laid aside his royal insignia and came to meet Caesar not merely as a private person but as someone actually on trial in a court – that is, he came dressed in public mourning. He asked Caesar for forgiveness that he had supported Pompey. He had done so, he said, under the constraint of command of Pompey's authority backed by menace of military force. It had been none of his concern to pass judgement on the disputes among the Roman people but merely to obey the commands of the authority present on his territory.

Caesar pointed out that when he was consul in Rome, he had conferred several benefits on Deiotaros. The Celtic ruler's excuses could not justify his mistake in supporting Pompey for 'as a man of such conscientiousness and intelligence' he should have known who was the rightful master of Rome and on which side the Senate and Roman people were. However, he was prepared to make allowances in view of Deiotaros' past services to Rome in the region and, significantly, because of Deiotaros' age, his reputation and the entreaties of his friends who had asked Caesar for clemency. It was undoubtedly the plea of Decimus Junius Brutus that won Caesar over. This Brutus had fought with Caesar in Gaul and Britain and Caesar had promised to make him governor of Cisalpine Gaul. Caesar told Deiotaros he could resume his royal dress and join him. He added that he would consider the complaints by the other Galatian chieftains at a later date.

The problem of Pharnaces now had to be dealt with.

Deiotaros could muster only one full-strength legion of trained Celts in the wake of the defeat of Calvinus and these he placed at

Caesar's disposal. Caesar incorporated Deiotaros' Galatians into his army. In spite of his age, Deiotaros and his son, Deiotaros junior, accompanied Caesar in person. The VI Legion, a veteran force, was so depleted that it consisted of fewer than 1000 men. There were also the survivors of the Roman legion which had been in battle with Pharnaces.

Pharnaces was, if anything, a diplomat, like his father. The velvet glove technique came first. He sent Caesar a gold crown as a present and promised he would submit to Caesar. Caesar replied:

'I myself am never happier than when pardoning supplicants; but I cannot overlook the public outrages against the provinces on the part of those who may have done me service. [Pharnaces had pointed out that, unlike Deiotaros, he had not sent troops to support Pompey against Caesar.] In any case, as for this good deed you speak of, it was far more profitable for Pharnaces, who avoided being defeated, than it was for me, to whom the immortal gods granted the victory. As for the great and dreadful wrongs done to the Roman citizens trading in Pontus, I cannot put these right, and so I am prepared to forgive Pharnaces for them. I cannot restore life to the slain nor manhood to the castrated – the torture worse than death, which Roman citizens have undergone. But Pharnaces must withdraw from Pontus; he must make speed to release the slaves belonging to the tax-gatherers and restore to the allies, and to the Roman citizens, the rest of the property in his possession. When he has done this, then he may send me the gifts and presents which generals are accustomed to receive from their friends after victory.'

Pharnaces replied that he would obey Caesar but wanted time for the withdrawal and terms for agreement; he presented all manner of delaying tactics. Pharnaces apparently knew that internal matters in Rome meant that Caesar could not afford a long, protracted campaign in Asia Minor. If Caesar was to hold power in Rome, he needed to be there to answer his critics. Pharnaces was confident after his victory over Calvinus: Rome was not so invincible, after all. He tried to keep negotiations going while he shifted his position, manoeuvring for more favourable ground. Caesar's patience wore out and, finding Pharnaces was positioned near Zela (Zile), a town in the midst of the mountains behind Trebizond, he advanced quickly towards him.

The Alexandrian War says:

Zela is a town in Pontus, fairly well defended considering its situation on a plain; for its wall is on a natural hillock, which has almost the appearance of an artificial construction and raises it to a considerable height on all sides. Round this town are many high hills, cut into by valleys. The highest of these, which is very well known in those parts because of the victory of Mithridates [when Mithridates the Great defeated Lucullus in 72BC] and the misfortune of Triarius [Gaius Valerius Triarius, Lucullus' lieutenant defeated by Mithridates at Zela in 67BC] and defeat of our army, is almost joined to the city by tracks over high ground and is not much more than 3 miles away. Pharnaces installed himself here with all his forces, after repairing the fortification of the old camp where his father had been successful.

Caesar made his camp 5 miles from the enemy. Having fortified his own position, Caesar ordered his legions to leave their baggage in the camp and set out lightly equipped. By a dawn attack he captured the very spot where Mithridates the Great had defeated the Romans, no more than a mile from Pharnaces' main position. He had his men begin to build new fortifications at this spot. On 2 August 47BC, while Caesar's troops were still making their new camp, Pharnaces suddenly attacked. He had made the rash gamble to move his men down the steep side of one hiil and across the valley floor, and to attack Caesar on the opposing hill. Says *The Alexandrian War*:

Caesar for some time was amazed at Pharnaces' vainglorious display and at the way in which his men were crowded together in a position into which no sane enemy would advance. Pharnaces began to climb up the steep hill opposite at the same speed as he had made that sharp descent, with his troops in order.

Caesar was astonished by this incredible recklessness – or self-confidence.

The attack was certainly unexpected. Yet, under the quiet command of Caesar and, not forgetting his ally, Deiotaros, the combined force of Romans and Galatians did not panic. They stopped work on the fortifications and assembled in their units. At first they were thrown into some confusion by the suddenness of the assault.

After hard, bitter fighting at close quarters, the first signs of victory appeared on the right wing where the veteran VI Legion was stationed. On that side the enemy were being pushed down the slope; meanwhile on the left wing Deiotaros and his Celts were routing Pharnaces' forces, much more slowly but with divine aid.

Together the combined forces drove Pharnaces' men down the slope and slaughtered them in the valley.

Our men, however, were exhilarated by their success and did not hesitate to clamber up the slope and attack the fortifications, and despite the resistance of the cohorts left on guard by Pharnaces they soon took the camp. The whole of Pharnaces' army was either killed or captured; he fled with a few horsemen, and if the assault on the camp had not made it easier for him to escape he would have fallen alive into Caesar's hands.

Caesar, too, was exhilarated that he had completed the campaign so quickly. He was able to send back his famous terse message to Rome: '*Veni, vidi, vici.*' (I came, I saw, I conquered.) Pharnaces fled back to Armenia where he was eventually assassinated. Caesar ordered the VI Legion to return to Rome with rewards and battle honours. Two legions were left in Pontus under the command of Caelius Vinicianus while Caesar himself, with his cavalry, accompanied Deiotaros and his son back to Galatia.

Caesar stayed as the guest of the Celtic king, firstly at his fortress at Peium and then at Blucium. We also hear that during his entire stay in Galatia, Deiotaros allocated one of his nobles, Hieras, to stay by Caesar at all times as a personal bodyguard. However, Castor, the grandson of Deiotaros, later claimed that his grandfather was plotting to assassinate Caesar at Peium and Blucium. We shall deal with these charges in the ensuing chapter.

With the threat of Pharnaces gone, Caesar was able to turn his attention to the complaints levelled against Deiotaros by the other Celtic chieftains. Caesar made some rulings. The chieftainship of the Trocmi was given to Mithridates, the nephew of Brogitaros of the Trocmi, who had saved him from his precarious position in Egypt. *The Alexandrian War* explains that Caesar 'assigned to Mithridates, by virtue of his race and kinship, the tetrarchy of Gallograecia which Deiotaros had seized and held a few years before'. Obviously this is again to misunderstand the structure of Galatia: it was only the chieftainship of the Trocmi that was in question. However, Caesar also appointed Mithridates as 'king of Bosporos which had been under the rule of Pharnaces'.

The Gallograeco met his end at the Bosporos because it was being held by a rebel governor named Asander, still loyal to Pharnaces, and Mithridates was killed attempting to take over the kingdom which Caesar had assigned to him.

It was clear that Caesar and Deiotaros were on cordial but less than friendly terms. Cicero, in his letters, goes so far as to say that no two men were less well disposed towards each other. Caesar deprived Deiotaros of authority not only over the Trocmi of Galatia but over the Tectosages, recognising Castor Tarcondarius as chieftain. The other territories which Pompey had ceded to him were also removed. So Deiotaros was now back where he had started, as a chieftain of the Tolistoboii. Although, Caesar allowed him to retain the title of 'king of Galatia', there was little power outside the territory of the Tolistoboii that went with it.

Within the year Deiotaros had recovered most of his losses. After the death of Mithridates of the Trocmi, he quickly asserted his rule over that tribe again. He also began to put pressure on the Tectosages. Castor, the son of Castor Tarcondarius, the chieftain of the Tectosages, responded by openly accusing Deiotaros of plotting to murder Caesar while he was in Galatian territory. This grave charge was something that the Romans could not overlook.

[16]

The Trial of Deiotaros

I N 45BC a young Galatian Celt named Castor, the son of Castor Tarcondarius (sometimes given as Saocondarius) and Deiotaros' daughter, arrived in Rome. Deiotaros had sent some emissaries to both Tarraco (Tarragona) and Rome that year in order to assure Caesar of his continued loyalty during Caesar's final campaign against the sons of Pompey. Perhaps he also hoped to seek Caesar's blessing on his reassertion of authority over the Trocmi following the death of Mithridates at the Bosporos. Whether Castor was one of these emissaries is not clear but it seems doubtful. Deiotaros' own physician, one Phidippus, was a member of the embassy to Rome. The leading members of the embassy were prominent Galatian chieftains – Hieras, Blesamius, Antigonus and Dorylaus.

It appears from later events that Castor was in Rome acting with the approval of his father, Deiotaros' son-in-law, who had obviously been one of those chieftains who had complained about Deiotaros to Caesar when Caesar was in Galatia. Castor accused his grandfather of attempting to murder Caesar and, as a witness, he presented Deiotaros' physician, Phidippus. The charges were that after the battle of Zela in 47BC, when Caesar had arrived at Deiotaros' fortress of Peium, the Galatian king had conspired to have him assassinated.

A room had been set aside in which presents for Caesar were placed; Caesar would be encouraged to go to view them on his own. Assassins would be hiding in the room and stab him to death. Caesar was saved, so Castor averred, only by the fact that he decided to have a bath and dinner before he went to the room and the assassins grew tired of waiting for him. A further attempt was made when Caesar moved on to Deiotaros' second fortress at Blucium. Assassins were said to have hidden in the bathroom which Caesar was to use after dinner but he was saved this time by the fact that instead of visiting the bathroom he went straight to his bedroom.

The charges were serious enough to have to be answered. Deiotaros' friend, Marcus Tullius Cicero, volunteered to undertake the defence. The hearing was conducted before Caesar himself at a private court held in Caesar's own residence beside the Forum – where Cicero complained that a lack of public audience was a handicap to his oratorical skill.

After the prosecution had presented the charges and the evidence, Cicero opened the defence by stating that a trial of more than usual importance always made him nervous; in this case he was not only defending someone charged with a capital offence, that of attempting to murder Caesar, but defending a king. For a king to be standing trial for his life was something quite unheard of, averred Cicero. He could think of no precedent throughout the whole of human history. Of course, Cicero obviously meant the trial of a king whose sovereignty had been recognised and endorsed by the Roman Senate. At least Deiotaros was lucky to have a trial. It was more than his fellow Celtic king, Vercingetorix, had. After surrendering to Caesar, Vercingetorix had been brought to Rome in chains, kept six years in the Tullanium, at the foot of the Capitol, before being taken out in 46 B C and, after twenty days of celebration for Caesar's victories in Gaul, publicly beheaded. Vercingetorix had no trial for seeking to maintain his people's freedom from Rome.

Cicero starts off by turning prosecutor against Castor whom he calls 'criminal and unnatural' for he was accusing his own mother's father. Castor's proper duty was to defend and protect Deiotaros in his old age but he had resorted to an abominable act of family disloyalty. Moreover, he had actually corrupted his grandfather's servant, the physician Phidippus. Cicero accused Castor of bribing Phidippus to make false allegations against his king.

When I saw the expression on the face of this servant, when I heard the terms in which he accused his master – a master who was not there to hear him, and is a profound lover of Rome – I sadly lamented the king's grave misfortune. But the sorrow I felt for the king was nothing to my dread of the trouble that this action was likely to bring down upon every one of us here in Rome.

Cicero's main task was to get Caesar in the mood to listen to the case without prejudice. He had to defuse Caesar's bias against Deiotaros by pointing it out. It had not escaped the notice of those who now accused Deiotaros, he said, that Caesar had been prejudiced towards him because of his support for Pompey. Caesar had already curtailed Deiotaros' territory. Deiotaros' accusers probably believed that since they claimed that Caesar's own life had been put in danger by Deiotaros, Caesar would welcome the chance to get rid of the Celtic king. Cicero now appealed to Caesar's vanity and belief in his own impartiality.

> You are someone who is accessible to appeals, Caesar, and once you have responded to an appeal that is always the end of the matter. Once you have reconciled yourself to an enemy, that enemy finds that you have banished every trace of animosity from your heart. Now the grievances that you harboured against Deiotaros are common knowledge. It is true that you never accused him in the same terms that you would have employed with an enemy. You merely remonstrated with him as a friend who had fallen short of his duty because he had laid more reliance on his friendship with Gnaeus Pompeius [Pompey] than a friendship with you. Even this you would have been prepared to overlook had not he also sent aid to Pompeius and troops commanded by his own son, Deiotaros [junior] because of his advancing years.

Cicero went on to remind Caesar that he had not punished Deiotaros for this because Deiotaros had only made the same mistake as many other people.

> A king, whom in the past the Senate often addressed by his royal title, in a whole series of highly complimentary decrees, a king who from his earliest youth saw that body as the very model of august dignity, had become the victim – foreigner as he was, in a far-off country – of the same circumstances which we ourselves proved unable to escape, even though we were born and spent our lives in the very heart of the Roman state itself.

Cicero now pointed out that when the civil war ripped Rome apart, the greater part of the Senate had, in fact, supported Pompey, and fled with him to Greece. This was actually a dangerous matter to raise before Caesar.

> Pardon Deiotaros, pardon him, Caesar, if he yielded to the prestige of the man we all followed, the man on whom every possible distinction had been heaped by gods and men alike, and by no one more generously and abundantly than yourself. For if your own great exploits have eclipsed the achievements of everyone else, that does not mean that we have forgotten all about Gnaeus Pompeius. His mighty name, his abundant wealth, his renown in every branch of war, the tremendous honours showered upon him by the Roman people, by the Senate, by yourself, these are matters of common knowledge. His glory surpassed everyone who came before him as completely as your own has surpassed the whole world. Admiringly we counted up all the wars, all the victories, all the triumph, all the consulships of Gnaeus Pompeius. Yours are beyond our power to count.

Cicero's skill is seen at its best here as he appeals to Caesar's vanity while heaping praise on Caesar's vanquished enemy.

He goes on to point out that Deiotaros had, after Pharsalus and Pompey's defeat, disassociated himself from Pompey. He had withdrawn to his own home and, indeed, helped Gnaeus Domitius Calvinus: he had held public auctions to raise money for the expenses of Caesar's campaigns and, Cicero adds, 'he risked his own life in the front line, fought by your side against Pharnaces, deeming your enemy his own.'

Cicero now gets down to the main charge. It was a deed that no one, not even a complete fool, could have thought of committing in the circumstances. His instant annihilation would have followed even if the act had been successful. How could someone of Deiotaros' intelligence and his outstanding record have even contemplated such an action? The charge could not begin to arouse the smallest element of doubt. Cicero is now in his element as he begins to tear the evidence of Castor to pieces.

Listen to the story which the prosecutor tells you: 'After Caesar had arrived at Deiotaros' fortress at Peium there was a room in which the presents that Deiotaros had set aside for Caesar were placed on view. After Caesar had finished his bath and before dinner, Deiotaros' intention was to take Caesar to this room. Inside it were armed men who would, at Deiotaros' command, strike Caesar down.' This is the charge, this is the claim which the renegade Castor makes.

Cicero says that when he heard that Castor was charging Deiotaros with attempted murder and had a witness in the person of Phidippus the physician, he had at first thought that the physician was going to claim that he had been asked to concoct some sort of poison for Caesar.

As it turned out, the doctor did not say anything about poison at all. And yet poison could have been introduced into your drink or food with very much less danger of detection than the violent methods which were actually charged. Besides it would have offered a better chance of escaping retribution because when poison has been administered it can be denied.

However, Cicero went on, if Deiotaros had been able to kill Caesar in the manner it was claimed he proposed to do, he would have easily been found out and a reprisal would have followed immediately. Phidippus was supposed to be an expert physician and loyal at that time to Deiotaros. If so, why had Deiotaros not seen fit to entrust Phidippus to poison Caesar when it could have been organised with so much greater secrecy and carried out discreetly? The court was being asked to believe that Deiotaros had no hesitation in confiding to Phidippus that there were warriors lurking in a room with daggers. Such an idea was a flight of fantasy.

The prosecutor had said that Caesar was saved by good fortune in that after his bath he had suddenly changed his mind and said he preferred to have his dinner and not inspect the presents until later. How long did dinner take? The court was now asked to believe that Deiotaros, having failed to lure Caesar to the room at that time, then gave up the plan for the assassination. It was incredible, observed Cicero. After the meal, Caesar had accompanied Deiotaros to the room. Surely if there had been a serious plot then the assassins would still have been there ready. What was so urgent that the assassins could not wait while Caesar had his dinner?

Instead, Caesar had eaten his meal and gone to inspect the goods. Deiotaros presented the gifts in person with kingly generosity and courtesy and then Caesar retired to his bedroom. There were no tensions, no problems. Cicero said that he was at a loss to know why Deiotaros would decide to kill Caesar after he had taken his bath and before he had eaten his dinner. And why had the whole plan fallen apart simply because Caesar said he wanted to eat his dinner first?

The prosecutor had said that Deiotaros put off the entire plan until the next day when he accompanied Caesar to his second fortress at Blucium. It was now his intention to carry out the assassination there. What on earth was the reason for this? demanded Cicero. For the sake of argument, let the court consider the possibility that this was the idea. After the meal following their arrival at Blucium, Caesar expressed a desire to vomit. (Cicero, in a letter to Atticus, implied that Caesar was in the habit of vomiting after a meal on medical advice.) Deiotaros' servants proposed to take Caesar to the bathroom where, the prosecutor had said, the assassins were now waiting ready to strike him down.

> However, your famous good fortune saved you as so often before, since you expressed a preference to retire for the purpose to your own bedroom instead. But let me tell his treacherous servant, Phidippus, curse him, that not content with showing himself to be an iniquitous scoundrel, he must be an absolute fool as well. He asks us to believe that the assassins posted by Deiotaros in the bathroom were made of solid bronze and it was thus out of the question to move them from the bathroom to Caesar's bedroom to do the job.

That was the sum total of the evidence brought by Phidippus who claimed that he was involved in the plot.

> You surely cannot mean that Deiotaros was lunatic enough to let someone into the secret of such an atrocious crime, someone who he then allows to go freely out of his sight and, in fact, actually dispatches him to Rome where he knew his grandson, Castor, to be – Castor, who hates him so bitterly? And, indeed, where Caesar, the very person against whom the king was supposedly plotting,

also was? The improbability increases further when you reflect that Phidippus was the only man in the world able to take advantage of his absence from Deiotaros in order to denounce him. Phidippus himself says that the king threw his [presumably Phidippus'] brothers into prison 'because they too were in the know'.

Phidippus is claiming, Cicero says, that on the one hand Deiotaros is imprisoning people to stop the secret of the attempted assassination coming out, while on the other hand he is letting a key and crucial witness travel freely to Rome where the very person he was attempting to kill was and where his enemies were.

There were now two other parts of the accusation to be dealt with. Firstly, that Deiotaros had raised a powerful army against Caesar, and secondly, that he watched incessantly for an opportunity to kill Caesar.

As to the matter of an army, Cicero said, Deiotaros' soldiers were only just numerous enough to protect his frontiers against raiders and brigands. The prosecutor claimed that Deiotaros had sent troops to Caesar's enemy Quintus Caecilius Vassus, a supporter of Pompey who, having submitted to Caesar after Pharsalus, had then incited the legions in Syria to mutiny in the cause of Pompey's sons. Further, the prosecution had claimed that when the Galatian troops said they did not want to join Caecilius, Deiotaros threw them into prison. Cicero said he would not bother to argue how unlikely it was that the king would have sent men or, had he sent them, that they would have been disobedient to his orders. He would not even stress the improbability that if his warriors had rebelled against his orders, they would have merely been imprisoned instead of being tried and executed for mutiny.

But this, Caesar, I really have to ask; is it in the slightest degree plausible to suppose that Deiotaros would have sent soldiers to Caecilius when he must have known perfectly well that Caecilius represented a lost cause? On the contrary, Deiotaros now has a profound understanding of Roman politics and must have taken a peculiarly low view of this man.

But, exclaims Cicero, what was insulting was the prosecutor's assertion that when Deiotaros had sent cavalry to help Caesar against

Pharnaces, they were not as well trained and as good as the Roman cavalry. Castor claimed that one cavalryman was actually a slave. This, of course, was not permitted in the Galatian forces. Cicero doubted whether this claim was true but subtly turned the point to ask how could Deiotaros' cavalry expect to be as good as the Roman cavalry?

Next, if Deiotaros hated Caesar so much, why was he supplying and helping the armies of Calvinus and Caesar and offering hospitality to them as well as sharing their dangers on the field of battle?

The prosecutor had said that Deiotaros was sending his agents to Nicaea (more likely to be Iznik than Nice) and to Ephesos to pick up the news of Caesar's campaign in Africa against the sons of Pompey. When a report arrived that Domitius Calvinus had perished in a shipwreck and that Caesar himself was being besieged at Ruspina, it was claimed that Deiotaros had jokingly quoted a Greek tag: 'Perish our friends, so long as our enemies perish too.'

Calvinus had not perished and was actually in the court to hear Cicero's defence.

Deiotaros, asserts Cicero, would not have made such a brutal remark for he was a kindly man, and how could he have called himself a friend of Calvinus had he not also been a friend of Caesar?

Castor claimed that Deiotaros was so pleased and excited by the news that he became very drunk and danced naked at a celebration. Cicero defied anyone to say that they had ever seen Deiotaros either dancing or drunk. Deiotaros was a man of the highest character and Caesar was well aware of it. Conspicuous among his merits was his sobriety. This was a quality not often praised in kings; to be called sober was not often seen as a fit compliment for a king. People were more often used to describing kings as brave, just, upright, dignified, magnanimous, philanthropic and so forth. Sobriety was a private characteristic and, in Cicero's view, an extremely valuable and significant virtue. Sobriety had figured prominently in Deiotaros' character from his early years; this was recognised throughout the entire province of Asia, and known by all Rome's officials and commanders who were engaged in business there.

Cicero goes on:

Deiotaros has won his present title of king because of a long series of services to our country in the field of public affairs. In addition, whenever he was able to find a little leisure from fighting Rome's wars, he liked to devote it to developing friendly relations and business connections with individual Romans. By this means he became well known to a great many of us, and we were able to learn that he was not only an illustrious prince but also an excellent head of a family, and at the same time, a hard-working farmer and stockbreeder. Moreover, even when he was still only a youth, before he had gained the success of his later life, his every action was already serious and dignified. Surely, then, we are not to suppose that such a man, after he had attained mature years and renown, could bring himself to take the floor and give a performance as a dancer!

Cicero turned to Castor and told him that he would have done far better to model himself on his grandfather's character than to use a treacherous servant, Phidippus, as a mouthpiece to malign a great and good man.

Cicero emphasised that Deiotaros was 'already in the evening of his days' and all the skills such as swordsmanship and horsemanship had already become things of the past: it took more than one man to lift Deiotaros into the saddle of his horse these days. 'All the same, we admire a man of his age for being able to stay in the saddle at all!'

Now Cicero turned his full venom on Castor. Castor had, he said, served under his command in Cilicia, when he was governor there. Cicero made no bones about the fact that he had supported Pompey and had gone to Greece at the time of Pharsalus in command of two legions raised in Cilicia. He pointed out that Castor's father, Castor Tarcondarius of the Tectosages, had sent Castor to Pompey with a picked unit of cavalry.

How well I remember him prancing about in our army at the head of his cavalry, showing off in the most boastful and ostentatious fashion, outbidding everyone in his enthusiasm and ardour for the cause. And later on, when the battle of Pharsalus had been fought and our army was destroyed, I, who had always advocated peace, urged that it was not enough to throw your weapons aside; they ought to be thrown away altogether. But I was entirely unable to convert Castor to such a view. He was still full of keenness for the war against you, Caesar, and he believed that this was the way he ought to live up to his father's expectations.

Cicero says that Deiotaros' greatest calamity was that he was being charged by his own flesh and blood. There was a feud between Deiotaros and his son-in-law Castor Tarcondarius of the Tectosages, and that was because Deiotaros had eclipsed him. 'Whoever heard of your father,' asked Cicero of Castor, 'until he had a father-in-law to his credit?' It remained impossible to excuse Castor and the way he had violated the right of the individual, the right of society and the right of humanity itself. He had seduced the physician Phidippus by bribes and promises and corrupted him.

Cicero recalled Gnaeus Domitius Ahenobarbus, who had held office as consul, censor and chief priest when Caesar and Cicero were boys. Ahenobarbus (bronze-beard) came from a distinguished Roman family. As tribune, he was prosecuting Marcus Aemilius Scaurus before a people's court. When a servant of Scaurus came to his home and offered to provide evidence against his master, Ahenobarbus ordered that the man should be arrested and handed over to Scaurus. While it was wrong to compare Ahenobarbus to Castor, Ahenobarbus had demonstrated that it was dishonourable to enlist a servant against his master.

At this point Cicero dealt his *coup de grace*.

Phidippus had confessed that he had been bribed to be a witness against Deiotaros and that Castor had bribed him. In fact, Phidippus had returned back to the embassy of the Galatian Celts and sought out Gnaeus Domitius Calvinus at his home. Calvinus was dining with the famous jurist and orator, and friend of Cicero, Servius Sulpicius Rufus, and Titus Manlius Torquatus. 'Phidippus admitted openly that you had bribed him and that yours were the promises which had induced him to tell all those lies.'

Not only was Domitius Calvinus in the court but so were his dinner companions, who had witnessed Phidippus' confession.

Cicero accused Castor of sheer, unbridled malice in his attack on Deiotaros. Castor's purpose in coming to Rome was nothing less than to overthrow the laws and traditions of Rome, to besmirch their humane society with the savage habits he was accustomed to at home.

Castor had claimed that a Celtic emissary named Blesamius,

acting between Caesar and Deiotaros, had written several times to Deiotaros claiming that Caesar was a tyrant and the Romans were against him. Could this name be a mishearing of Belosamos, 'Bel-like'? Belinus, 'the shining one', was an important deity and in Gaul his name was linked to Apollo. Cicero asked whether Blesamius could possibly have written such nonsense. Castor's charge had been scratched together, and he was now slandering a reputable emissary of the king.

In fact, Blesamius and other Celtic nobles, Hieras and Antigonus, were in court that day. Also Dorylaus, another Galatian noble who was known to Caesar. Each one of these ambassadors was a loyal friend of Deiotaros and they offered to give themselves up that very day as hostages for the deliverance of Deiotaros and his son. Caesar could ask Blesamius himself if he had ever written such letters. Indeed, Blesamius was ready to offer himself as defendant in the place of Deiotaros. If so, Blesamius, or Belosamos, was truly virtuous and 'Bel-like'.

Cicero appealed to Caesar's reputedly excellent memory to recall that Hieras had always been at his side in Galatia and particularly at Deiotaros' fortresses. Hieras (perhaps named after Antiochos Hierax, who had been an ally of the Galatians) had been appointed body-guard to Caesar by Deiotaros himself. He had been in the dining-room and, further, had accompanied Caesar and Deiotaros to the room to inspect the presents. When Caesar went with Deiotaros to Blucium, Hieras was at Caesar's side once again. If the allegations were considered to be authentic, Hieras stood prepared to accept the entire blame on his own shoulders.

I do not believe that I have left anything out. One point I have kept to the last, however, that is my hope that this defence will result in your complete reconciliation with Deiotaros. I am not worried that you harbour a grudge against him. I am afraid that you may suspect that he harbours a grudge against you. Believe me, nothing could possibly be farther from the truth.

He ended his defence by saying:

You showed how willing you were, Caesar, to give Deiotaros his full due, when you granted him and his son the designation of king.

Retaining and cherishing that title he feels that the benefactions he has received from the Roman people, and the high opinion he has earned from the Roman Senate, are still his proud possessions, of which nothing has been lost. He is a man of nobility and courage, and neither his enemies nor the blows of fortune will ever bring him down. He has many assets, he believes, that can never be taken away from him. He has earned them by his deeds in the past – and his valiant spirit has kept them intact.

For many a complimentary resolution in praise of Deiotaros has been decreed by many a Roman general and no evil stroke of fortune, no vicissitude, no unjust blow could ever erase these commendations. Ever since Deiotaros was old enough to serve in the field, no Roman commander who has ever fought a war, whether in Asia or Cappadocia or Pontus or Cilicia or Syria, has failed to cite his services in honorific terms. And the honours which the Senate, too, has repeatedly lavished upon him, honours recorded in the official archives and public memorials of Rome, will never be effaced throughout all the centuries of future time. If everything else that has ever happened was consigned to total oblivion, those glorious citations would still be remembered. And his personal bravery, his noble heart, his moral strength, his unfailing integrity – what can I say about those? They are qualities of character which wise and learned men, without exception, have pronounced to be the highest virtues of all. Indeed, some have even declared that they are the only true virtues that exist and have asserted that if a man possess them he has everything he needs, not only to lead a good life but to lead a happy life as well.

Cicero was quoting Stoic philosophy.

Cicero then slyly revealed that he had a copy of a letter which Caesar had given Blesamius at Tarraco to deliver to Deiotaros. Cicero observes that Caesar was not in the habit of writing letters without meaning every word of what he said in them. Cicero does not go so far as to quote Caesar's praise for Deiotaros but says that this letter must have reassured Deiotaros about their relationship. Cicero cleverly reminded Caesar of its existence.

Cicero was reaching the end of what was to become one of his most famous defence speeches.

I must tell you that I feel a strong sense of personal involvement in Deiotaros' case. Public life has brought us together as friends. The ties of hospitality have been strengthened by mutual regard. Our association has developed into intimacy. The invaluable assistance he provided to myself and my army has attached me to him with unbreakable bonds.

He asks Caesar to give a sympathetic thought for Deiotaros and his son, Deiotaros junior. They were not in court for Caesar to see but Cicero urged Caesar to imagine the terrible nature of their predicament. 'Our opponents are cruel, what they are after is the ruin of Deiotaros and his son. But you are a clement man, and I implore you to come to their rescue ... There are many memorials of your mercifulness, Caesar, but none are more glorious than the lives that you have seen fit to spare.'

It was one of Cicero's best defences, a well-constructed one although Cicero wrote about it in modest terms in a letter to his son-in-law, Publius Cornelius Dolabella (c.80–43BC), husband to his daughter, Tullia.

Caesar adjourned the hearing without making a decision. It seemed that he preferred to keep political suspects in suspense. Additionally, he was planning to return to Asia Minor in the following year. The idea was to undertake a military operation against the Parthians and he probably thought that this would present him with an ideal opportunity to visit Galatia and deal with Deiotaros at first hand. There seemed little doubt, however, that he would exonerate the Galatian king.

His return to Galatia never came. On 15 March 44BC, Caesar was stabbed to death in the Senate house. Cicero himself was to be killed after delivering his fourteen speeches, the *Philippics*, against Mark Antony, who aspired to assume Caesar's mantle. These speeches cost Cicero his life for, on 7 December 43BC, Antony's soldiers caught Cicero and executed him. His head and hands were taken to be displayed on the Rostra, the platform at the Forum in Rome from which speakers usually addressed the people.

We are told that Deiotaros was no doubt delighted by Caesar's death. It was certainly no great loss for the Galatian king, who was now free to exact his own retribution on his accusers. He immediately sent his warriors to the fortress of Gorbeous, south of Ancyra near modern Ogulbey. They found his grandson Castor, who had levelled the charges, and killed him. There is some confusion for in another report this is said to be Castor Tarcondarius, and it is claimed that Deiotaros had his own daughter killed as well. Having taken over control of the Trocmi and now the Tectosages, Deiotaros was once again the sole ruler of Galatia.

[17]

Amyntas, Last King of Galatia

DEIOTAROS was asked to pay Rome 10 million *sesterces* in return for the Senate's approval of him reasserting authority over the Trocmi and Tectosages. Deiotaros, in his old age, was trying to play the wary game of keeping on the winning side of Roman political faction fighting. But a confusing picture was emerging from Rome as differences between Brutus and Caesar threatened to split the Roman empire into a civil war again. Deiotaros was not prepared to declare on one side or the other. He had made a mistake by siding with Pompey and nearly lost everything. But Caesar was assassinated. Who should he support now? There was Mark Antony, and Caesar's adopted son Octavian. Then there was Marcus Junius Brutus, who had fought for Pompey at Pharsalus, and now led the anti-Caesar faction. When one of Caesar's assassins, L. Tillus Cimber, was appointed as governor of Bithynia, Deiotaros was persuaded to supply him with cavalry which helped him inflict a defeat on Cornelius Dolabella, the Roman governor of Syria: the same Dolabella who was Cicero's son-in-law. But as the lines of conflict became clearer, Deiotaros refused to help another of Caesar's assassins, Gaius Longinus Cassius. However, Marcus Junius Brutus finally succeeded in persuading Deiotaros that his star was in the ascendant. He asked the Celtic king to send Galatian troops to reinforce his army at a place called Philippi, in Macedonia. There, in 42BC, Brutus was facing the combined armies of Mark Antony and Octavian.

Being very elderly now, Deiotaros sent his chief adviser, Amyntas, with units of cavalry and infantry. Presumably Deiotaros' son, Deiotaros junior, was needed at home to help the old king govern Galatia. The Galatians joined the republican forces of some twenty legions (100,000 men). On 27 October the battle commenced. Octavian was ill and Brutus was able to rout him but Antony, who had learnt his tactical skill from Caesar, drove back Cassius' wing and surrounded him. Cassius, hearing a report that Brutus had been defeated, committed suicide. At this point Amyntas and the Galatians decided, tactically, to change sides. However, Brutus was able to regroup and two weeks later, on 16 November, a second battle took place. This time Brutus' forces were defeated and Brutus took his own life.

Octavian returned immediately to Rome to secure his position. He, Mark Antony and Marcus Aemilius Lepidus had formed the Second Triumvirate to govern the empire. Mark Antony was to stay in Asia Minor to re-establish Roman rule over the eastern provinces. He eventually arrived in Egypt, and his affair there with the Ptolemy queen, Cleopatra VII, has become part of world folklore. Like Caesar's affair with her before him, it scandalised Roman society.

Deiotaros died about this time. He had been one of the longest serving and, perhaps, the greatest of the Galatian rulers, keeping Galatia independent amid the warring kingdoms and the designs of Rome, struggling to keep a balance between the different Roman factions. He had produced out of the conflicts a centrally governed state.

He was succeeded by his son Deiotaros II. Deiotaros II approved of the policy of the Galatian chieftain, Amyntas, in changing sides at the battle of Philippi and soon afterwards issued some coins to commemorate the victory of his Galatians in the battle. A good politician, he ensured that the head of Mark Antony's wife Fulvia was on the coin; one of the towns of Galatia, Eumeneia, now changed its name to Fulvia. The town magistrate at this time bore a good Celtic name, Zmertorix, son of Philonides, and significantly Zmertorix accepted the personal political patronage of Mark Antony.

Mark Antony approved these measures and confirmed that Rome recognised Deiotaros II as 'king of Galatia', also returning to him ownership of lands in Lesser Armenia which had been taken away by Caesar. But Deiotaros II did not survive long on the throne. Perhaps, in view of the length of his father's reign, he was also elderly when he came to assert his rule over Galatia. Before Mark Antony had passed through Asia Minor on his way to Egypt, Deiotaros II was also dead.

His successor was Amyntas, the Galatian chieftain who had fought at Philippi. He became the first major Galatian leader to emerge who did not bear a Celtic name. Dr Mitchell points out: 'There is, however, no real reason to doubt his Celtic origins.' Amyntas often appears as a favoured name among the Galatians; C. Julius Severus of Ancyra in the 2nd century AD numbered two Galatian chieftains called Amyntas in his ancestry, one the son of Dyitalus (perhaps 'of the world') and the other the son of Brigatus (perhaps 'the high one'), two obvious Celtic names.

Mark Antony was clearly concerned about the possibility of invasion by the Parthians and was intent on setting up strong kingdoms to protect the eastern provinces of Rome. He gave Amyntas lands in Pisidia, Phrygia and even Antioch and Apolloniato to govern as new territories of the Galatian kingdom as well as formerly recognising Amyntas' right to the title 'king of Galatia'. Amyntas was able to mint his own coins. At one time he is reported as having a personal fortune which included 300 flocks of sheep. According to Strabo, Deiotaros Philadelphus, a son of Castor and great grandson of the original Deiotaros, was made king of Paphlagonia with Gangra as his capital. A new chieftain of the Trocmi appeared at this time with the clearly Celtic name of Ateporix. The name means 'king' or 'leader of cavalrymen'. A list of high priests of the imperial cult at Ancyra during the reign of Tiberius lists the son of a Celtic chieftain named Brigatus for whom no territory is given. This was, perhaps, another chieftain of the Trocmi.

Another appointment at this time was that of Adiatorix, son of Domnecleius who became governor of the city of Heracleia Pontica on the Black Sea. He was confirmed in his position by Mark Antony. It is thought that Domnecleius might be identical with Domnilaus, the Tectosagean chieftain who is mentioned as sending his son to Pharsalus. Cicero mentions an Adiatorix as someone of high position in this area about 50BC.

Having consolidated Rome's suzerain authority in Asia Minor, Antony decided to deal directly with the Parthian threat. In the spring of 36BC he led an army of two Roman legions into Parthia. He sent a second army consisting of Galatian Celts supplied by Amyntas, including levies from Pontus and Armenia, through the valley of the Araxes (Araks) river. Antony launched an attack on Phraaspa, the Parthian capital. The Romans were repulsed with heavy losses. The new Parthian king, Phraates IV, ambushed the second army of Celts and almost annihilated it while Antony was trying to besiege the town. He gave up at the onset of winter and made a forced retreat back to Armenia, harassed all the way by Phraates. Total losses were said to be 30,000 men.

The Parthian fiasco saw the turning point in Mark Antony's career. His generosity to the Galatian Celts was to ensure that he had their full support in his growing conflict with Octavian. Mark Antony and Octavian's relationship had never been good and when, coinciding with the Parthian disaster, Lepidus was forced out of the triumvirate, the arguments began to take a more forceful turn.

The thirty-two-year-old Octavian had consolidated his position in Rome and the west. Fulvia, Mark Antony's first wife, who had delighted over the corpse of Cicero because he had attacked her for her political attitudes in his speeches, had died in 40BC. This allowed Mark Antony a momentary reconciliation with Octavian when he married Octavian's sister, Octavia. But in 36BC he went through a form of marriage with Cleopatra in Antioch while still married to Octavia. She became the mother of his three children, including twins. Mark Antony settled in Alexandria, where he lived like an oriental king, bestowing large parts of Rome's eastern provinces as gifts on Cleopatra and her children. These were Caesarion, the nickname of Ptolemy XV, her son by Caesar, who had been appointed co-ruler of Egypt in 44BC. As we have seen, the original Ptolemy XV Neoteros, Cleopatra's youngest brother, had only survived a short time after Caesar had appointed her as co-ruler. Caesarion was now thirteen years old. Mark Antony's son by Cleopatra, Alexander Helios, aged six, was appointed king of Armenia, Parthia and Media; his twin sister Cleopatra Selene received Cyrenaica and Libya; and the two-year-old Ptolemy Philadelphios obtained Syria and Cilicia. Moreover, in 32BC, Antony struck a coin bearing both his own head and that of Cleopatra and declaring her as 'queen of kings and of her sons who are kings'.

When Mark Antony declared that Caesarion was the legitimate son of Caesar, he threw down a direct challenge to Octavian. In 33BC, Octavian and Mark Antony's agreement as joint governors of the Roman empire ended and in May 32BC Mark Antony further insulted Octavian by divorcing Octavia. Octavian then published Antony's will, showing how Antony was squandering Rome's possessions as gifts. In fact, Mark Antony had split the empire in two, giving most of the eastern territories to Cleopatra. Roman sentiment became so hostile that the Senate demanded that Octavian declare war on Egypt and Mark Antony's eastern possessions.

Early in 31BC Octavian landed an army of 40,000 men in southern Epiros. On the promontory of Actium, Mark Antony's army of similar numbers was gathered. Off the coast stood the two opposing fleets. For a long time the two men faced each other without giving battle. Then, in August, Antony decided to attempt a sea battle because Octavian's ships had cut his supply lines back to the Peloponnese. It was not until dawn on 2 September that the 480 ships of Antony sailed into the Ionian Sea to do battle with the 400 ships of Octavian. Antony commanded the right squadrons with Marcus Octavius in the centre and C. Sosius on the left. Octavian split his fleet into three squadrons. The left was commanded Marcus Vipsanius Agrippa (64–12BC), regarded as one of Rome's best naval tacticians, the centre was held by an officer named Aruntius and the right wing by Octavian himself.

At first each side tried to turn the other's flanks but during the afternoon the battle was becoming a stalemate. It was then that Cleopatra, with some sixty Egyptian warships which had been in reserve, suddenly, for no apparent good reason, left the battle, breaking through the Roman fleet and standing out to sea. Mark Antony, seeing this, transferred to a fast quinquereme, with five banks of oars, and fled after Cleopatra. He caught up with her ship and boarded it.

However, his fleet was now leaderless. Octavian's ships, dodging the rams and missiles of the enemy, managed to set fire to many of the warships. Ten hours after the engagement began, there were few survivors of Antony's burning ships: some 5000 men were dead.

On land, P. Crassus Canidus, the commander of Antony's army, decided to flee to Egypt as well. By 9 September, Mark Antony had no army left. The flight of Cleopatra and Mark Antony has become one of the great mysteries of history. What made them flee the battle?

Octavian followed them to Egypt. Mark Antony sought peace terms which were rejected by Octavian. On 1 August, 30BC his fleet arrived at Alexandria. Mark Antony had eleven legions ready to face him but they deserted *en masse* to Octavian. Mark Antony committed suicide. Cleopatra was ordered to leave for Rome but also committed suicide in order to avoid the shame of being taken to Rome as a captive. With her died the last of the Ptolemaic rulers and, indeed, the last of the Macedonian monarchies set up in the wake of Alexander's conquests.

Octavian, the adopted son and heir of Caesar, now had Caesarion, his father's natural son by Cleopatra, executed in case the boy-king grew into a rival. The children of Mark Antony and Cleopatra were allowed to survive and disappeared from history. At the age of thirty-three, Gaius Octavius was now sole master of Rome. He was elected consul and swore to restore the republic. He would pursue his ambition to become the first Emperor, Augustus Caesar.

As mentioned earlier, the historian Josephus refers to Cleopatra's élite bodyguard of 400 Celts. Octavian, in 'pacifying' the area previously dominated by Antony, took these Celts to Judaea. The king of Judaea was Herod the Great (c.73–4BC), the son of a local Hellenic governor of the south of Judaea. He was both a Hellene and a Roman citizen. He had risen to obtain the title of 'king' from Mark Antony, a title approved by Rome in 37BC. He ruled Judaea as a Hellenistic kingdom under the patronage of Mark Antony. After Mark Antony's defeat at Actium, Herod found himself in a precarious position.

According to Josephus:

Because of his friendship for Antony, recently defeated by Octavian Augustus at Actium, Herod was uneasy about the security of his power. Yet he was more alarmed than hurt, since Octavian did not consider his victory complete so long as Herod continued to aid his rival. Resolving to confront danger, Herod sailed for Rhodes where Octavian was staying, and appeared before him without his diadem and in the dress and character of a private man but with the spirit of a king. He concealed nothing of the truth, addressing Octavian candidly: 'I was made king of Judaea by Antony, and I acknowledge, Caesar, that I have, as a king, in all things studied his interests: I unhesitatingly avow that had not insurrection prevented me, you would most certainly have found me in arms, an inseparable companion of Antony. According to my ability, however, I supported him with some troops and with many thousands of measures of grain; nor did I desert my benefactor ever after his defeat at Actium. When I could no longer help him as an ally, I gave him the most prudent counsel: I told him that there was but one remedy for his disasters – to kill Cleopatra. I promised him money, ramparts for his security, an army, and myself as his confederate in the war against you were she to be destroyed. But his passion for Cleopatra closed his ears. Together with Antony, therefore, I too have been conquered, and with his defeat I lay down my crown. To you, however, I come, founding my hope of safety on my integrity, foreseeing that it will be asked how firm a friend, rather than whose friend, I have been.

Apparently, Octavian was impressed by his speech and decided to confirm Herod as king in Judaea under his suzerainty. Later in 30BC, Octavian went to Ptolemaic (Acco) and Herod entertained him there before he went on to Pelusium. In fact, Octavian decided to hand over to Herod control of some territories which Cleopatra had previously ruled, such as Gadara, Hippos, Samaria and Gaza, Anthedon, Jaffa and Strabos' Tower (later Caesarea). In addition, says Josephus, Octavian 'presented him with Cleopatra's bodyguard of 400 Celts'.

Herod, who became known as Herod the Great, died in 4BC having ruled Judaea for thirty-four years. Josephus says that the Celts were in attendance at the funeral observances.

The bier was solid gold, studded with precious stones, and the bed was of variegated purple. On it lay the body, also covered with purple. A diadem was on Herod's head, and over it a crown of gold. At his right hand was a sceptre.

Herod's sons and numerous kin surrounded the bier. Next came the guards, the Thracian units, Germans *and the Celts* [my italics], all of them equipped as for war. The rest of the army, preceded by its commanders and subordinate officers, marched in front, armed and in order. They were followed by 500 of Herod's servants and freedmen bearing sweet spices. The body was conveyed to Herodium, a distance of 200 furlongs, Herod having left orders to be buried there. So ends the history of Herod.

It hardly seems likely that the same men who constituted Cleopatra's bodyguard had survived in Herod's military service for twenty-six years. It is obvious that Herod, as a Hellenic king, continued the practice of recruiting the Celts to his bodyguard; one wonders whether Celts continued to serve the heirs of Herod during the next decades, which were to be the most fascinating and turbulent in Judaean history.

It is also intriguing, returning to Octavian's conquest of Egypt in 30BC, that a Romanised Celt then became prefect and first Roman governor of Egypt. This was Gaius Cornelius Gallus (c.69–26BC), who was born in Narbonese Gaul, which is now Fréjus in Provence, his cognomen being simply 'the Gaul'. He seems to have gone to Rome at an early age and risen to equestrian rank. He fought on Octavian's side in the civil war and was appointed to redistribute the appropriated lands of Cisalpine Gaul among army veterans. He was a poet and friend of Virgil, who, if not of Celtic origin himself, was certainly raised among the Cisalpine Gauls. Gallus wrote love elegies, a genre he appears to have originated, and his work was influenced by Hellenistic poets such as Callimachos and Euphorion. Some of Gallus' literary work has been recovered from an Egyptian papyrus. He was governor for four years but Octavian recalled him after he fell out of favour and Gallus was forced to commit suicide. It is said that his friend Virgil then had to rewrite the latter half of the fourth *Georgic* which had been a eulogy to Gallus.

After the defeat of Antony at Actium, Octavian turned his attention to Asia Minor to examine the loyalties of Mark Antony's friends there. Certainly Amyntas and his Galatian kingdom were prime suspects because of the gifts Mark Antony had showered on them. But Amyntas survived Octavian's 'inquisition'. It is recorded that Octavian had Adiatorix and his second son executed at Heracleia Pontica. Adiatorix tried to defend himself by arguing that Mark Antony had been placed in charge of the area by Rome and it was therefore his duty to obey him. His defence did not work. But Adiatorix's eldest son, Dyteutus (whose name seems to mean 'of the people' or 'of the tribe'), was spared: he had impressed Octavian with his organisational qualities and was soon appointed governor of Comana Pontica.

In 25BC Amyntas was killed. He had been campaigning along the Tauros, suppressing tribal groups hostile to his rule. By this time the Roman world was rapidly changing. Octavian had received the title, at the proposal of L. Munatius Plancus, of 'Augustus' (Greek – *sebastos*, reverend), setting him above the entire state. This became the title of the new dynasty of Roman emperors founded by Octavian.

The republic was ended and when he died in AD 14, Augustus was acclaimed as a god.

Amyntas was the last king of Galatia to be acknowledged as such by Rome. The only hint of a legal transfer of authority in Galatia from Amyntas to Rome is when Strabo mentions that a commission had been sent by the Roman Senate to deal with a bequest by Amyntas. This implies that Amyntas, like other kings of Asia Minor such as the mad Attalos of Pergamum or Nicomedes of Bithynia, actually left his kingdom to Rome when he died. But why would he have done so? In the case of the other kings making their will in favour of Rome, the absence of an undisputed heir was a common factor. The employment of Rome as a guardian to ensure that a young heir's rights were safeguarded until he came of age was not unusual. This would presuppose that the Galatian Celts were by now so Hellenised that they accepted this form of inheritance by primogeniture. However, it could well be argued that they had not yet discarded their electo-hereditary system of appointing chieftains: only twenty years before, they had complained to Caesar about Deiotaros, accusing him of seizing previously unheard-of power in Galatia. And even if they did now accept hereditary kingship, there was an heir in the person of one Pylaemenes, son of Amyntas.

What made Rome step in and, ignoring local claimants to the kingship, annex Galatia to make it a Roman province?

Are we witnessing a parallel to the situation which arose eighty years later in Britain? Prasutagus of the Iceni had accepted the Roman conquest and become a client king of Claudius. When Prasutagus died he made a will in Roman fashion and left half of his kingdom to the Emperor Nero and Rome, and the rest to his widow Boudicca and his children. The Romans, not satisfied, tried to seize it all and thus pre-empted the uprising of the British tribes.

Galatia and the possessions of Amyntas might simply have become a test case for changing the borders of the kingdoms of Asia Minor in order to unite them into one major Roman province. This certainly seems to have been the policy of Rome over the next century. That there was initial dissatisfaction is demonstrated by the fact that the new province had to be garrisoned. In 25 BC M. Lollius arrived as *legati Augusti pro praetore*. He was to be the first of many governors of Galatia over the succeeding centuries, during which the fortunes of Galatia greatly changed.

Galatia, a Roman Province

THE first legion to be sent to Galatia to act as garrison troops was the veteran VII Legion. Their battle honours included fighting for Octavian at Mutina, at Philippi and in the Perusine War. It appears that the legion was stationed in southern Galatia and that as and when its soldiers retired new recruits were enrolled from the local population. This meant that after a short time the legion would have consisted entirely of Galatian troops. Auxiliary units were also recruited locally and we know of two local cavalry regiments, the Antiochiensium and the Augusta Colonorum. There are also references to a legion designated the XXII Deiotariana, formed around 15BC, and named after the late Galatian king. Perhaps this was the only Roman legion named after a Celtic king.

It was at this time that the Romans had to conduct a military campaign along the borders of southern Galatia against local tribes who had become restless and were causing problems by recourse to banditry. The campaign was conducted by the new governor of Galatia, P. Sulpicius Quirinus. The fighting lasted between 12BC and AD1. The principal problem was a tribe called the Homonadeis, apparently not a Celtic people, who were said to terrorise the area. It took Quirinus several campaigns to pacify the district, round up the Homonadeis, transplant them and introduce more peaceful settlers to the region from other parts.

Troops raised in Galatia from the Celtic population were used in 11–9BC to suppress a rising in northern Thrace. From this period on, Celtic cavalry would appear throughout the empire in the service of Rome.

Rome started building new cities in Galatia. The old Celtic settlements, hill-forts and strongholds fell into disuse. The cities at Pessinus, Ancyra and Tavium were rebuilt. Coins carried new Roman designations such as Sebasteni Tolistoboii Pessinuntii,

Sebasteni Tectosages Ancyrani and Sebasteni Trocmi Taviani, echoing the names of former tribal capitals. The first element of the name gives a clue as to the date of the foundation of the new city by Augustus (Sebastos). There is evidence that the old tribal lands began to be redefined by the Roman administration. The creation of the new cities seems to be a deliberate act to urbanise Galatia immediately after its annexation.

By 3BC there were still Celtic chieftains claiming kingship in Galatia, such as Brigatus in Amaseia, Dyteutus in Comana, and Ateporix in Zela (Megnopolis). Significantly, all bore Celtic names instead of Hellenic forms. This year of 3BC was the year when Ateporix died and his territory, lying to the east of the main Trocmi tribal lands, was immediately annexed by Rome. Almost at once a new Roman city called Sebastopolis (Augustus's city) was founded in the centre of that territory. Brigatus in Amaseia died soon after and Rome annexed his territory, renaming it Pontus Galaticus (Celtic Pontus). It was not until AD 34/5 that Dyteutus died and Comana was merged into Pontus Galaticus.

When Octavian accepted the title Augustus, Nicolaus of Damascus wrote:

> Because men call him by this name as a mark of esteem for his honour, they revere him with temples and sacrifices, organised by islands and continents, and as cities and provinces they match the greatness of his virtue and the scale of his benefactions towards them.

Indeed, within a year of his accepting the title, in 27BC, temples began springing up to the new imperial cult. By 3BC the imperial cult was widespread in Galatia and an oath of loyalty to Augustus and his family was being administered. The first centre of worship was the 'Temple of Rome and Augustus' at Ancyra. At Pessinus a Corinthian-style temple was built and this seems to have become the chief temple and headquarters of the high priesthood of the cult in Galatia. Several other major temples were erected throughout the Roman province.

It is curious how the various parts of the Celtic world involved themselves in the cult of Augustus. At Lugdunum in Gaul the first priest of 'Rome and Augustus' was one C. Julius Vercondaridubnus, an Aedui Celt. He was succeeded by C. Lucterius Leo of the Cadurci, who surely must have been a descendant of Lucterius ('the mouse'), one of Julius Caesar's bitter enemies during the war of independence led by Vercingetorix. At Ancyra we find a similar story of Celts accepting the worship of Augustus.

The high priests occupied their position for one year and could serve more than one term. The first priest whose name we can recognise was Castor, a son of the chieftain Brigatus. Then we find Pylaemenes, the son of the last Galatian king, Amyntas. He was high priest of the cult in AD 22/23 and again in AD 30/31. Pylaemenes was succeeded by Albiorix son of Ateporix in AD 23/24 and he served again in AD 26/27. In AD 34/35 we find the son of Albiorix, Aristocles, is high priest. An Amyntas, son of Gaesatodiastes, served the temple in AD 24/25. In AD 28/29 Musanus son of Articnos was high priest and so on.

We can see from this name list that Celts, moreover with Celtic names, were still able to hold high office in the Roman province and were therefore culturally influential.

A fascinating aside about the temple of Augustus in Ancyra is the inscription on the partial remains of a monument. This records the 'achievements of the Divine Augustus' and was set up in AD 14. The memorial records the names of two British Celtic kings, Dubnovellaunos and Tincommius, who apparently travelled to Rome to visit the Roman emperor nearly thirty years before the Roman invasion of Britain. Dubnovellaunos was king at Camulodunum (his name is also given as Dumnovelaunuos) and he ruled the Trinovantes, while Tincommius appears to be the son of Commius of the Atrebates, who helped Caesar during his attempted invasions in 55 and 54BC. Both kings are known from coins that they struck. Dubnovellaunos was a chieftain of a Cantii sept before he became king of the Trinovantes. He appears to have been displaced about AD 7 by Cunobelinos (the hound of Belinos – Shakespeare's Cymbeline).

It is clear that in Galatia, at least, the ruling families were beginning to be Hellenised, but with the changes under the Roman administration, many turned to Romanisation. The most influential Galatian Celt in the second half of the 2nd century AD bore the name C. Julius Severus, and he boasted descent from the Celtic chieftains Brigatus and Dyitalos. He was known to have had a distinguished civic career and his hospitality was proverbial. He became high priest of the imperial cult. When the Emperor Trajan (AD 98–117) embarked on his war against the Parthians, Severus played host to the XXXII pia Victrix Legion which passed through Ancyra during the winter of AD 113/114 and his generous hospitality astonished his guests.

The difficulty of identifying who was a Celt and who was a Greek simply by their names is now followed by the problem of who was a Celt and who was a Roman. Names had first become submerged in the Gallograeco culture and now they were merging in a Graeco-Romano culture. Yet sometimes we can still recognise them. A Celt named A. Caesennius Gallus became governor on the Euphrates frontier in the period AD 80–82. An auxiliary regiment, the Cohors II at Dascusa, set up a dedication to him. He is recorded as building many new roads in both Galatia and Pontus.

The Emperor Claudius (AD 41–54) separated Paphlagonia from the Galatian province but his successor Nero, in AD 64, incorporated eastern Pontus into Galatia. After the fall of Jerusalem, in AD 70, the Emperor Vespasian placed Cappadocia and Lesser Armenia under the governorship of Galatia. The borders of the province then remained static until Trajan's period.

Among those who joined the army of Lucius Ceionus Commodus Verus, the co-emperor, in a war against the Parthians in AD 163–164, was the I Adiutrix Legion, a legion recruited from the Aedui of Gaul. We find a centurion of that legion buried at Ancyra: a sad and curious example of a western Celt arriving in the territory of his eastern cousins and dying there.

In AD 242 the new Emperor Gordianus III, and his wife Tranquillana, set forth with his praetorian prefect, C. Furius Timesitheus, to lead an army through the Balkans and Asia Minor to Syria and Mesopotamia. Here the son of Ardashir (the Parthian emperor), an able leader named Shapur, had made great territorial gains and was threatening to capture Antioch. Galatia, like the rest of the eastern Roman provinces, was worried by the threat. It could be argued that this was the beginning of the end of stable Roman government in the area. Timesitheus died of a disease and the young Gordianus placed his affairs in the hands of Romanised Arab called M. Julius Philippus, who stirred up a mutiny, murdered the emperor, and negotiated a deal with Shapur which allowed Syria and much of Anatolia (Asia Minor) to be overrun. He marched back to Rome declaring himself emperor. He reigned for four years before he was assassinated.

There began a new tradition of Roman officers using their troops to seize power and declaring themselves emperor by assassinating the resident emperor. This unsettled period saw the Goths, Huns and Vandals beginning to change the face of the Roman empire. Ravaging armies wrought havoc among the communities of Galatia.

In the 6th century A D the Chinese noticed a nomadic people whom they designated as Turks, which name found its way into Arabic, Greek and Latin. They were a numerous and widely spread people, occupying central Asia, and speaking an Ural-Altaic or Turanian family of languages. As Rome's power receded, they pressed forward into Anatolia (Asia Minor). The vast Ottoman or Osmanli Turkish empire was founded in the 13th century, spreading into Europe as well as Asia and Africa. Byzantium (which had become Constantinople) was conquered in 1453 and renamed Istanbul. Greece was unable to reassert its independence until the 19th century and many areas of modern Greece, such as Lesbos, even had to wait until the 20th century. But in the Greek cities of Anatolia, the Greek populations were driven out or absorbed into the new Turkish nation. And as for the Galatian Celts, they had certainly disappeared in the initial settlements of the Turks.

[19]

'The Foolish Galatians'

BEFORE the Celts of Galatia resigned themselves to the absorbing fortunes of more powerful peoples, they bequeathed one more fascinating chapter to world history and to one of the major religions of the world. In 4BC Archelaus, son of Herod the Great, succeeded to the kingdom of Judaea. Alas, we do not know whether he continued to employ his father's Celtic bodyguard. He was already in dispute with his brothers Philip and Herod Antipas. Moreover, the Jewish population were rebelling against the Hellenic kings who ruled under the patronage of Rome.

P. Quinctilius Varus, the governor of Syria, was faced with an explosive situation. A Roman legion of 5000 men with 5000 auxiliaries, under Sabinus, marched in to take control and entered Jerusalem, fortifying themselves in Herod's palace. Full-scale insurrection broke out and Varus sent two more legions as reinforcements. He began to round up the Jewish rebels, and introduced crucifixion as a form of execution for them, crucifying as many as 2000 people. Archelaus was sent to Rome to face charges of incompetence before Augustus. The charges were brought by his brothers as well as by leading representatives of his Jewish subjects.

Augustus gave his judgement. Archelaus was to rule one half of the kingdom, comprising Idumaea, Judaea and Samaria. His brother Herod Antipas received Peraea and Galilee, while Philip would rule Baanaea, Trachonitis, Auranitis and Panias. Archelaus' territory included Jerusalem, Jaffa, Sebaste and Caesarea. Augustus annexed the towns of Gaza, Gadara and Hippos to his Syrian province.

Archelaus had no sooner arrived in Jerusalem when he started to inflict retribution on the rebellious Jews. In AD6 Augustus stepped in and banished him to Gaul, seizing his property. His kingdom was made a Roman province and P. Sulpicius Quirinus, the former governor of Galatia, was sent to become governor of Syria. In turn he ordered an officer named Coponius to proceed to Judaea as procurator. One of the first things Quirinus arranged with his procurator was a census of the inhabitants of Judaea and Samaria so that Rome, in imposing direct rule, might know how much wealth was available. The Roman administration wanted to have a property valuation, so that they could start to levy a new system of taxes. The census was only to apply to landowners and was ordered in AD 6. The New Testament wrongly places it twelve years earlier and also wrongly attributes it to an order of Augustus applying to all the Roman world.

Quirinus and Coponius' census provoked armed revolt in many areas of the new province. Galilee was a hotbed of revolution. Judah of Gamala and Zadok, a Pharisee, according to Josephus, 'exhorted the nation to assert its freedom'. Judah's father has been identified as Ezekiah, a Galilean rebel executed by Herod. The resistance movement became known as the Zealots. They took their name from Phinehas the Zealot, the son of Aaron 'who was zealous for his God' (Numbers xxv, 13). The Jews believed that Phinehas had never died and was identical with the prophet Elijah who would also come back to life and tell of the coming of the Messiah (Malachi iv, 5). Judah himself is mentioned in the New Testament (Acts). According to Josephus, a Pharisee himself, when the Romans burned one of the Jewish temples, 'in consequence, the customs of our fathers were altered . . . for Judah and Zadok, who introduced among us a fourth philosophic sect, which had numerous followers, filled our state with increasing turmoil and laid the foundations of future miseries with their system of philosophy, a system formerly unknown among us.' It should be pointed out that Josephus was pro-Roman; after the fall of Jerusalem he settled in Rome and spent his life there as a Roman citizen.

Archelaus' brother, Herod Antipas, was ruling over Galilee (4BC–AD 29) and he had married Herodias, wife of one of his half-brothers who had left her husband to marry him. According to Josephus, a religious teacher, 'John the Baptist', rebuked Herod for this marriage which was against religious law. Herod's daughter Salome is, according to Mark, supposed to have encompassed John's execution. According to Josephus:

For Herod had John executed though he was a good man and commanded the Jews to exercise virtue through justice toward one another and piety towards God and by so doing to arrive at immersion [baptism], for immersion would be acceptable to God only if practised not to expiate sin but for purification of the body after the soul had first been thoroughly purified by righteousness.

Herod Antipas' army was defeated by an Arab king, Arteas, father of his first wife whom he had deserted. Josephus says the Jews believed that the destruction of the army was a just punishment for what Herod had done to John. There is, unfortunately, once again no reference as to whether Herod Antipas retained his father's Celtic bodyguards and whether they played any part in these matters.

But against this background of unrest in Galilee, a young boy was growing to manhood. He had been named Yeshua, 'the red-handed hero', usually transcribed as Joshua, but in later Greek texts his name was to be written in the form of Jesus. Josephus says: 'Now about this time lived Jesus, a wise man, if indeed he should be called a man. He was a doer of wonderful works, a teacher of men who received the truth with pleasure, and won over many Jews and many Greeks.'

The young Jesus was about ten years old when Judah the Galilean and his Zealots captured the city of Sepphoris, the capital of Galilee, and held it against the Romans. In the modern world, the Zealots would be called either 'terrorists' or 'freedom fighters' depending on which perspective one took. They believed in direct action; a guerrilla campaign against Rome to win freedom for their people. The Pharisees, however, were moderates, believing that the time was not right for a war. The Sadducees, another faction, co-operated to a great extent with the administration of the Roman occupation.

The Zealots' full-scale war was not to come about until AD 66–73 and ended with the heroic last ditch defence of Massada conducted by a descendant of Judah of Galilee, Eleazar ben Jair.

During this period of the continuing guerrilla war with Rome, the procurator Coponius was replaced by Marcus Ambivius (AD 9–12), Annius Rufus (AD 1–15) and Valerius Gratus (AD 15–26). The fifth procurator arrived in AD 26 and was Pontius Pilatus (Pilate). He had allowed his soldiers to march into Jerusalem bearing the portrait of Caesar on his standards and the Jews protested that their religious laws permitted no image to be paraded in the city. Pilatus ordered his soldiers to draw their swords but when he saw the Jews would rather die than submit he ordered the removal of the offending standards.

Against such tensions Jesus the Galilean grew up; to those who have analysed his teachings, comparing them with the Hebrew religious texts, it seems obvious that he was trained as a teacher. Such teachers were called a master or rabbi. Without an understanding of Judaism and the history of the time it is almost impossible to understand the tensions of his background. The title Messiah (Christos in Greek) was not a divine title to the Jews. It simply meant 'anointed'. The king of Judaea and his high priest were 'anointed' and every Jewish king of the House of David had the title Messiah. The high priests throughout the Roman period also used such a title. Today the Greek form Christ has become so imbued with divinity that it is almost impossible to appreciate what the word actually meant in Jesus' day.

Most Biblical scholars and scholars of the history of this period agree that Jesus was brought up in an area that was the centre of an idealistic resistance to Rome and that he must have been keenly aware of this. He became a wandering teacher from about the age of thirty years. There are grounds for an argument about just how pacifist he was. Sometimes the records of his teachings let down the modern Christian image. 'I came not to send peace but a sword' (Matthew x, 34), and he certainly distributed swords to his disciples after the Last Supper, a fact mentioned by Luke.

Some scholars have argued that his disciples were actually members of the Zealot group which would surely make him at least a Zealot sympathiser. Simon Bar-Jonah, more popularly known to modern Christians as Peter, is said to have been called Simon 'the Outlaw' (Baryona), not the more innocuous 'Son of Jonah'. In Luke (vi, 15) Simon is clearly called 'the Zealot' (*zelotes*). Judas Iscariot bears a name derived from the word 'assassin'; *sicarius* was a Roman term of contempt for a Zealot, as 'terrorist' is used by English people to denote an Irish Republican who believes in physical force to win Irish reunification. James and John are nicknamed 'Boanerges', glossed as 'sons of thunder' (Mark iii, 17), but the meaning is *benei ra'ash*, 'sons of martial thunder', which was also applied to Zealots. Mark and Matthew called Simon 'the Canaanite' but, as Canaan no longer existed at the time, the Hebrew word for Zealot, *kanai*, has probably been mistranscribed as *kena'ani* (Canaanite).

Whatever the teachings of Jesus, Rome and her client king, Herod Antipas, saw him as a political threat. We are told that a cohort (500 men) of Roman soldiers was sent to arrest him. He was handed over to the officers of the high priest. It was standard procedure for the Roman authorities to leave a preliminary examination of political suspects to the Jewish collaborationist authorities. The idea that Jesus was tried for blasphemy before the Synhedrion at night demonstrates a lack of knowledge of Jewish law and custom. Calling oneself Messiah was not blasphemy and the law expressly forbade the Synhedrion to meet at night. Neither could it meet during Festival time. As for its members spitting at and striking Jesus, it would be as incredible as if one read a report that the High Court judges of England or the judges of the Supreme Court of the US had spat at and struck a defendant appearing before them.

The accounts were written decades later and by people who were anti-Jewish. The charge against Jesus was obviously one of sedition, a political charge. Josephus makes this clear, as does the historian Tacitus. Religious offenders were dealt with by the Jews but political offenders had to be handed over to the Romans. Jesus was tried and executed in AD 30. Pontius Pilatus remained procurator until AD 36 when he was dismissed by the governor of Syria, L. Vitellius, for a pointless massacre of Samaritans on Mount Gerzim.

In the years following Jesus' execution a sect arose known as the Nazarenes, under the leadership of Jesus' brother Jacob (James). This sect was not considered heretical to Judaism and, indeed, remained within the Pharisee party until AD 90. At the time of the fall of Jerusalem, Ananus, the high priest, a Sadducee collaborating with Rome, decided to smash the Nazarenes.

> He brought before the Synhedrion Jacob [James], the brother of Jesus who was called Messiah, and some other men whom he accused of breaking the [religious] law, and delivered them to be stoned. But those who seemed to be the most moderate of the citizens and strictest in the observance of the laws disliked the deed and secretly sent a message to king Agrippa beseeching him to bid Ananus to refrain from similar actions in the future, because what he had done was not right.

So writes Josephus, who was a witness in Jerusalem at the time. Ananus, who was later assassinated by his countrymen, was responsible for getting Josephus dismissed from office in Galilee.

The Nazarene movement won a new convert about the year AD 36, six years after Jesus' execution. This was a Hellenised Jew from Tarsus, not far away from the borders of Galatia. His name was Saul, which apparently meant 'asked of God' but which was later more easily rendered in the Latin form, Paul, meaning 'little'. He was born about AD 3 and it is claimed that he was taught by the great liberal Pharisee rabbi Gamaliel in Jerusalem. While born in the Jewish diaspora, he was a Roman citizen which was of tremendous help to him in his later wanderings and settlement in Rome.

In spite of claims that he was a Pharisee, in all likelihood he was a Sadducee. Not only did he lack the liberal attitudes associated with the philosophies of the Pharisee group but he openly worked as an agent for the high priest as a Roman collaborator. His work at the time was tracking down and arresting Nazarenes, among other 'terrorist' suspects: this would have been anathema to any Pharisee and openly opposed by them. More telling is the fact that Paul implies that he was a member of the Synhedrion itself. The Synhedrion comprised seventy-one scholars acting as supreme court and legislature over Jewish religious matters under Roman civil authority. At this time it was composed of Sadducees as representatives of the rich and powerful.

In Acts 26 (v.9–10) Paul tells King Agrippa:

I myself once thought it my duty to work actively against the name of Jesus of Nazareth; and I did so in Jerusalem. It was I who imprisoned many of God's people by authority obtained from the chief priests [i.e. the Synhedrion] and when they were condemned to death, my vote was cast against them.

As only a member of the Synhedrion would be able to cast such a vote, Paul was obviously such a member. 'In all the synagogues I tried by repeated punishment to make them renounce their faith, indeed my fury rose to such a pitch that I extended my persecutions to foreign cities.'

It seems that Paul was also present at the execution of Stephen c.AD 35. Stephen is recorded in Acts as one of the seven leaders of the Nazarenes who were appointed to look after the welfare of

Greek-speaking widows within the Nazarene movement. He was tried and executed for blasphemy.

Within a year or so Paul became an eager convert of the Nazarene sect, but he also had his own ideas about improving its philosophy and began to propound teachings which were considered inconsistent by the Nazarene-Pharisee followers of Jesus who had actually known him in life. Paul gave divine status to Jesus; he declared that the Jewish religious law (the Laws of Moses) had been abrogated and that the sect should be opened up to non-Jews, or Gentiles, who would not have to convert to Judaism and be circumcised. He also interpreted Jesus' death in terms of Gnostic soteriology (salvation doctrine). He had not as yet developed the full non-Jewish Christian doctrine but had certainly laid the foundations for it.

That Paul was a missionary of genius for his new philosophies is undisputed. But his critics pointed out that he had never known Jesus and had begun to preach a philosophy that the original followers found unacceptable. The Nazarenes were loyal members of Judaism. Jesus' brother Jacob (James) was appalled by Paul's activities. Paul began to use his knowledge of pagan Hellenistic culture in order to help develop his new theology. A great schism took place about AD 60 between the Paulinists (followers of Paul) and the original followers of Jesus, the Nazarenes.

Only one Nazarene document survives into modern Christian literature, the Epistle of James (Jesus' brother) which has, of course, been revised by Paulinists. Nevertheless, there are indications of its origin when it aligns itself with the doctrines of the Zealots in attacking the vices of rich people, combats some of Paul's key philosophies and calls a community a *synagogue* instead of an *ecclesia*. It is also monotheistic and contains no Gnosticism. The Nazarenes took part in the defence of Jerusalem against the Romans and most of them died in the subsequent massacre, including Jacob. A few survived and were sometimes called Ebionites, a Latinised term from the Hebrew word *ebyon* meaning 'poor'.

The Nazarenes came into conflict with their fellow Pharisees in AD 90 and were expelled from the Jewish synagogue. The Nazarenes continued to exist until AD 400. They taught that Jesus was not divine but a Messiah and that he had never abrogated Jewish (Mosaic) law. They also claimed that Paul was the one who had perverted Jesus' teachings.

It is now that the Celts of Galatia once more enter the historical scene and become the focal point of the conflict between Paul of Tarsus and Simon Bar-Jonah (Peter), who was one of the leaders of the Nazarene movement.

Paul, three years after his conversion, says he went to stay for a fortnight with Peter in Jerusalem. It is here that later translators and copyists of Paul's works deliberately set out to disguise the realities of what was happening. Jesus had, according to the teachings of the sect, made Simon Bar-Jonah his special disciple, nicknaming him 'the Rock' which in Greek is *cephas* and in Latin is *petra*. Paul, in spreading his teachings, needed the authority of one of Jesus' original disciples – someone who had known Jesus in life because Paul had not. It would be unseemly for Paul to be seen arguing with Peter, to whom, Paul had taught, Jesus had given the keys to the gate of the Christian heaven. So in subsequent texts, translated out of the Greek, the name was left as Cephas without translation so that it might appear that Paul was arguing with someone else. He also met Jacob, Jesus' brother and the leader of the Nazarene movement. In his Epistle to the Galatians Paul clearly calls him 'the Lord's brother'.

It was fourteen years later that Paul, with his own two disciples, Barnabas and Titus, arrived in Jerusalem again. Paul, as he admits in his letter to the Galatians, had begun to develop his new theories and particularly the idea of making converts to his creed outside Judaism without requiring the converts to convert to Judaism. He says that he met with the leaders of the Nazarene movement. They, of course, raised objections to what he was doing. As Paul interprets this in Galatians:

These men wanted to bring us into bondage, but not for one moment did I yield to their dictation.

But as for the men of high reputation (not that their importance matters to me: God does not recognise these personal distinctions) – these men of repute, I say, did not prolong the consultation, but on the contrary acknowledged that I had been entrusted with the Gospel for the Gentiles as surely as Peter had been entrusted with the Gospel for Jews. For God, whose action made Peter an apostle to the Jews, also made me an apostle to the Gentiles.

Recognising, then, the favour thus bestowed upon me, those reputed pillars of our society Jacob, Peter and John accepted

Barnabas and myself as partners and shook hands upon it, agreeing that we should go to the Gentiles while they went to the Jews.

This is, of course, Paul's version of the agreement; it seems unlikely that the Nazarene leadership would really have agreed on this unless they had merely dismissed Paul, thinking he would have little impact with his preaching in the non-Jewish world.

Paul's next confrontation with Peter took place at Antioch. Here he reports a public confrontation with Peter in front of the Nazarene/Christian community. Paul's version is that Peter arrived in Antioch and stayed with non-Jewish converts. A message arrived from Jesus' brother Jacob reminding him that unless non-Jews converted to Judaism they could not be regarded as members of the sect. Peter, says Paul, was afraid of Jacob. He accepted Jacob's decision as did Barnabas, on whom Paul also rounded in anger. Paul challenged Peter face to face at Antioch. Alas, we do not have Peter's version of the affair.

Sometime in the AD 40s Paul returned to his native town Tarsus in Asia Minor. Tarsus was capital of the region of Cilicia where Cicero had once been governor and it was close to the southern borders of Galatia. Paul and his group were thought to be heading towards the cities on the northern coast, along the Black Sea. It has been argued that Paul passed through the main three cities of Galatia, Pessinus, Ancyra and Tavium. But, in fact, there is little evidence of exactly where Paul conducted his mission of conversion except that a long tradition has it that he stayed among the Tolistoboii in or around Pessinus. We are told that Paul did not intend to remain in Galatia at all but stayed simply because he was overcome by an illness. His 'thorn in the flesh' remark has been interpreted to mean that he was suffering from malaria. If this is true then his move from the low-lying country to the higher plain of Galatia was a wise one.

The date of this mission is likely to have been about AD 46 or 47.

It should be pointed out that Galatia now had a mixture of cultures within its cities: the original Phrygians, the Greek settlers, Jews of the diaspora, the Celts and the Romans. The religions of the area ranged from the Phrygian nature worship, with which the Celts probably felt much at home, to Hellenistic religious cults, Roman imperial cults and Judaism. Under Rome, Galatia now had a thriving commerce. The wealthier Celts had become Hellenised or were, most likely, bilingual while the poorer Celts, still dwelling in rural locations, retained their language and religious attitudes.

Galatia was a fertile ground for Paul's Gnostic message based on Hellenic cultural concepts.

It should be pointed out, however, that some scholars argue that Paul's Galatians were not Celts. Dr Mitchell, for example, says that there is virtually nothing to be said for arguing that the *ecclesia* to whom Paul was writing were in the cities of Celtic Galatia, and that Galatia had expanded at this time to take in the cities of Antioch, Iconium, Lystra and Derbe which were more Hellenic, Jewish and Roman. But equally there is nothing to be said to support the view that Paul was confining his remarks to these recent additions to the growing Roman province. As a Hellenic Jew of Anatolia, Paul would obviously be aware that a Galatian was regarded as a Celt. He knew the area too well to call Greeks, Roman and Jewish settlers 'Galatians'. And, indeed, a Roman inscription around A D 68 identified Calpurnius Asprenas as legate for 'the provinces of Galatae, Paphlagonia, Pamphyliae Pisidiae'. Therefore, the geographical entities were still clearly defined at this time.

Paul is clearly writing to the *barbaroi* who gave their name to the province. Dr Mitchell contends that he is doing so sarcastically, insulting the Jews and Greeks to whom he is writing. This is an intriguing idea but not one that is very credible. There is no evidence for this. The 'foolish Galatians' were none other than the Celtic Galatians. There is no reason at all to presume that the Celtic Galatians would not be receptive to Paul's teaching. In fact, about a decade after Paul's visit we find that in the town of Acmonia, an area where the Tolistoboii spread themselves, a *synagogue* (as opposed to an *ecclesia*) had been built by Julia Severa, a Gentile Christian who traced her ancestry back to the chieftains of the Tolistoboii.

It is likely that the Jewish communities, hearing about Paul's teaching to the Galatians, contacted the Nazarenes in Jerusalem and that Jacob sent out a mission to teach the true Nazarene doctrines. The basic teaching was that one could only be a member of the Nazarene sect if one accepted Judaism and Mosaic Law. This mission arrived in Galatia some time after Paul's visit there. The sort of criticism Paul was receiving from Peter and Jacob is clear, from his letter to the Galatians. All he knew of Christianity he had learnt from those who had known Jesus and this he was now perverting. Where was the proof Jesus had rejected Judaism? Those who had known Jesus and now preached his teachings did not regard him as divine and had never done so. Only Paul did. And Paul was always changing his arguments. He had once preached in favour of circumcision and appealed only to Jews. Now he told the Galatians that they need not be circumcised to be admitted into Judaism. If he rejected circumcision why had he circumcised Timothy and Titus?

The newly converted Galatians, impressed by the Nazarene missions from Jacob and Peter, began to question Paul's representatives about his teaching. Paul was now in Rome but soon learnt about the dissension. He was angry that his teaching was being questioned and in his rage wrote to the *ecclesia* of Galatia one of the earliest Christian documents, a document which has become one of the most powerful icons of the Christian movement and of which Martin Luther once wrote: 'The Epistle to the Galatians is my Epistle; I have betrothed myself to it; it is my wife.'

Paul begins with little preamble:

I am astonished to find you turning so quickly away from him who called you by grace and following a different gospel. Not that it is in fact another gospel; only there are persons who unsettle your minds by trying to distort the gospel of Christ. But if anyone, if we ourselves or an angel from heaven, should preach a gospel at variance with the gospel we preached to you, he shall be held outcast. I now repeat what I have said before, if anyone preaches a gospel at variance with the gospel which you received, let him be outcast!

Does my language now sound as if I were canvassing for men's support? Whose support do I want but God's alone? Do you think I am currying favour with men? If I still sought men's favour, I should be no servant of Christ.

I must make it clear to you, my friends, that the gospel you heard me preach is no human invention. I did not take it over from any man; no man taught it me; I received it through a revelation of Jesus Christ.

Paul gets right down to basic dogma. 'Believe in me and my revelation.' He attacks Peter and Jacob and almost loses his temper: 'You stupid Galatians! You must have been bewitched . . .' I think 'foolish' is a less emphatic way of rendering the Latin *stolidus*. Paul ends his letter by hinting at the anti-Judaism which his Gentile Christian movement would soon develop.

> You see these big letters? I am now writing to you in my own hand. It is all those who want to make a fair outward and bodily show who are trying to force circumcision upon you; *their sole object is to escape persecution for the cross of Christ* [my italics]. For even those who do received circumcision are not thorough-going observers of the [Judaic] law; they only want you to be circumcised in order to boast of your having submitted to the outward rite.

Gentile Christianity eventually became a strong movement in Anatolia and Pliny the Younger remarked on the large numbers of Christians in the areas of Pontus and Bithynia in about AD 110. Interestingly, it seems that the Celtic areas of Galatia have only produced, so far, a few early Christian inscriptions. In Ancyra in the 4th century AD, a lady named Aquilina, daughter of Archedemos, set up an inscription for her sons Theotimus (Timothy) and Paulus (Paul) and her husband Memnon. Her children had presumably been named after the two evangelists of Galatia.

There is little evidence to show how widely Paul's Gentile gospel had spread among the Celtic Galatians at this period. But there is evidence that the Celtic Galatians later organised missions to their fellow Celts in Gaul and that the early Galatian *ecclesia* had links with Gaulish *ecclesia*.

It was not until the 4th century AD that Christianity began to take a dominant hold throughout the region. One of the great proselytising missionaries of the area was Theodore, born in north-west Galatia around AD 210. He went to study Christian philosophy in Caesarea in Palestine. The school he went to had just been founded by Origen (c.AD 186–255), an Alexandrian who had fled from the persecution of Severus (AD 202–203). It was after he had settled in Caesarea that Origen wrote an attack on the philosopher Celsus, *Contra Celsum*, significantly mentioning the Druids of the Celts and Getae and referring to these peoples as 'very wise and ancient nations'. He also comments on the fact that there were no known survivals of any books of learning written by Druid philosophers. Could Origen have picked up this information from his pupil Theodore from Galatia?

In AD 240, Theodore returned home to be bishop. He took a new name, Gregorios, 'the reawakened one'. It is said that when he died in AD 270 there were only seventeen pagans in Anatolia not converted to the Christian faith.

By the 3rd century AD a monastic system of wandering holy men, hermits and other mystics proliferated in Galatia. An early church historian, Sozomen, mentioned the monks, describing them as ecclesiastic philosophers, who travelled around Galatia espousing the Christian doctrines. We hear from Epiphanos of Salamis, in the 4th century, that there was a particular sect of Galatian Christians called the Tascodrougitai. It has been argued that the *tasco* element in the name signifies a 'peg'; others argue that it might mean a 'firm wedge'.

Apart from St Jerome's visit to Ancyra in the 4th century and the story of the monk of Ancyra in the 6th century, in which we find a Celtic language still being spoken in the region, it is not until the mid-7th century that we find a written account of the life of a Christian Galatian. This is the *Life of St Theodore of Sykeon*.

Theodore was born during the reign of Justinian (AD 527–565). The *Life*, written a hundred years later, says that Theodore was twelve when he survived the bubonic plague. We know this plague reached its height in AD 542, which gives an approximate date for his birth of AD 530. Sykeon was a little village on the great road running from Ancyra to Constantinople near Juliospolis in northwest Galatia. It was an area of the Tolistoboii.

From the names we have no way of knowing whether Theodore's family were Celts or Greek settlers. From the hints given by the author of the *Life* it seems likely that they were Celts. His mother Maria, aunt Despoinia and aunt Elpidia ran a tavern and a brothel for travellers, serving as prostitutes as well as hosts. Theodore's uncle was said to be a local official called Cosmas. The *Life* says that the family were not poor and that Theodore's mother later married an official from Ancyra called David, implying that he was either a Jew or a Christian.

Theodore spent two years as a recluse before being admitted to the priesthood at the age of eighteen. He had predicted (by what means of divination is not clear) that Maurice would become emperor in AD 582. He became bishop of Anastasiopolis and served there for eleven years before making his first visit to Constantinople. He made three trips to the city. He built a monastery at Sykeon, with money inherited from his family, there he died on 22 April AD 613. His biographer was a monk there, one Georgius, who was not quite eighteen years old when Theodore died. He finished the biography in AD 641.

The history of Galatia during these later centuries of Rome had been one of the cosmopolitan cities of Ancyra and Pessinus. Therefore, the *Life of St Theodore*, presenting a picture of a rural setting, in an area which seemed to be one of the last that might have retained its Celtic identity, shows us a different and interesting side of life. Indeed, Theodore's biographer was also based in this rural setting and so does not distort the account.

We find the governor, Euphrantes, c.AD 600, sending his soldiers to arrest people he suspected of robbing ancient tombs in the area. And we find Theodore siding with the local population when a petty official of the governor abused his position of authority.

After Theodore's life, Galatia began to sink into obscurity. Perhaps isolated pockets of Celtic speakers might be found during the next century or two but certainly no more than that. The Celts had become absorbed into the mixture of races of Anatolia which were to finally emerge as the Turks.

[20]

Celtic Retreat to the West

BY the beginning of the 3rd century BC, the Celts had reached their furthest eastward expansion in Europe. Galatia in Asia Minor was established but Celtic enclaves could also be found along the coast of the Black Sea even as far north-east, according to Plutarch, as the Sea of Azov. The question, why did these settlements disappear, is perhaps inappropriate. The better question might be, why did they last so long? In the same manner as the Celts had suddenly erupted in an expansion in the middle of the first millennium BC, it was the turn of the Germanic and Slavic peoples to start pushing out in search of new lands. To these Germans and Slavs, the Celts – and, indeed, the Latins as well – were 'foreigners'. They were called Vlachs (Old Slavonic), corresponding with Walkholz (Gothic). An early form of this word even became an acceptable appendage to the name of the Tectosages, who are listed in the Slovakian area as Volcae Tectosages, with the same designation later occurring in Gaul itself. The same word root occurs in the Anglo-Saxon word for foreigner, *welisc*, applied to all British Celts and today surviving in 'Welsh/Wales' and 'Cornwall' (Kern-*wealhas*).

The Germanic people, the ancestors of the Germans, Anglo-Saxons, Franks, Frisians, Dutch, Flemings and Scandinavians, first appeared in recorded history in 222BC. They are mentioned in the Roman *Acta Triumphalia* which records the battle of Clastidium (Casteggio) when the Romans achieved a victory over the Insubrian Celts of Cisalpine Gaul. The Germans are shown serving in the army of Virdomaros, who bears a distinctly Celtic name meaning 'the great man'. It is possible that they were fighting at Clastidium as mercenaries hired by the Celts, although this would have been highly unusual, but it is more likely that they were a people who were under Celtic political domination at the time of their emergence into written history.

According to Professor Eoin MacNeill:

A number of words of Celtic origin are found spread through the whole group of Germanic languages, including Scandinavian languages and English, which was originally a mixture of Low German dialects. Some of these words are especially connected with the political side of civilisation and are therefore especially indicative of Celtic political predominance at the time of their adoption into Germanic speech.

These words include *reich*, from the Celtic *region*, a royal dominion; *amt*, office, charge, employment, from the Celtic *ambactos*, a retainer of a Celtic chieftain, originally signifying 'one sent in the chieftain's place', a minister or envoy, from which an adoption into Latin led to the word *ambassadeur* entering Norman-French from Low Latin, and then English as 'ambassador'; and the word 'town' itself, from *dunon*.

The Germans and Celts had long mingled along the northern Celtic border and it has been argued by Professor MacNeill and others that this mingling produced a mixed Celto-Germanic people who became Celtic in speech. Hence the confusion of Roman writers as to who was and was not a German. Strabo, for example, says that the Nervii, who led the Belgae confederation against Caesar, were Germans while Tacitus claims that 'the Treveri and the Nervii are especially forward in asserting their German origin, as though by this boast of race to be distinguished from the pacific character of the Celts.' The Treveri were clearly Celtic-speaking. Dio Cassius says that 'the Boii are a nation of Germans' while elsewhere clearly talking of them as Celts. Was it merely confusion on the part of the Romans or was there something to be confused about?

The argument that there was a Celto-German-speaking borderland between the Celts proper and the Germans would seem acceptable. Of the Aestyi, dwelling on the northern seaboard of Germany, Tacitus says that their language resembled that of the British Celts. Celtic place-names are certainly found throughout central Germany. When the Germans began to expand in the 2nd century BC, they began to displace these Celto-German tribes. Tacitus observes that the Tungri were pushed westward over the Rhine. The Belgae seemed also to have been a mixed Celto-German people and they were among the first to be displaced. The hostile pressure from the German-speaking tribes pressed the Celts increasingly westward over the Rhine and down into the Danube valley. There is still argument as to whether the Cimbri and Teutones were Germans or Celto-Germans. Caesar, in the middle of the 1st century BC, regarded the Rhine as the dividing line between German tribes and the Celts.

In the extreme east, those Celts who had settled around the mouth of the Danube, including the settlements in the valleys of Mures, Somes and Cris in Transylvania, Moldavia and Thrace, were all coming under new pressure. Most of them were absorbed by the beginning of the 1st century BC into the Geto-Dacian population. These Celtic tribes, who were skilled in iron exploitation and processing and also introduced the potter's wheel into the area, contributed to the acceleration of the development of the local tribes as we have previously mentioned. Prosperous Celtic communities had spread over the whole territory of modern Romania.

According to Pompeius Trogus, a king named Oroles had arisen around 200BC. He was a Dacian king resisting the intrusion of the Bastarnae, a population generally now considered to be of Germanic origin but which was in fact Celto-Germanic, speaking, as Livy points out, a Celtic language. They moved from Silesia into what is now central and northern Moldavia. Dr Hoddinott affirms the Celtic element: 'Described as Celtic or Germanic in the [Classical] sources, the Bastarnae seem to have migrated from a mostly Germanic but partly north Celtic homeland, assimilating Baltic and other elements on their way.' In response to pressure from them, Oroles organised a strong kingdom as a means of defence.

Early in the 2nd century BC, when Mithridates the Great of Pontus extended his rule over the northern coast of the Black Sea and along the coastline of Moldavia, Romania and Bulgaria, further pressure was put on the area. A balance seems ultimately to have been established for a short time between the Geto-Dacian groups, the Bastarnae to the north and Celts to the south-west. Professor Otetea states:

The Getae and Dacians, singly or co-operating with the Celts and Bastarnians, carried on unceasing attacks against the new power [of Rome] that had been established in the middle of the Balkan Peninsula. Indeed, they were its most implacable enemies.

M. Municius Rufus, the Roman governor of Macedonia, attempted an attack on Dacia which then made an alliance with the Celtic Scordisci, south of the Danube, in 110/109BC. There was obviously still a strong Celtic presence in this area. But with Rome accelerating its attacks to gain control from the south and the rise of the Geto-Dacian civilisation to the north, the Celts were rapidly disappearing. The 1st century BC saw the start of a classic period of the Geto-Dacian La Tène culture, centred around the city of Sarmizegetusa Regia in south-west Transylvania.

The Romans continued to push forward and in 75/74BC the legions of proconsul Gnaeus Scribonius Curio reached the Danube as Alexander had done 300 years before him. But Curio was no Alexander. He feared to cross the river and, as Julius Florus says, 'was scared of the dark woods there'.

In reaction to the Roman incursions, a Geto-Dacian king named Burebista began to unify the tribes. Strabo says that he was supported by a priest named Decaeneus and that he enforced a military order among his warriors, ordering them not to drink too much wine. Strabo says:

> Burebista, a Getan, having become the leader of his people, exhausted by frequent wars, raised them to a new height through drilling, abstention from wine and obedience to orders, that he achieved a powerful state within a few years and subjected to the Getae, the major part of the neighbouring populations, coming to be feared even by the Romans themselves.

Archaeologists have found on numerous sites a burnt layer dated to the 1st century BC and believe this to be connected with the rise of Burebista. To add further weight to the argument, through the Hungarian Plain and the Tatry mountains a plethora of small Celtic hill-forts began to appear during the early 1st century. After living for centuries in the area in settled conditions, we can ask why the Celts would suddenly need to build hill-forts. The fortresses starkly contrast with the previous prosperous open farming settlements. A similar contrast exists in Slovakia, Bohemia and Moravia although in the Czech republic we can find remains of Celtic fortresses dating back to the preceding centuries, of which Závist is the oldest.

Jordanes (in his *Getica*) says that Burebista consolidated the Getic tribes during the time of Sulla (82–79BC) although most scholars date his activities to the middle of the 1st century BC.

One thing has become noticeable in the area, as Dr Hoddinott says:

> The coinage of the four main Geto-Dacian groups ceased after the first decades, when Burebista forbade minting presumably to assert his authority, possibly also to diminish Celtic influence, and preferred to use Roman *denarii*, easily available through the growing trade with the west or minted locally.

There is soon no further sign of any Celtic populations in this region and by 60BC Burebista was launching an offensive against the Celtic peoples in Pannonia (Hungary) and Slovakia, in an attempt to expand the frontiers of his new empire. These Celtic tribes were basically the Boii and Taurisci. Burebista was also extending his rule over the Greek colonies in the area, and these too were disappearing.

Sometime around 60/55BC Burebista defeated the Celts of the Boii and Taurisci. Instead of absorbing them, he began to push them out, first out of Pannonia and then from Slovakia, forcing them increasingly westward. This occurred at the very time when the Germanic tribes were pressing the Celts from the north and were pushing them southward. The Boii had already repulsed the Cimbri and the Teutones in 120BC. But now Burebista stood master of a territory from the Black Sea to the middle Danube valley and the Slovakian mountains. He did not enjoy his victories long; soon after Julius Caesar was assassinated he died or was himself killed.

As Dr Hoddinott says:

> As pursuit of the Celts was not pressed so far as Gaul, and Dacian troops were too late for the battle of Pharsalus, no confrontation with Roman forces took place. But in his last years Julius Caesar determined to remove the Dacian danger. The many coins from Histria found in the Transylvanian forts of Piatra Rosie and Cosesti suggest that Burebista, aware of Caesar's plans, strengthened his defences with technical help from the Greek cities. Then, in 44BC, came the almost simultaneous assassination of Julius Caesar and the death, natural or otherwise, of Burebista. The Dacian state

disintegrated into tribal groups and it was nearly 150 years later that Dacian and Roman forces met in Transylvania.

However, the Dacian thrust against the Celts of Hungary and the area of the Czech and Slovakia republics caused a 'knock-on' effect which did eventually reach Gaul. The Celts were now pushing back upon one another. There began a flight from Bohemia, the land named after the Boii. According to Caesar some 32,000 men, women and children of the Boii fled from Bohemia and moved into Noricum (Austria) where they mauled a Roman army, joined with some of the local Celtic tribes and pushed on into the land of the Celtic confederation known as the Helvetii (Switzerland). The Helvetii were also under threat from the Germanic tribes to the north. The chieftain of the Helvetii confederation was named Orgetorix (king of killers) and his daughter was married to a chieftain named Dumnorix (king of the world) of the Aedui. They entered into an alliance by which they sought to avoid the expansion of the Germanic tribes.

According to Caesar, Orgetorix, in 61 BC, came up with the idea of a migration *en masse*, the like of which had not been seen for some centuries.

Orgetorix died, but the new chieftains of the Helvetii confederation, continually squeezed by the advances of the Germanic tribes, and now finding the Boii, Rauraci and Taurisci as well as the Tigurini seeking refuge in their lands, decided to continue the plan for mass migration.

Some 400,000 men, women and children, of whom 92,000 were warriors, gathered with wagons and horses. They were simply looking for 'living space' away westward out of the path of the Germans. Dumnorix of the Aedui had persuaded Casticos of the Sequani to allow the Helvetii to pass through his tribal lands. On the appointed day the Celts fired their villages, towns, farmsteads and fields, to prevent them falling into the hands of the incoming German tribes, and began to trek slowly westward, south of the Jura mountains, passing Lake Geneva to the Pas de l'Ecluse.

Caesar reported:

> ... they burnt all their twelve towns and four hundred villages as well as the isolated buildings belonging to private individuals, and also the whole of their grain, except what they intended to carry

with them; for they thought that, if there was no possibility of returning home, they would be more willing to face all the perils that awaited them. Every man was directed to take with him from home three months' supply of flour for his own use. They persuaded their neighbours the Rauraci, Tulinigi [sic] and Latovici to follow their example – to burn their towns and villages and go with them – they were joined also by the Boii who formerly lived on the other side of the Rhine, but had recently migrated into Austria and attacked the town of Noreia.

Obviously Caesar was not aware of or concerned with the main reasons behind the migration. Of the 400,000 who started out on that exodus only 100,000 were to survive, thanks to Caesar.

The brother of Dumnorix, Diviciacus (he who avenges) was pro-Roman. Diviciacus had sent word to the Romans about this movement, thus giving Julius Caesar the excuse that he had been waiting for to invade Gaul proper and begin its conquest.

The Helvetii and the other tribal leaders did not want a conflict with Rome. The majority of them were old men, women and children – an entire nation on the march. On 28 March 58 BC, they began their movement. Caesar rushed his legions to confront them. The Helvetii sent two chieftains, Nammeius (one with a physical blemish) and Verucloetius (he of great renown) to Caesar, saying they sought his permission to move peacefully through Narbonesis Gaul and promised they would not damage any persons or property. Caesar refused this passage.

To avoid the Romans they then turned north-west into the territory of the Sequani who allowed them through and where they passed without harming anyone or doing any damage. Then they moved into the Aedui territory where Dumnorix welcomed them. His brother, Diviciacus, however, being pro-Roman had given the Romans permission for a 'hot pursuit'. It was all the same to Caesar; he was going to attack the Helvetii whichever way they turned. He followed them into Aedui territory, ostensibly at the invitation of Diviciacus.

He came on the slow-moving columns of refugees crossing the river Saône near Lugdunum (Lyons) and found the Tigurini still crossing. He launched his attack and cut the tribe to pieces. In satisfaction, Caesar recalled:

Fifty years earlier, the men of this clan had engaged in battle with the consul Cassius and defeated his army, killing him. Thus, whether by accident or divine providence, the section of the Helvetii that had inflicted a singular defeat upon Rome was the first to suffer for it. In thus punishing the Tigurini, Caesar also avenged a private injury as well as that done to his country, for a general named Lucius Piso, grandfather of the Lucius Piso who was Caesar's father-in-law, had been killed in the same battle as Cassius.

It was true that in 107 BC the Tigurini had allied themselves with the Tectosages of Gaul and defeated the army of L. Cassius Longinus. The Celts had released Cassius' second-in-command, C. Popillius Laenas, but humiliated the Romans by marching the survivors of the 'invincible legions' in chains.

Caesar now marched his army towards Bibracte where the Helvetii warriors fought desperately to keep Caesar away from the women and children of the columns. Some 6000 were killed in one day of fighting alone. The next day Caesar surrounded the rest of the tribe at Langres. He massacred an estimated 200,000 Celtic men, women and children. Some prisoners were taken, including one of Orgetorix's sons and a daughter. The 130,000 survivors, still keeping together, marched all through the night to avoid Caesar's marauding troops and, after three days of non-stop marching, arrived in the country of the Lingones.

'We were not able to pursue immediately,' says Caesar, 'because we spent these days in attending to the wounded and burying the dead.'

Needless to say, the attention was to the Roman wounded and dead, not the Celts.

The Helvetii leaders realised that they could not find any sanctuary from the Romans. They were running out of supplies and had lost most of their warriors. There was simply nowhere to go. They sent emissaries to Caesar who 'prostrated themselves before him and, with tears of supplication, begged him to grant them peace'. Caesar ordered the survivors of the Helvetii to stay put until he could march his army up to them. That night some 6000 from a sept called the Vernigeni, fearful that Caesar intended to massacre them, fled towards the Rhine. Caesar sent out troops to hunt them down and bring them back. He is straightforward in his account: 'When they were brought back he put them to death.'

Here was ethnic cleansing on a grand scale.

Having collected arms and hostages from the remaining Helvetii survivors, Caesar marched them forcibly back to their homeland where they were subjugated by the incoming Germanic tribes and eventually vanished as a distinct Celtic people. Only the word Helvetica remains as a name for modern Switzerland to mark their passing. The survivors of the Boii, however, were allowed to settle in the country of the Aedui because the Aedui intervened with Caesar and pleaded their cause. Boulogne bears the stem of their name.

A significant piece of information was given by Caesar in the following passage:

> Some documents found in the Helvetian camp were brought to Caesar. They were written in Greek characters and contained a register of the names of all the emigrants capable of bearing arms, and also, under separate heads, the numbers of old men, women and children. The grand total was 368,000 comprising 263,000 Helvetii, 36,000 Tulingi [*sic*] 14,000 Latovici, 23,000 Rauraci and 32,000 Boii; and the list of men fit for military service contained 92,000 names. By Caesar's order, a census was taken of those who were forced to return home, and the number was found to be 110,000.

Caesar was now able to show his real ambition. Having managed to get his Roman armies into Gaul on the pretext of protecting Gaul from the invading Helvetii, he unleashed his legions on the Gaulish tribes and began his vicious conquest of the Celtic heartland. In doing so, of course, it can be argued that he kept the German tribes on the east bank of the Rhine for another 400 years. That is, presupposing that the Gauls would not have been able to do so. But in all parts of the world the Celts were being absorbed or killed off. They were being steadily pushed back until finally it would be only in the north-west corner of Europe, on the Continental peninsula of Armorica (Brittany) and in the islands of Britain and Ireland, that the remnants of this once vast and fascinating civilisation would survive, albeit barely, into the modern world.

Of the centuries of the close relationship between Celt and Greek, apart from archaeological and antiquarian survivals, what remains to mark it? Perhaps it is sadly significant that, representative of the few Celtic words which were absorbed into the Greek language from this fascinating period, are: λειούσματα or λελούσματα, a type of body armour; κάρνος, a trumpet and ἔμβρεκτον, a soup or porridge.

Acknowledgements and Select
Bibliography

I WOULD claim a lengthy gestation period for the idea for this particular work. It was in 1971 that I first talked about the story of the Celtic invasion of Greece with my good friend, the Greek composer, Christos Pittas. I would like to acknowledge my thanks to him for occasionally reminding me over the years about the sack of Delphi. I would also like to express my thanks for advice over the years from the late Professor Kenneth H. Jackson (former Professor of Celtic languages, literature, history and antiquities at the University of Edinburgh); Professor Gearóid Mac Eoin (former Professor of Old and Middle Irish and Comparative Celtic Philology at University College, Galway); Professor Per Denez (former Professor in the Celtic Department of Rennes University); Professor David H. Rankin (now Professor of Philosophy at Southampton University); to Maria Soteriades and to Elizabeth Murray.

My aim in this work, as with my previous works, is to present a history for the general reader and thus copious footnote references have been dispensed with although references, and sometimes their validity or otherwise, are made clear within the text itself.

Obviously, the primary sources for this work have been from the Classical authors. The texts of all those referred to are available in English translations. Such translations have appeared in various editions over the years. For example, the Loeb Classical Library, published by Heinemann of London, is one good source. J. M. Dent's Everyman Library is another excellent set of translations. Similarly, the Penguin Classics Library has a commendable series of modern translations currently in print. In this series, and highly recommended, is *Pausanias' Guide to Greece* (2 volumes), translated and edited by Peter Levi (1971); Livy's *The History of Rome from its*

Foundation, translated by Henry Bettenson and introduced by A. H. McDonald (1976) (another good translation of Livy is one by Spillane and Edmunds, published by George Bell & Sons, London, 1919); the works of Polybius, translated by Ian Scott-Kilvert (1979); the works of Cicero, translated and edited by Michael Grant (1975); *Caesar: The Civil War* (including the important text of *The Alexandrian War*) translated by Jane Gardner (1967). Jane Gardner also translated *Caesar: The Conquest of Gaul* (1951). Xenophon, Plutarch, Diodorus Siculus, Strabo, Arrian, Herodotus, Thucydides, and others are all to be found in the series. An excellent translation of the writing of the Jewish historian, Flavius Josephus, which covers this period is Professor Nahun G. Glatzer's *Jerusalem and Rome: The Writings of Josephus*, Collins, London, 1966.

General

Allen, D. F. *The Coins of the Ancient Celts*, Edinburgh University Press, Edinburgh, 1980.

Audouze, Françoise and Büchsenschütz, Olivier. *Towns, Villages and Countryside of Celtic Europe*, B. T. Batsford, London, 1991.

Benoit, F. 'The Celtic Oppidum of Entremont, Provence', in R. Bruce Mitford ed., *Recent Archaeological Excavations in Europe*, London, 1975.

Bertrans, Alexandre L. J. and Reinach, Salomon, *Les Celtes dans les vallées du Pô et du Danube*, Paris, 1894.

Bittel, K. *Die Galater in Kleinasien archäologisch gesehen, Assimilation et résistance à la culture gréco-romaine dans le monde ancien*, Bucharest/Paris, 1976.

Bourmet, F. 'Les tombeaux de Vix et la mont Lassios', *Revue Historique* No. 234, Paris, 1965.

Bury, J. B. and Meiggs, Russell. *A History of Greece*, Macmillan, London (4th edition, 1994 reprint).

Childe, V. Gordon. *The Dawn of European Civilization*, Routledge & Kegan Paul, London, 1957.

Cunliffe, Barry. *Greeks, Romans and Barbarians*, Batsford, London, 1988.

Cunliffe, Barry. *The Celtic World*, Constable, London, 1992.

Danov, C. M. 'The Celtic Invasion and Rule in Thrace in the Light of Some New Evidence', *Studia Celtica*, Dublin, 10–11, 1975/76.

D'Iakonov, I. M. 'On the Original Home of the Speakers of Indo-European', *Journal of Indo-European Studies*, Vol. XIII.

Dressler, W. 'Galatisches' in *Beiträge zur Indogermanistik und Keltologie, Julius Pokorny zum 80*, Geburstag Geuridmer, Innsbruck, 1967.

Dunbabin, T. J. *The Western Greeks*, Oxford University Press, Oxford, 1948.

Duval, D. M. 'Les inscriptions gallo-grecques', *Actes du Collogue sur les influences helléniques en Gaule*, Dijon, 1957.

Ellis, Peter Berresford. *The Celtic Empire: The First Millennium of Celtic History 1000 BC to AD 51*, Constable, London, 1990.

Ellis, Peter Berresford. *Dictionary of Celtic Mythology*, Constable, London, 1992.

Ellis, Peter Berresford. *The Druids*, Constable, London, 1994.

Ellis, Peter Berresford. *Celtic Women; Women in Celtic Society and Literature*, Constable, London, 1995.

Evans, David Ellis. *Gaulish Personal Names*, Clarendon Press, Oxford, 1967.

Evans, David Ellis. 'The Labyrinth of Continental Celtic', Rhys Memorial Lecture, 1977, in *Proceedings of the British Academy*, London, 1981.

Evans, David Ellis. 'Celts and Germans', *Bulletin of the Board of Celtic Studies*, No. 29, Cardiff, 1982.

Filip, Jan. *Celtic Civilization and its Heritage*, Publishing House of the Czechoslovakian Academy of Sciences, Prague, 1962.

Gerasimov, T. in *Izvestiya na Bulgarskiya Arkeologicheski Institut*, No. 25, Sofia, 1962.

Green, Miranda J. ed. *The Celtic World*, Routledge, London, 1995.

Green, Miranda J. *Dictionary of Celtic Myth and Legend*, Thames and Hudson, London, 1992.

Griffith, G. T. *The Mercenaries of the Hellenistic World*, Cambridge University Press, Cambridge, 1935.

Gwynn, Edward J. *Poems from the Dindshenchas*, Dublin, 1900.

Hänsel, B. in *Germania*, 47, Bonn, 1969.

Hoddinott, Ralph F. *The Thracians*, Thames and Hudson, New York (USA), 1981.

Hornblower, J. *Hieronymus of Cardia*, Oxford University Press, Oxford, 1981.

Hubert, Henri. *The Rise of the Celts*, Kegan Paul, Trench, Trubner & Co, London, 1934. New edition and introduction by Professor Gearóid Mac Eoin, Constable, London, 1987.

Hubert, Henri. *The Greatness and Decline of the Celts*, Kegan Paul, Trench, Trubner & Co, London, 1934. New edition and introduction by Professor Gearóid Mac Eoin, Constable, London, 1987.

Hull, Eleanor. 'Observations of Classical Writers on the Habits of the Celtic Nations', *Celtic Review*, vol. III pp 62–76 and 138–154, Edinburgh.

James, Simon. *Exporing the World of the Celts*, Thames and Hudson, London, 1993.

Jerem, Elizabeth. 'An early Pottery Workshop in North Western Hungary: some Archaeological and Technical Evidence', *Oxford Journal of Archaeology*, No. 3, 1984.

Jerem, Elizabeth. 'Celts of Eastern Europe' etc. See Miranda J. Green, *Celtic World* (1995).

Joubert, P. *Macedonian Imperialism*, Kegan Paul, Trench, Trubner & Co, London, 1928.

Katsarov, G. I. in *Spisanie Bulgarskiya Akademia Nauk*, No. 18, Sofia, 1919.

Klindt-Hensen, O. 'Foreign influence in Denmark's Early Iron Age', in *Acta Archaeologia*, No. 20, Copenhagen, 1950.

Kovács, T., Petres, E., Szabó, M. 'Corpus of Celtic Finds in Hungary, I', *Transdanubia 1*, Budapest, 1987.

Launey, M. *Recherches sur les armées hellénistiques*, 2 vols, Paris, 1949 and 1950.

Lloyd, S. *Early Highland Peoples of Anatolia*, Thames and Hudson, London, 1967.

Maccoby, Hyam. *Revolution in Judaea: Jesus and the Jewish Resistance*, Ocean Books, London, 1973.

MacNeill, Eoin. *Phrases of Irish History*, M. H. Gill, Dublin, 1968 (first published, Dublin, 1919).

Mihailov, G. *Trakite*, Sofia, 1972.

Mitchell, Stephen. *Anatolia: Land, Men, and Gods in Asia Minor*, 2 vols. Clarendon Press, Oxford, 1993.

Moscati, Sabatino *et al. I Celti* (catalogue of the 1991 Venice exhibition of Celtic artefacts) 798pp, Gruppe Editoriale Fabbri Bompiani, Sonzogno. Etas SpA, Milano, Italy, 1991.

Müller-Karpe, A. 'Neue galatische Funde aus Anatolien', *Istanbuler Mitteilungen*, No.38, Istanbul, 1988.

Nachtergael, G. *Les Galates en Grèce et les Sôtéria de Delphes*, Brussels, 1977.

Nash, Daphne. *Coinage in the Celtic World*, B. A. Seaby, London, 1987.

Ó hÓgáin, Dáithí. *Myth, Legend and Romance: An Encylopaedia of the Irish Folk Tradition*, Ryan Publishing, London, 1990.

O'Laverty, James. 'Remarkable Correspondence of Irish, Greek and Oriental Legends', *Ulster Journal of Archaeology*, vol. VII n.d., Belfast.

Olmsted, Garrett. *The Gaulish Calendar*, Dr Rudolf Habelt, Bonn, 1992.

Olmsted, Garrett. 'Gaulish and Celtiberian Poetic Inscriptions', *The Mankind Quarterly*, XXVIII no. 4, pp 339/387, 1988.

Olmsted, Garrett. 'The Meter of the Gaulish inscription from Larzac', *The Journal of Indo-European Studies*, XVII nos 1–2, 1988.

O'Rahilly, Thomas F. *Early Irish History and Mythology*, Dublin Institute for Advanced Studies, Dublin, 1946.

Otetea, Andrei, ed. *The History of the Romanian People (Istoria Poporuli Roman)*, Scientific Publishing House, Bucharest, 1970.

Parvan, Vasile. *Dacia*, Cambridge University Press, Cambridge, 1928.

Piggott, Stuart. *Ancient Europe*, Edinburgh University Press, Edinburgh, 1965.

Pleiner, Radomir. *The Celtic Sword* (with contributions by B. G. Scott), Clarendon Press, Oxford, 1993.

Pollitt, J. J. *Art in the Hellenistic Age*, Cambridge University Press, Cambridge, 1986.

Powell, T. G. E. *The Celts*, Thames and Hudson, London, 1958.

Ramsay, W. M. *A Historical Commentary on St Paul's Epistle to Galatians*, Hodder & Stoughton, London, 1900.

Rankin, H. D. *Celts and the Classical World*, Croom Helm, London, 1987.

Rhŷs, John. 'Celtae and Galli', *Proceedings of the British Academy*, 1905.

Rhŷs, John. 'Celtic Inscriptions of France and Italy', *Proceedings of the British Academy*, 1906.

Rhŷs, John. 'The Celtic Inscriptions of Gaul', *Proceedings of the British Academy*, 1911/12.

Ridgeway, Sir William. *Early Age of Greece*, Cambridge University Press, Cambridge, 1901.

Rose, H. J. *A Handbook of Greek Literature*, Methuen, London, 1934.

Sandars, N. K. *Prehistoric Art in Europe*, Penguin Books, Harmondsworth, 1968.

Schmidt, K. H. 'On the Celtic Languages of Continental Europe', *The Bulletin of the Board of Celtic Studies*, XXVIII, Cardiff, 1979.

Sherwin White, A. N. *Racial Prejudice in Imperial Rome*, Cambridge University Press, Cambridge, Mass, USA, 1967.

Szabo, Miklós. *The Celtic Heritage in Hungary*, Budapest, 1971.

Szabo, Miklós. *Les Celtes en Pannonie: contribution à l'historique de la civilisation celtique dans la cuvette des Karpates*, Paris, 1988.

Tierney, J. J. 'The Celtic Ethnography of Poseidonius', *Proceedings of the Royal Irish Academy*, Vol. 60, 1959/1960.

Walbank, F. W. *A Historical Commentary on Polybius*, 3 vols, Oxford University Press, Oxford, 1957–79.

Weisgerber, Leo. 'Galatische Sprachreste', *Natalicium Johannes Geffcken*, Heidelberg, 1931.

Weisweiler, J. 'Die Stellung der Frau bei den Keltenund das Problem des Keltischen Mutterrechts', *Zeitschrift für Celtische Philologie*, 21.2, 1953.

Whatmough, Joshua. 'Continental Celtic', *Proceedings of the Second International Congress of Celtic Studies*, Cardiff, 1966.

Index